"Today I am sending you with My mercy to the people of the whole world."

(From the diary of Sister Faustina #1588)

MERCY MY MISSION

Life of
Sister Faustina H. Kowalska, S.M.D.M.

Sister Sophia Michalenko, C.M.G.T.

Divine Mercy
Library

MARIAN PRESS
Stockbridge, Massachusetts 01263
1987

On the part of the St. Stanislaus Kostka Province
Congregation of Marians:

NIHIL OBSTAT:
Rev. Joseph J. Sielski, MIC

IMPRIMI POTEST:
Rev. Richard J. Drabik, MIC
Provincial

Stockbridge, Massachusetts
May 20, 1987

On the part of the Diocese of Springfield in Massachusetts:

NIHIL OBSTAT:
Most Rev. George H. Pearce, S.M.

IMPRIMATUR:
Most Rev. Joseph F. Maguire
Bishop of Springfield, Massachusetts

August 1987

The NIHIL OBSTAT and IMPRIMATUR are a declaration
that a book or pamphlet is considered to be free from doctrinal or
moral error. It is not implied that those who have granted the
NIHIL OBSTAT and IMPRIMATUR agree with the contents,
opinions or statements expressed.

Library of Congress Catalog Card Number 87-090692

ISBN 0-944203-02-7

CONTENTS

ACKNOWLEDGEMENTS
CONTENTS
INTRODUCTION
THE EARLY YEARS (1905-1925)
    Home Life 1
    Housemaid.. 8
    The Call 10
THE NOVITIATE YEARS (1925-1928)
    Postulancy (1925-1926) 16
    Novitiate (1926-1928) 18
    "Darkness"....................................... 22
THE YEARS OF TEMPORARY PROFESSION (1928-1932)
    Warsaw 26
    "Pray for Poland"................................ 28
    New Assignments 29
    Untarnished Chastity 30
    Assignment to Plock 30
    Revelation of the Image of The Divine Mercy 31
    The "Visionary" 32
THIRD PROBATION AND PERPETUAL VOWS (1932-1933)
    Blessed Assurances 35
    "Victim Soul" 39
    Return to Cracow................................ 44
    Perpetual Vows.................................. 47
THE VILNIUS YEARS (1933-1936)
    Between Assignments.............................51
    The Promised Spiritual Director 52
    A Vision Put on Canvas 56
    Gift of Knowledge 57
    An Act of Oblation............................. 59
    A Predicted Illness 61
    A "Troublesome Vision" 65
    A Special Feast of Mercy 66
    Advent and Christmas 1934 66
    The Lord's Secretary and Apostle 69
    An Eight-day Retreat, 1935...................... 72

A Visit to the Family 73
Lent and Easter, 1935............................. 77
First Exposition of the Image of The Divine Mercy ... 79
Urgencies and Apparent Obstacles.................. 83
A New Congregation? 84
God and Souls.................................... 86
Special Graces................................... 89
The Chaplet of The Divine Mercy 91
Eight-day Retreat and More on the New Congregation. 93
Christmas 1935 97
A YEAR OF MANY CHANGES (1936)
The New Congregation Again..................... 99
An Understanding of the Mystery of Suffering 100
A Time of Trials and Graces 101
New Assignments: Walendow and Derdy 104
Further Testing 109
Warning for Poland 111
Opportunities for Trust in Mercy 112
An Unusual Eight-day Retreat 117
Vision of Hell 117
True Worship of Divine Mercy.................... 118
The Invisible Stigmata 121
Vision of Heaven 122
A Lesson from the Mother of God................. 123
The Sanatorium 125
A Time of Intercession.......................... 127
Her Work and Mission 128
Christmas 1936 131
The Glory of The Work of Mercy 132
INTERCESSORY SUFFERING
AND CONSUMING LOVE (1937).................... 134
The Value of Obedience......................... 137
A Sacrifice for Sinners.......................... 138
Lent and Easter 1937 141
The Feast of The Divine Mercy 148
Compassionate Suffering........................ 150
Return to Joseph's Place 153
A Sudden Healing 156
Divine Urgings 157

The Divine Tutor 159
The Growth of Sacrificial Love 163
Gatekeeper...................................... 169
Atonement for Abortions 170
Mystical Graces................................. 171
Mother Irene's Role 174
Hidden Mysteries 175
The Hour of Great Mercy 177
The Making of a Saint........................... 178
Source of Strength in Suffering 183
Love for Mary Immaculate 186
Suffering for Souls 188
Christmas 1937 190
TOTAL SUBMISSION (1938)
Acceptance of More Suffering 195
Devotion to The Divine Mercy................... 204
Sacrificial Host 208
A Lesson in Humility........................... 209
A Blessing for a "Saintly" Secretary........... 212
The Hour of Great Mercy 214
On Calvary with Jesus 215
Moments of Respite 217
In the School of Suffering 221
Holy Week and Easter 226
Return to the Sanatorium 229
The Power of Union with God 236
The Last Days.................................. 243
EPILOGUE....................................... 249
BIBLIOGRAPHY 255

ILLUSTRATIONS

Sister Faustina H. Kowalska, S.M.D.M. (1905-1938)-   Frontispiece
Novitiate House (St. Joseph's) in Cracow 15
Sister Faustina in Plock (1929)........................... 34
A visit to the family (1935).............................. 50
The Rev. Michael Sopocko, confessor and spiritual
    director of Sr. Faustina in Vilnius (1933-1936) 98
The Rev. Joseph Andrasz, S.J. confessor of Sr.
    Faustina during the last years before her death 194
Faithful visiting the grave of Sr. Faustina, seeking to
    obtain graces through her intercession 248
Latest version of the Image of The Divine Mercy 254
Places where Sister Faustina lived and worked 256

ACKNOWLEDGEMENTS

The author is deeply grateful to all those who have in any way helped make this book a reality, but especially to the Congregation of Marians of the St. Stanislaus Kostka Province who sponsored it; to her brother, Fr. Seraphim Michalenko, M.I.C., and sister, Mary Adamczyk, for their time spent in proofreading and advising; to Sr. Dolores Liptak, R.S.M., for her invaluable suggestions and comments; to Fr. George W. Kosicki, C.S.B., for his added insights; and to Maureen Digan for suggesting the title.

INTRODUCTION

Throughout human history, whenever a crisis of a spiritual, social, or political nature threatened humankind, God in His mercy raised up visionaries to help the people survive it and even profit from it. Recall just a few: Francis of Assisi, Catherine of Siena, Joan of Arc, Margaret Mary Alacoque, Bernadette of Lourdes, and Therese of Lisieux. In the twentieth century, to counteract atheism, materialism, and humanism, God sent the Blessed Virgin Mary to three children in Fatima; and when Hitler was rising in power, Jesus Himself came to a Polish peasant girl, known in religion as Sister Faustina.

She was born Helena Kowalska, in the obscure village of Glogowiec, near Lodz, Poland in 1905, the third of ten children. Responding to the graces of God, she entered the Congregation of the Sisters of Our Lady of Mercy in Warsaw, Poland, at the age of twenty. Because she was uneducated, Faustina performed ordinary convent chores—that of a cook, baker, gardener, and gatekeeper. In such a humble setting, she underwent extensive mystical experiences, unknown to even her closest companions. She accepted the invitation of Jesus to become His apostle and secretary, and to announce anew to mankind the Gospel message of God's mercy.

In 1934, obeying her spiritual director, her superiors, and Jesus Himself, Sister Faustina began to record her experiences. After some time, while her spiritual director was away in the Holy Land, Sister Faustina burned the then existing notebook, supposedly at the prompting of an angel. When her director returned and learned of it, he ordered her to rewrite the destroyed portion and, at the same time, to continue writing her ongoing experiences. Then, too, the Servant of God did not always date her entries, but merely began with the words "At one time....," and she often repeated herself, for she seldom reviewed what she wrote. For the reader of the diary of some 600 printed pages, the result could become confusing.

This new biography of Sister Faustina, unlike the thematic or personal commentary approach of previous biographies, is a chronological presentation. The author has carefully selected passages which most clearly reveal the life and mission of Sister Faustina, and has rearranged them in proper sequence, in so far as possible. The quoted sections are linked together with commentaries based on other sections of the diary and on researched accounts of people who knew her.

Finally, this presentation may help those who want to make a more detailed study of the Diary. For this reason, the author has provided easy references. The numbers in parentheses correspond to the numbers of the paragraphs as found in both the Polish and English editions of the Diary. Just as in the Diary, the words spoken by the Lord are printed in bold print, those of Our Lady, in italics. Diary excerpts, for the most part, are indented.

The words of Sister Faustina and the Lord Jesus, as recorded in the Diary, are quoted extensively, with little or no comment from the author, for they are powerfully effective in themselves.

Jesus told His secretary: **Mankind will not have peace until it turns with trust to My mercy.... My daughter, be diligent in writing down every sentence I tell you concerning My mercy, because this is meant for a great number of souls who will profit from it.**

May this work touch the hearts and spirits of those who read it, fill them with trust, and inspire them to promote this apostolate of The Divine Mercy by word and deed.

THE EARLY YEARS (1905-1925)

Home Life

The servant of God, Sister Mary Faustina of the Blessed Sacrament, known simply as Sister Faustina, was born near the geographical heart of Poland not far from the textile city of Lodz. Within the county of Lodz, in the district of Turek, was an obscure little village of Glogowiec, no longer to be found on a map of Poland. It has become a part of Swinice Warckie.

Stanislaus Kowalski, Sister's father, was born in the village of Swinice on May 6, 1868; her mother, Marianna Babel, in a nearby village of Mniewie, on March 8, 1875. There seems to be no information concerning their childhood years. After their marriage on October 28, 1892, they settled in Glogowiec.

"Glogowiec" comes from the word "glog," a hawthorne berry; or, in a larger sense, weeds or brambles. The hawthorne is a spring shrub or tree of the apple family, noted for its pink and white fragrant flowers. Whether the name describes the village accurately is immaterial; but in God's providence, a "flower" did blossom from the "weeds and brambles" of this humble village. Her message of The Divine Mercy, represented in the Image of Jesus from whose Heart stream forth red and pale rays, is already widely known throughout the world. Now is the time to make the life of the messenger better known.

The village road from Swinice to Glogowiec, a distance of about three kilometers, wound among sandy plains intersected occasionally by forests and clumps of trees. In the poor soil, only potatoes and rye grew with any success. There were also pastures on which cows were allowed to graze, but only after the second haying. Earlier, the cows were confined to the grassy paths between the rows of growing grain or to the grassy lanes that formed the boundaries of the various properties.

A spruce forest dominated the rich tree line. Against this background stood the village itself. Some cottages, with their neat little gardens, lay scattered among the fields. Others were lined up along the road. It was in one of these roadside homes that the Kowalski family resided.

Their home was a typical cottage built of stone with a small admixture of brick. Wooden shingles covered the roof. The building consisted of two rooms separated by a hallway, and a kitchen with an earthen flooring. The house and two barns surrounded a courtyard on three sides.

For nine years the Kowalskis remained childless. But both Marianna and her mother stormed heaven that God would bless the marriage with children. At last, in 1901, their prayers were answered. After three days in labor and a complicated delivery that almost took her life, Marianna gave birth to a girl whom she named Josephine. Two years later another daughter was born, but only after a second complicated delivery. It was little wonder that Marianna became very apprehensive during her third pregnancy. To her surprise, however, the delivery of a third baby girl on August 25, 1905, was without complications. Two days later Father Joseph Chodynski, pastor of the parish church of St. Casimir in Swinice, baptized her "Helena." Her godparents were Marcin Lugowski and Maria Szewczyk Szczepaniak.

After Helen's birth, the subsequent seven births were likewise uncomplicated. With the passage of time, Marianna would say with conviction, "Helenka (diminutive for Helen), that blessed child, she sanctified my womb." Two girls, Casimira and Bronislava died in infancy. The surviving eight children, according to their ages were: Josephine, Genevieve, Helen, Natalie, Stanislaus, Mecislaus, Mary, and Wanda.

The early 1900s were years full of unrest, revolutionary activities and general strikes, but news of these events rarely reached the quiet hamlet of Glogowiec. A farmer like Stanislaus was only concerned with making ends meet. Though he owned about seven acres of arable land and five acres of pasture land, it was hardly enough means to sustain the ever-growing family. Thanks to his skilled hands, however, it was possible for Stanislaus to supplement the family income with carpentry.

Though he did carpentry work during the day, and attended

to his farm work afterwards, often working well into the night, nevertheless, Stanislaus was known to rise very early and begin each day with the singing of the traditional Little Hours of the Immaculate Conception, popularly known as "Godzinki." During the Lenten Season he would substitute them with the Lamentations of the Lord's Passion called "Gorzkie Zale."

When Marianna would try to silence him with, "Stop your singing. You will awaken everyone," he paid no attention to her.

"The first duty is to God," he would sometimes retort, no doubt echoing the sentiment embodied in a popular morning hymn of praise, the "Kiedy Ranne," which also was a part of his daily ritual:

> When the dawn from sleep is winging
> All the earth of Thee is singing
> Of Thee sings the boundless ocean:
> "Praise the Lord of all creation!"
>
> Man endowed beyond all measure,
> With Thy goodness and full treasure,
> Who created and saved by Thee,
> Why should he not also praise Thee!

These practices were characteristic of Stanislaus' personal faith—simple but deep. He himself would never miss Mass on Sunday and the feasts of the Church; and, as was the custom then, he would receive Holy Communion on the feasts of Easter and Christmas and perhaps some of the other major feast days. Later, when age would keep him from going to church, he would hang a watch over his bed so that, in spirit, he could participate in the Sunday Mass that was being celebrated in the church. Stanislaus likewise managed his household according to the commandments of God and of the Church, an age-old Polish heritage. One of his sons who was later the organist of the parish church stated, "As to religion, Father was very demanding of us and of Helen, for which we are now very grateful."

As for discipline, his son Stanley recalled being severely punished as though for a grave transgression when, as a little boy, he broke off an armful of twigs from a neighbor's willow. It is no wonder that the boys were happy that their father's severity was tempered by a mother's understanding love.

According to her sons, Marianna was a courageous, hard-working mother, full of self-denial. She helped her husband as much as possible while bringing up her children. Every day she brought him a hot meal, no matter where he was working. Returning, she invariably carried a load of firewood on her back. Even during winter, with the snow up to her knees, the routine was the same.

Thus, these poor, uneducated but upright parents taught their children by word and example the love of God, obedience and diligence. Helen's whole life was characterized by these virtues.

Very early in life Helenka was taught to say short prayers. As she grew older, she prayed together with the entire family. The attention span of children is ordinarily very short. It is not easy or natural for a child to spend long periods in prayer. Yet Helenka was drawn to commune with heaven at a very early age. An indication of this was a dream that she had when she was only five years old. Her mother recalled that at that time Helenka told the family, "I was walking hand in hand with the Mother of God in a beautiful garden." Many times, even before the age of seven, the child would awaken during the night and sit up in bed. Her mother could see that she was praying. To put an end to such extraordinary zeal she would say to her, "Go back to sleep or you'll lose your mind."

"Oh, no, Mother," Helenka would answer, "my guardian angel must be waking me to pray."

God was already attracting her at this tender age. When she was seven years old, Helenka experienced an invitation from God to a more perfect life. This occurred at Vespers during the exposition of the Most Blessed Sacrament. Later in life she commented, "But I did not always obey the call of grace. I did not know anyone who might have explained these things to me."

When she was approximately nine years old, Helenka was prepared for the sacraments of Confession and Holy Communion by the parish priest, Father Pawlowski. Often the eager child prolonged the time of prayer during the night. Her parents frowned upon this practice which they regarded as being unhealthy. Her mother remembered that before leaving home on her First Holy Communion Day, Helenka kissed the hands of both parents to show her sorrow for having offended them. From then on she went to Confession weekly, and each time would beg her parents' forgiveness and, following an old Polish custom, kiss their hands. This she did even though none of her brothers or sisters imitated her.

Helen helped around the house as soon as she was able to do so, putting things in order, helping in the kitchen; later, she took care of the younger children and encouraged them to be obedient and diligent in the work they were told to do. Mild of character, obedient, quick to help others and anticipate their needs, it is no wonder that Helen became the parents' favorite child.

Having learned from her pastor what her religious duties were, Helen became very serious about keeping holy the Lord's Day and never wanted to miss Holy Mass on Sunday. But the cows had to be pastured and milked even on that day. In order to make it easier for all the members of the family to get to Mass, on one occasion Helen got up very early in the morning, climbed out a bedroom window which she had unlocked the night before, went to the barn, opened the doors, unlocked the gates and led the cows to pasture on the grassy path between the rye. In the meantime, her father checked the open barn and not seeing the cows thought someone had stolen them. Suddenly he heard Helen singing the "Godzinki" with all her heart. There she was, bringing in three cows from the far end of the field. Angered at the thought that the cows must have ruined his crop of rye, he unbuckled his leather belt and held it ready to thrash his daughter for being the cause of such mischief. As he walked towards her, however, he was amazed to see the three cows tied to one rope, the grass on the pathway eaten, but not a blade of rye touched on either side. Awkwardly, he hid the belt behind his back.

"Daddy," she called to him, "may I go to Mass today?" He could not chide, nor could he refuse her. She took the cows to the barn and sang for joy as she began to milk them. She could go to Mass!

"To tend to one cow would have been difficult enough, but to manage three on one rope! That is beyond all belief!" he exclaimed as he later recounted to the family this unforgettable incident.

Helen's brother Stanislaus noted that she would often let the cows graze on the narrow grassy lanes that marked the boundary of their property. The cows likewise did no damage to the neighbors' fields. For this reason and also because she always had something nice and pleasant to say to them, Helen earned the good will and affection of their neighbors.

Whenever it was her turn to take the cows to pasture, Helen had a large following of children who were attracted by her natural goodness. They were an eager audience for the many stories she had to tell. It was her father's love for books and the stories he read to his children from his modest library of religious books (the Bible, magazines about missionaries, and biographies of saints), which provided the source materials for her stories. Later, when Helen was able to read, he turned the task over to her. These were the stories that she later dramatized, with such zeal and deep emotional involvement, that the children would hang on to every word. Often she would tell them that someday she also would leave home to either join the hermits in the forests and live on roots and berries, or become a missionary and teach the faith to pagans. The children were so fired with her enthusiasm that they were ready to follow her anywhere.

Being of a sociable and creative nature, Helen would make things from bits of paper and cloth and then play "store," selling the things she made to her companions. She gave the few pennies earned to help the "poor" children. The animals also received her love and compassion. If a dog fell ill or a chicken was hurt, Helen was quick to aid.

Once the World War began, all of Poland suffered destruction, great famine and poverty. The Kowalski family was almost destitute; they could not afford the proper clothing to attend church. This caused Helen much grief. When she could not go to Mass on Sunday (the girls took turns wearing the one good dress they possessed), she would take her prayerbook and find a suitable hiding place to pray while the Mass was being celebrated in church. If her mother happened to call her to do some chore at that particular time, Helen would not answer her until she felt the Mass was ended. Then she would go to her mother and kiss her hand, saying, "Don't be angry, Mother. I had to fulfill my duty towards God."

According to Regional District School records, Helen began

to attend school in Swinice in 1917, when she was already twelve years old. This was so because schools were closed during the Russian occupation of Poland. As she was already able to read, she was placed in the second grade. Helen was a good student. Her principal remembered with pride that on the day of the inspector's visit she won a prize for her fine recitation of Adam Mickiewicz's poem "Powrot Taty" (The Father's Return). She completed only three terms when in the spring of 1919, all the older students were told to leave school. The authorities decided that room had to be made for the younger children.

During the next two years Helen worked at home. As she carried out her tasks, her mind and heart were preoccupied with other thoughts and desires. She had no inclination to remain at home because another type of life was attracting her. She wanted to serve God exclusively and totally. Although she had no idea of convent life as such, she was certain it existed somewhere and that it was for her. Her desire to pray intensified and she continued her nightly prayerful vigils. When at one time she told her parents that she often saw strange bright lights, they ordered her to stop imagining such things and talking nonsense. She then no longer spoke about her extraordinary experiences but she could not stop thinking about them.

Only once did Helen sadden and anger her father. She was then fourteen. Her eldest sister Josephine had been invited to a party in Swinice, sponsored by some gentlemen farmers. As Mr. Kowalski was very careful regarding social matters, he told Helen to accompany her sister. It was already after midnight when both sisters returned home with one of these young men. Helen's uncle saw them and informed the father, giving him a somewhat exaggerated account of what he had seen. Mr. Kowalski flew into a rage, severely reprimanded and cruelly punished both daughters because of the shame they brought him by staying out so late. They tried in vain to explain. Helen could not forget the fact that her father was forced to deal with his favorite daughter in this fashion. "For this sadness I caused him, I must make up a hundredfold by bringing him honor, not shame," she resolved.

8

Housemaid

In the spring of 1921, the fifteen-year-old Helen said to her mother, "Mom, Daddy works so hard and yet I still have nothing to wear. Of all the girls, I have the worst-looking dress. I should be going out to earn something for myself."

The mother, who had already allowed her two older daughters to go to work as housemaids, thought a moment and then said, "Well then, my child, go in the name of God." It was then that Helen left home and went to work for her neighbor's sister, Mrs. Helen Goryszewska, who lived in Aleksandrow near Lodz.

As a maid, Helen was accommodating, obedient and cheerful at her work. She accomplished all her duties well. Mrs. Goryszewska was particularly pleased with the way she entertained her little son with her gift of story-telling. Before the year was up, however, Helen gave notice that she was leaving. Because she wanted Helen to stay, the unhappy woman asked, "Why are you leaving?"

Helen answered, "I can't tell you why I am leaving, but I can't stay any longer." And with this mysterious reply she gave up her first means of earning money.

What Mrs. Goryszewska did not know was that Helen's prayer life was expanding. She prayed during the day while she worked and often late into the night. She could not sleep due to a strange brightness that kept her awake. Her yearning and longing for God increased. She knew she had to make a decision.

Helen first broke the news to her mother. "Mother, I must enter the convent."

Both parents refused to pay any attention to her pleas. Her father gave the excuse, "I have no money for a dowry (the money and/or wardrobe expected of a person entering religious life) and I still have many unpaid bills."

"Daddy, I don't need any money," she replied. "Jesus Himself will lead me to a convent." But the parents, overly attached to this favorite daughter, remained firm in their refusal to allow her to enter the convent.

It was in the fall of 1922 that a disappointed Helen left home again. This time she went to look for work in Lodz. She lived with her cousins, the Rapackis, but worked for three women who belonged to the Third Order of St. Francis. Although her pay was modest she was content because they allowed her to attend Mass daily and visit the dying people in that vicinity. Strange requests from a seventeen-year-old girl! She also asked to be a penitent of their confessor, Father Wyzykowski. Her uncle, Michael Rapacki, aware of her desire to be a religious, teased her about it continually but she would not be sidetracked. Her firm and steadfast reply always was, "I will go and serve God because that is what I resolved to do since my childhood and that I will do."

Despite the advantageous arrangement, Helen decided to look for work elsewhere. In the meantime, thoughts of consecrating herself totally to God persisted as an inner voice kept urging her to "leave the world and go to the convent." Helen went home and again begged for permission to enter the convent. Still her parents refused. Broken in spirit, Helen now decided to abandon the spiritual life and began "to live a distracted, worldly life," as she called it. She tried not to pay attention to the promptings of God's grace and even made attempts to suppress them by indulging in such pleasures as caring more for her outward appearance, buying fashionable clothing and going to dances with her girl friends. Yet none of this activity made her happy or gave her satisfaction of soul.

With the help of an employment agency, Helen found a position in the home of Mrs. Marcianna Sadowska in Lodz. She began work on February 2, 1923. Mrs. Sadowska remembered that day because she later recounted, "Helen came to me so fashionably dressed that I hesitated to hire her as a maid. I purposely lowered the amount of salary so that she would go away, but Helen accepted my proposition."

Mrs. Sadowska, busy with her grocery store, was happy with her new maid and babysitter. She too perceived in Helen a talent for taking care of children. In the evenings, the maid would seat the three small children near herself, telling them such interesting stories that she had them totally absorbed. At other times the children would burst into laughter, with Helen joining in. Mrs. Sadowska found Helen to be very reliable; so whenever she had to take a trip, she was at peace because she knew that Helen would do the housework better than she herself could do it. Sometimes they would go shopping together. Helen would always want to carry the shopping bag. Seeing how exhausted the young girl was from fasting, Mrs. Sadowska tried, unsuccessfully, to take the bag from her.

Mrs. Sadowska could not help but notice that Helen abstained from meat every Wednesday, Friday and Saturday. During Lent, she ate no meat at all, and also abstained from dairy products on those three days.

One day, Helen's sister Josephine, now Mrs. Jasinska, came to visit her. Mrs. Sadowska suggested to Helen to treat her sister with a snack, so she ran to the store and returned with a honeybun. "Helen, why didn't you get some meat?" asked Mrs. Sadowska.

"Not today, Mrs. Sadowska. It's a fast day," Helen replied.

Mrs. Sadowska turned to Mrs. Jasinska saying, "What kind of people are you and how were you brought up that you fast so strictly? Helen won't touch any meat during all of Lent."

"That's how it is with us," answered Mrs. Jasinska. "That's how our father brought us up."

According to Mrs. Sadowska, Helen was always devout, prayerful and a regular participant in the services in the cathedral. But she also noted that Helen was of such good humor and so witty that she easily could have become a professional comedienne. Her goodness, helpfulness and joyous laughter made her a very lovable person.

Without sharing her future plans with her employer, Helen left her position on July 1, 1924. "She would have left sooner," said Mrs. Sadowska, "but she was so good and caring. I knew she waited until my baby was born."

The Call

Shortly after leaving Mrs. Sadowska, Helen attended a dance with her sister Josephine. Although everyone was having a good time, Helen was beset with great torment. As she began to dance, she had the following mystical experience. Suddenly she saw Jesus standing next to her. He was stripped of His clothing and covered with wounds. Jesus glanced at her reproachfully and said to her, **How long shall I put up with you and how long will**

you keep putting Me off? (Diary 9) At that moment she no longer heard the pleasant music; she saw no one around her. She was alone with Jesus. She walked off the dance floor, went to sit beside her sister, and pretended that the abrupt change in her was due to a headache. Then she slipped away from the dance hall unnoticed and directed her steps toward the Cathedral of St. Stanislaus Kostka. It was already dusk. Only a few people were in the church. Unaware of everyone around her, Helen prostrated herself before the tabernacle. From the depths of her anguished soul she implored the Lord to enlighten her as to what was His will and what her next step should be. Suddenly she heard the words: **Go at once to Warsaw; you will enter a convent there.** (10)

She arose from her prayers and went to pack her belongings. In the morning she went to say good-bye to her sister and then returned to her uncles' home and said to him, "I am going to Warsaw to enter a convent."

"My God, Helen! What are you doing!" her uncle cried out. "You know that this will make your dear mother and father very sad and break their hearts!"

Helen answered, "Well then, Uncle, tell them nothing now. When you do get to visit them later, give them these clothes."

"And what will you have?" he asked.

"What I am wearing is enough. Jesus will take care of all my needs," she replied.

Helen left for Warsaw with only the set of clothes she was wearing. Her uncle took her to the train station. She was courageous until she sat down in her compartment. Then came the tears. "Mother will say I ran away from home when she finds out about this," she sighed. It made her sad for she knew that her action would hurt her parents, but she felt more deeply the need to be obedient to Him whom she had come to love so much ever since the time she was a small child of seven.

It was already late afternoon when the train arrived in Warsaw. As she stepped into the milling crowd at the railroad station she suddenly was terror-stricken. What should she do? Where should she go? She knew no one in Warsaw. In her dejection she prayed to the Mother of God, "Mary, lead me, guide me." (11)

At once she heard, in the depths of her soul, that she should ride out beyond the city to a nearby village where she would find safe lodging. Helen obeyed and found everything just as the Mother of God had told her.

Early next morning she returned to the city and entered the first church she saw. It was the Church of St. James in the suburb Ochota. She knelt down and began to pray that God would reveal His will to her. The Holy Sacrifice of the Mass was being celebrated by one priest after another. During one of these Masses she heard the words, **Go to that priest and tell him everything; he will tell you what to do next.** (12) After Mass she went to the sacristy, told the priest all that had transpired in her soul and asked him to advise her as to which convent to enter.

At first, the priest was astonished; but then he told her to really trust and await further direction from God. "For the time being," he said, handing her a note, "I shall send you to a pious lady with whom you will stay until you enter the convent." (13)

Thus, during that summer of 1924, the Reverend Canon James Dabrowski, pastor of St. James Church in Warsaw, sent Helen to Mrs. Aldona Lipszyc. As a good friend of her husband, Father Dabrowski knew that Mrs. Lipszyc, who had four children, was looking for a maid. The Lipszyc family lived in Ostrowek, not far from Warsaw. Helen arrived there with the note from the Reverend Canon Dabrowski on which was written, "I do not know her, but I hope she will qualify."

Mrs. Lipszyc took a liking to Helen who impressed her as being a healthy, good-natured and cheerful person. She noted that all of Helen's possessions were tied in her kerchief; so, for a start, she gave her a dress and some other clothing. Helen explained to her that she left home because she wanted to become a religious and as soon as she made enough money for her dowry she intended to enter a convent.

Helen's love for children was again quite evident. She enjoyed being with them. When the children wanted to masquerade she too would dress up and play with them. This family also recalled her happy, healthy laughter.

Depending upon the advice and directions of Mrs. Lipszyc, Helen began to knock on one convent door after another in the big and "terrifying" city of Warsaw. Her somewhat neglected appearance, her lack of education, her extreme poverty, and present occupation as a maid must have been the reason why she met with refusal at each convent where she applied. "We do not accept maids here," they would say.

Heartbroken, Helen called to the Lord Jesus, "Help me. Don't leave me alone." One day Helen came to the convent of the Sisters of Our Lady of Mercy at 3/9 Zytnia Street. With trepidation gripping her heart, she stood before the door of the austere-looking building. She knocked. The portress leaned out and asked, "What do you want, my child?" (See 13)

"I wish to enter the convent," Helen replied.

"Come in and wait here. I will call the Mother Superior."

After a while, Mother Michael Moraczewska entered the room. Unknown to Helen, the superior was observing her from the doorway and also unimpressed by her appearance intended to send her away immediately after she had heard her petition for entrance. However, she decided it would be more charitable to ask the girl a few general questions before sending her away. In the course of the conversation, Mother Michael noticed that the candidate did have some merit: a pleasing smile, a likeable countenance, much simplicity and sincerity; and her speech revealed much common sense. Mother decided to accept her.

It is interesting to note that Helen recalled something entirely different of that first meeting. She wrote later in her Diary:

> When Mother Superior, the present Mother General Michael, came out to meet me, she told me after a short conversation to go to the Lord of the house and ask whether He would accept me. I understood at once that I was to ask this of the Lord Jesus. With great joy, I went to the chapel and asked Jesus: "Lord of this house, do You accept me? This is how one of these sisters told me to put the question to You." Immediately I heard this voice: **I do accept; you are in My Heart.** When I returned from the chapel, Mother Superior asked first of all, "Well, has the Lord accepted you?" I answered, "Yes." "If the Lord has accepted, [she said] then I also will accept." (14)

Helen's poverty proved to be a major obstacle to her entry. She had no dowry. The Holy See easily could dispense her from that, but she needed a wardrobe, and the community had no funds set aside for that purpose. Mother suggested, therefore, that Helen continue to work and set aside a few hundred zlotys for a wardrobe. The new candidate was very pleased with this idea. It was agreed that periodically she would bring her saved money to the convent for safekeeping. The interview over, Mother Michael said good-bye and forgot all about that encounter. Helen returned to the home of Mrs. Lipszyc and continued her work as a maid in order to earn the required sum.

A few months later, while on a visit to the congregation's house in Vilnius, Mother Michael was quite surprised when she received a letter in which it was stated that a certain young lady brought sixty zlotys "for safekeeping, as agreed." After searching her memory Mother Michael did recall what it was all about. From then on, Helen's deposit kept increasing, and within a year she had turned in the required sum.

Two particular situations challenged her during this time. The first was caused by her employer, Mrs. Lipszyc, who liked the pleasant, freckle-faced redhead with such a happy, healthy outlook on life. This kind woman, not understanding the happiness of religious life, began to make marriage plans for her maid. Had she paid attention to the themes of the songs and hymns her maid liked to sing, she would have realized that marriage was out of the question for her. Of course, she did not know that Helen had already made a major decision that would influence her life. It happened at Vespers during the Octave of Corpus Christi, June 25, 1925. When she turned to God with all the longing of her soul, He filled her with an interior light of a deeper knowledge of Himself as Supreme Goodness and Supreme Beauty. She experienced the depth of God's love for her from all eternity. Using simple words, from her inmost being, Helen made a vow of perpetual chastity. (See 16) It was no wonder that her favorite hymn at this time was "The Hidden Jesus" ("Jezusa Ukrytego"):

> Jesus hidden in the Blessed Sacrament
> Him I must adore;
> Renounce everything for His sake,
> Live only by His love.

The other challenging situation for Helen arose when her sister Genevieve came to visit her. Though Helen never again returned home, she did write her parents from Warsaw, disclosing the fact that she would be admitted to the convent after she had earned enough money for a wardrobe. Genevieve was sent by her parents to try to dissuade Helen from entering the convent and to persuade her to return home with her. When Genevieve realized how firm Helen was in her decision to enter the convent, she relented in her persuasions. After spending the night in Warsaw, Genevieve returned home to Glogowiec. It was a sad moment for her parents when they saw her returning home without Helen.

All obstacles out of the way, Helen Kowalska finally entered the convent on the eve of the Feast of Our Lady of the Angels, August 1, 1925. Several years later, she wrote of this moment in her Diary, "I felt immensely happy; it seemed to me that I had stepped into the life of Paradise. A single prayer was bursting forth from my heart, one of thanksgiving." (17)

THE NOVITIATE YEARS (1925-1928)

Postulancy (1925-1926)

The Congregation of the Sisters of Our Lady of Mercy, to which Helen Kowalska was accepted, took its roots from Laval, France, where it was founded by Teresa Rondeau in 1818. The spirit of this Congregation was brought to Polish soil by Ewa (Sulkowska) Countess Potocka in 1862. The chief aim of the Congregation was, and still is, the imitation of Christ in His mercy towards all types of spiritual misery of humanity; the special goal, the rehabilitation of wayward women and girls; the characteristic trait, a special devotion to Mary, Mother of Mercy, patroness of the entire Congregation, and to the Mercy of God, the inspiration of its apostolic work.

Until 1962, the Congregation consisted of two groups of sisters—the Directresses and the Co-adjutors. Instructing and training the women and girls in a Christian spirit was the work of the Directresses. The Co-adjutors helped them by performing the household chores, and by their prayers, sacrifices and mortifications. Helen was accepted into this latter group.

Helen spent only three weeks with the Sisters when she experienced a strong temptation to leave the community. Her appraisal that too little time was devoted to prayer, combined with other conditions she disliked, led her to consider entering a more austere congregation. One night she resolved to tell the Mother Superior of her decision to leave, but God so arranged things that she could not get to see her.

Because the main chapel was a separate building some distance from the sisters' residence, the Blessed Sacrament was reserved in a small room in the house where the sisters lived. They referred to this room as "the little chapel." Before going to bed that night, Helen went to the little chapel to pray for God's guidance and enlightenment. She received none. Instead, a strange uneasiness, which she could not understand, enveloped her. In spite of that, she made up her mind to approach Mother Superior the next morning, immediately after Mass, to tell her of her decision.

The sisters were all in their beds, the lights were out. Full of anguish and discontent, she entered the dormitory. Not knowing what to do or where to turn, she threw herself face down on the floor. She begged God to help her recognize His will. As she prayed, a brightness filled her sleeping area. On one of the curtains which served as a partition between beds in the dormitory, she saw the deeply sorrowful Face of Jesus. There were open wounds on His Face and large tears were falling on her white bedspread. Not knowing what all this meant, she asked the Lord, "Jesus, who has hurt You so?"

And Jesus answered, **It is you who will cause Me this pain if you leave this convent. It is to this place that I called you and nowhere else; and I have prepared many graces for you.** (19) Deeply moved, Helen begged pardon of the Lord and resolved to remain where she was.

The next day Helen went to confession and related to the confessor all that had taken place. He told her that evidently it was God's will that she remain in this congregation and that she had no right to even think of leaving to another. Hearing this, she felt happy and at peace about the matter.

As a postulant, Helen became acquainted with the spiritual exercises and the duties that she would be called upon to perform as a future member of the congregation. She was assigned to kitchen duty; her other task was to clean the room of Mother Jane Barkiewicz, and to take care of her during any illness. Mother Jane had, for many years, been a superior and even Vicar General, of the Congregation. As Directress of Postulants, this elderly and experienced religious carefully observed the conduct of the newest members. Of Helen she said briefly and to the point, "Helen is an interior soul."

Due to her inner conflicts, intense spiritual zeal, and change of life-style, Helen's health began to decline. The Superior, alarmed by her complete exhaustion, sent her for a rest, in the company of two other sisters, to Skolimow. It was a rented summer home for the sisters who were living in Warsaw and for the girls in their charge. Helen's duty was to prepare the meals for the three of them.

While there, Helen asked the Lord for whom else she should pray. Jesus told her that on the following night He would let her know. It was then that Helen had the first mystical vision revealing the condition of the souls in Purgatory. When she was told to write her Diary, she recorded this incident as follows:

> I saw my Guardian Angel who ordered me to follow him. In a moment I was in a misty place full of fire in which there was a great crowd of suffering souls. They were praying fervently, but to no avail, for themselves; only we can come to their aid. The flames which were burning them did not touch me at all. My Guardian Angel did not leave me for an instant. I asked these souls what their greatest suffering was. They answered me in one voice that their greatest torment was longing for God. I saw Our Lady visiting the souls in Purgatory. The souls call her "The Star of the Sea." She brings them refreshment. I wanted to talk with them some more but my Guardian Angel beckoned me to leave. We went out of that prison of suffering. [I heard an interior voice] which said, **My Mercy does not want this but justice demands it.** Since that time, I am in closer communion with the suffering souls. (20)

Novitiate (1926-1928)

The Congregation of the Sisters of Our Lady of Mercy maintains a huge educational institution for wayward girls at Lagiewniki, a part of Cracow. It was founded in 1890 by the Reverend Alexander Lubomirski. The large buildings with the surrounding orchards and gardens were placed under the patronage of St. Joseph, and the sisters referred to it simply as "Joseph's Place." This was also the site of the novitiate in which future members of the Sisters of Our Lady of Mercy received thorough training in the religious life which they intended to embrace voluntarily until death.

Helen and her companion candidates completed the remaining three months of their postulancy here, and then made an eight-day retreat in preparation for entrance to the novitiate.

The ceremony of receiving the habit and the veil took place on April 30, 1926. It was already on this occasion that God revealed to Helen the extent of her future sufferings. In an instant she was given to understand to what she was committing herself. The piercing suffering of this revelation lasted but a moment. Then God filled her soul again with great consolation.

Sister Clemens Buczek, who was chosen to assist Helen at this ceremony, remembered that when she was telling her "to hurry and put on the habit," Helen seemed to have fainted. Sister immediately ran for the smelling salts. Later, Sister Clemens admitted that she used this incident to tease Helen no end about her "loathing to leave the world." Only after Helen's death did she learn that this incident was more than just a fainting spell. (See 22)

With the reception of the habit and the white veil, the sisters were given a new name to symbolize the beginning of a new life. From that moment Helen Kowalska was known as Sister Mary Faustina or, simply, as Sister Faustina. The name Faustina means the fortunate, happy, or blessed one.

To this day, in the Congregation of the Sisters of Our Lady of Mercy, the novitiate period lasts two years. During the first year, called canonical, the novice has the opportunity to deepen her spiritual life by meditation and other religious practices, and to study the rules of convent life, the Constitutions, as well as the meaning of the vows and the practice of the virtues, especially the virtue of humility. The novices also study the fundamentals of the faith so that they will know them well enough to impart them to others. During this time the novices may not attend school for formal study, nor may they have any excessively absorbing duty.

During the second year of novitiate, the novices may take up studies, or work under the direction of a professed sister, in addition to performing their religious and spiritual exercises. If this trial period proves satisfactory to the Congregation and the novice, she will be admitted to the profession of vows, which will bind her for one year. She would renew them annually for five years before being admitted to perpetual profession.

For about two months, Sister Faustina's Directress of

Novices was Sister Margaret Gimbutt, an exemplary woman: meek, humble, prayerful, full of the spirit of sacrifice and self-denial. On June 20, 1926, however, she was replaced by Sister Mary Joseph Brzoza. The new Directress of Novices had been sent to Laval, France, to observe the formation of novices and to absorb the spirit of the Congregation while there. She, too, was an exemplary Directress and, providentially, a great discerner of souls. She was demanding, but also full of motherly care and good will towards the novices.

A few vignettes gathered from this period of Sister Faustina's life reveal some aspects of her special character, already noticed at that early stage in her life as a religious. Sister Regina Jaworska, who lived with Sister Faustina in the novitiate for a year and a half, recalled that the sisters loved to be in her company. Jokingly, they called her their "lawyer" because she would use hand gestures to enhance her talks. God was ever the theme of her conversations. Her demeanor at prayer evoked a greater reverence for the majesty of God in the rest of the novices.

Sister Regina worked with Sister Faustina in the kitchen where they prepared meals for the girls in the institute. Often they both worked long and hard in the cellar where the food was stored. While they worked, they prayed aloud, or, with permission, conversed about spiritual matters. One day Sister Faustina abruptly stopped talking and walked out. She went to the Mother Directress because she remembered that she had not asked for the necessary permission.

Sister Placida also worked in the kitchen with Sister Faustina. When the sister-in-charge became ill, Sister Placida debated as to who should take charge. She remembered that Sister Faustina immediately gave way, saying, "Sister dear, let's not lose holy peace over such things. Let us work to satisfy Jesus."

The same Sister Placida admitted that during recreation she liked to be near Sister Faustina, who always had something uplifting to say. In fact, the novices would joke among themselves saying, "Let us go to our theologian." She often talked to them about the virtues of faith, hope and love, or about the souls in purgatory, encouraging them to pray for the poor souls. Recreation periods were very happy times for Sister Faustina, especially when they took place out of doors. Delighted by the beauties of nature she would often lift her hands to heaven and call out loudly, "O infinitely good God, how marvelous are Your works!"

During one such recreation period, while Sister Faustina was admiring some insects near the pond and was leaning over the water, Sister Placida threw a stone into the water close to her. Sister Faustina's face and veil were splattered with mud. The Directress saw this and ordered Sister Placida to exchange her veil for Sister Faustina's soiled one. Sister Faustina begged the Mother Directress to ignore the incident. When the Mother refused to respond to her plea to retract the order, Sister Faustina calmly told Sister Placida, "I will pray for you to accept this trial for the sake of Jesus who knows how much it is costing you."

Sister Faustina was assigned to the kitchen during her novitiate. This upset her very much because the pots used in the kitchen were very large and she was unable to manage them. The most difficult task for her was to drain the big pot of potatoes. In the process, she would sometimes spill half the contents. When she spoke to Mother Directress about it, she was told that with time she would acquire the necessary skill. The task, however, did not become any easier because she was getting weaker with each passing day. So she began to avoid that work. It didn't escape the sisters' notice! They could not have known that, in spite of all her willingness to do the work without sparing herself, she found herself unable to do it. One day at noon, during the examination of conscience, Sister Faustina complained to the Lord about her weakness. She heard these words in her soul: **From today on you will do this easily; I shall strengthen you.**

That evening, trusting in God's words, she hurried to get to the pot first. She picked it up with ease and poured off the water perfectly. When she lifted the lid to let the steam escape, instead of potatoes she saw bunches of roses, beautiful beyond description. Never before had she seen such roses! As she stood there, astonished by this vision and trying to understand its meaning, she heard a voice within her saying, **I change such hard work of yours into bouquets of most beautiful flowers, and their perfume rises up to My throne.** From then on she was eager to drain the potatoes, not only during the week assigned to her but also during the weeks assigned to the other sisters. Because she understood how pleasing this was to God, she willingly went to the aid of the sisters in this work and in every difficult task. (65)

The fruit of this lesson endured. In January of 1937, when she was already gravely ill, she wrote a prayer which reflected what already was a part of her general practice of mercy. The following is an excerpt of it:

> Help me, O Lord, that my hands may be merciful and filled with good deeds, so that I may do only good to my neighbors and take upon myself the more difficult and toilsome tasks.
>
> Help me, that my feet may be merciful, so that I may hurry to assist my neighbor, overcoming my own fatigue and weariness. My true rest is in the service of my neighbor. (163)

"Darkness"

Towards the end of the first year of novitiate, Sister Faustina began to experience the trial of the soul known as the "Dark Night." This lasted six months. During this time she found no joy and no consolation in prayer; meditation became virtually impossible; fear enveloped her. Looking deeper into her own being she saw nothing but great misery and, at the same time, she understood the great holiness of God so clearly that she dared not lift her eyes to Him. Falling into the dust at His feet, she continually begged for mercy. Even the encouragement of the Mother Directress during this difficult period proved unsuccessful. Her sufferings continued.

Then there arose some interior difficulties linked to some exterior problems. Sister did not explain what they were; but as they grew steadily worse, she found she was unable to cope with them and did not know how she could go on living. She made many novenas to various saints but the situation grew more difficult. Suddenly the thought occurred to her to pray to St. Therese of the Child Jesus. Before her entrance to the convent, Sister Faustina had had a great devotion to her, but for some reason had grown somewhat negligent in it. On the fifth day of the novena St. Therese appeared to her in a dream, but as if she were still living in the world. She concealed from Sister the fact that she was a saint and began to comfort her, saying, "Do not be worried about this matter, but trust more in God. I suffered greatly, too."

Sister Faustina, who did not believe her, replied, "It seems to me that you have not suffered at all."

But St. Therese convinced her that she had suffered much. She then said, "Sister, know that in three days the difficulty will come to a happy conclusion." Because Sister Faustina still refused to believe her, St. Therese revealed herself to her as a saint. The ending of this encounter is taken directly from her diary:

> ... At that moment, a great joy filled my soul, and I said to her, "You are a saint?" "Yes," she answered, "I am a saint. Trust that this matter will be resolved in three days." And I said, "Dear sweet Therese, tell me, shall I go to heaven?" She answered, "Yes, you will go to heaven, Sister." "And will I be a saint?" To which she replied, "Yes, you will be a saint." "But, little Therese, shall I be a saint as you are, raised to the altar?" And she answered, "Yes, you will be a saint just as I am, but you must trust in the Lord Jesus." I then asked her if my mother and father would go to heaven... And she replied that they would. I further asked, "And will my brothers and sisters go to heaven?" She told me to pray hard for them, but gave me no definite answer. I understood that they were in need of much prayer.
>
> This was a dream. And as the proverb goes, dreams are phantoms; God is faith. Nevertheless, three days later the difficulty was solved very easily, just as she had said. And everything in this affair turned out exactly as she said it would. It was a dream, but it had its significance. (150)

The second year of Sister Faustina's novitiate was fast approaching. Just the thought that she was to take the vows made her shudder. How could she make her profession of vows? She found it difficult to understand what she was reading, she could not meditate. It seemed to her that God was displeased with her prayer life. Her soul was in anguish.

One day just as she was placing herself in the presence of

God, there came the overpowering thought that God had rejected her. Despair flooded her soul. She experienced the torture suffered by the damned. Throughout the morning she fought the complete darkness of soul as best she could. In the afternoon she was seized by such deadly fears that she was completely physically exhausted. She remained helpless for three quarters of an hour. Fortunately, one of the sisters came to her cell. Finding her in such a strange condition the sister immediately went to inform the Directress.

Mother Directress went to her at once. As soon as she entered the cell she said, "In the name of holy obedience get up from the ground." Sister Faustina felt that some force immediately raised her up from the ground; she stood up. With kind words the Directress began to explain to her that this was a trial sent to her by God. "Have great confidence; God is always our Father, even when he sends us trials," she told her.

When she began to agonize again during the evening service, Sister Faustina prayed, "Jesus, who in the Gospel compare Yourself to a most tender mother, I trust in Your words because You are Truth and Life. In spite of everything, Jesus, I trust in You in the face of every interior sentiment which sets itself against hope. Do what You want with me; I will never leave You, because You are the source of my life." That night the Mother of God visited her, holding the Infant Jesus in her arms. Strength and great courage sprang up anew, but only for a day. It seemed to her that these spiritual torments would be her lot for the rest of her life. (See 24, 25)

The days of her novitiate were coming to an end but Sister Faustina's sufferings did not diminish; rather, they brought about physical weakness. Mother Directress dispensed her from all common spiritual exercises and told her to substitute them with brief exclamatory prayers.

On Good Friday, which in 1928 occurred on April 16, Sister wrote:

> ... Jesus catches up my heart into the very flame of His love. This was during my evening adoration. All of a sudden, the Divine Presence invaded me, and I forgot everything else. Jesus gave me to understand how much He had suffered for me. This lasted a very short time. An intense yearning—a

longing to love God. (26)

On April 30, 1928, Sister Faustina and her companions made the profession of simple vows for one year. On this day she expressed to the Lord her desire to empty herself for His sake by an active love, but a love that would be imperceptible even to the sisters closest to her.

She did not know then that her prayer was acceptable to the Lord. The darkness of soul persisted for another six months. Faustina had no spiritual director to guide her, and the lack of help from her confessors added to her agony. These priests tried to comfort her by saying that she was more pleasing to God in this present state than she would be if she were abounding in great consolations. However, they failed to help her realize that this state of soul conformed to one of the stages in the spiritual life which saintly souls experience on their journey to God, and so the dark night continued.

After her first profession Sister Faustina remained in the novitiate house at Lagiewniki until the end of October. Meanwhile, at the General Chapter of the Congregation, held from October 6 to 10, 1928, Mother Michael Moraczewska, the Mother who admitted Sister Faustina, was elected Superior General. As major superior throughout Sister Faustina's lifetime, Mother Michael was her chief support and source of consolation.

THE YEARS OF
TEMPORARY PROFESSION (1928-1932)

Warsaw

On October 31, 1928, Sister Faustina arrived in Warsaw, at the same convent where she was a postulant, eager to begin work in her new assignment—kitchen duty. However, her health soon began to fail. Despite the kind and solicitous care of her superiors and the medical treatments she received, Sister's condition remained unchanged. While confined to the infirmary for about a month, she suffered much unpleasantness on the part of some of the sisters and found refuge only in contemplating the sufferings of Jesus in His sorrowful passion. She then wrote: "When the Lord Himself wants to be close to a soul and to lead it, He will remove everything that is external... The superiors were indeed very solicitous for the sick, but the Lord ordained that I should feel forsaken."

One day Mother Michael herself told Sister Faustina, "Sister, along your path, sufferings just spring up out of the ground. I look upon you, Sister, as one crucified. But I can see that Jesus has some business in this. Be faithful to the Lord." (149)

Rumors that she was only pretending to be ill reached the ears of Sister Faustina. These rumors persisted for a long time and were the cause of much suffering. She complained to Jesus that she was a burden to the sisters. Jesus told her, **You are not living for yourself but for souls, and other souls will profit from your sufferings. Your prolonged suffering will give them the light and strength to accept My will.** (67)

When one of the elderly sisters learned of Sister Faustina's close relationship with Jesus, she bluntly told her that she must be deluding herself because God associates in such a manner only with saints and not with sinners like herself. It is no wonder then that this young sister began to somewhat disbelieve Jesus. During her morning talk with Him she once asked Him, "Jesus, are You not an illusion?"

He answered, **My love deceives no one.** (29)

As people began to sow doubts in her soul, she became more frightened; she thought herself to be an ignorant person, without knowledge of many things, let alone things spiritual. When these doubts increased, Sister Faustina sought light and counsel from her confessor or superiors, yet she never seemed to derive any satisfaction from them.

One superior in particular seemed to understand her soul and the road God intended for her. When Faustina followed her advice, she made quick progress towards perfection. But this did not last long. When she opened her soul more completely, the superior thought such graces were improbable and was no longer able to help her. "It is impossible that God should commune with His creatures in such a way," her superior told her. "I fear for you, Sister; isn't this an illusion of some sort? You'd better go and seek the advice of a priest."

But the confessor likewise did not understand her and said, "You'd better go, Sister, and talk about these matters to your superiors." And so she went from the superiors to the confessor and back again, and found no peace. The Lord's grace became for her a source of great suffering.

More and more she would tell the Lord, "Jesus, I am afraid of You; could You not be some kind of a phantasm?" Even though Jesus kept reassuring her, she remained ever diffident. It was a strange thing: the more distrustful she became, the more proofs Jesus gave her that these things were His doing.

Sister Faustina continued to endure many sufferings because her advanced spiritual experiences were being misunderstood by superiors and sisters alike. For quite a long time she was regarded as one obsessed by an evil spirit. She was looked upon with pity, and the superior even took certain precautions concerning her. When it reached her ears that even her fellow sisters regarded her as being possessed, she became increasingly pessimistic.

Whenever she tried to shun God's graces, she found it was

beyond her power to do so completely. In spite of herself she would be suddenly enraptured and immersed in God and completely dependent upon the Lord. (See 122-123)

"Pray for Poland"

As with St. Catherine of Siena, St. Joan of Arc, and others, so also Sister Faustina's spiritual experiences appear to intimate that the lives of holy people are closely bound with the lands of their origin. She often heard Jesus and his Mother Mary telling her to pray for her native land, Poland. On one occasion, Jesus told her to ask the Mother Superior for permission to make an hour's adoration daily for nine days and during this adoration to unite her prayers with those of His Mother. **Pray with all your heart in union with Mary, and try also during this time to make the Way of the Cross,** He told her. She did not receive permission for the whole hour but for as much time as she could spare over and above her duties. The novena was to be offered for her country. On the seventh day she had a vision of the Mother of God clothed in a bright robe, standing between heaven and earth, praying with her hands folded on her bosom and gazing towards heaven. From her heart issued forth fiery rays, some pointing towards the heavens, others enveloping her native land. (See 32-33)

At another time Jesus told Sister Faustina that He would punish the most beautiful city in Poland with the kind of punishment that had fallen on Sodom and Gomorrah. As Sister witnessed in a vision the greatness of God's wrath, a shudder pierced her heart. She prayed in silence. After a few moments Jesus said to her, **My child, unite yourself closely to Me during the Sacrifice and offer My Blood and My Wounds to My Father in expiation for the sins of that city. Repeat this without interruption throughout the entire Holy Mass. Do this for seven days.** On the seventh day she saw Jesus in a bright cloud and she began to implore Him to look graciously upon her city and country. Jesus gave her a benign look. When she saw His kindness she begged Him for a blessing. He said, **For your sake I bless the entire country.** And He traced the sign of the cross over the whole country of Poland. Her heart leaped with joy at the goodness of God. From then on, she prayed daily for her beloved country with even greater fervor. (See 39)

New Assignments

On February 21, 1929, Sister Faustina was sent to Vilnius to replace Sister Petronela who returned to Warsaw for her Third Probation (a time of preparation before the taking of perpetual vows). Sister's duty was a two-month assignment in the kitchen. The Mother Superior, Sister Irene Krzyzanowska, did not know then that she would be seeing more of Sister Faustina in the future.

Sister Faustina returned to Zytnia Street in Warsaw on April 11. But in June, she was again assigned to work in the kitchen in "Jozefinek," at 44 Hetmanska Street, in Grochow, a section of Warsaw. This newly-formed home was under the administration of the superior on Zytnia Street.

Then in July, after only a few weeks, Sister Faustina was sent to another one of their homes in Kiekrz near Poznan, to replace the sickly Sister Modesta Rzeczkowska. There she worked in the kitchen until October. When she returned to Grochow she was put in charge of the garden. Her attitude toward the girls who helped her with the work must have been very positive for when they learned that Sister Faustina was to return to Zytnia Street, they threatened to pack up their belongings and go with her.

"Why such frequent changes?" one might ask. Some sisters were of the opinion that she liked them. However, Sister Faustina confided to one of the sisters that these frequent changes were difficult for her, but that she would never resist them because she saw in them the Will of God. Mother Michael, the Superior General, later remarked that the only one she could reassign, without a fuss being made, was Sister Faustina.

Soon after her return to Warsaw, Sister Faustina again suffered physical ailments which continued to school her in patience. Only Jesus knew what great efforts of will she exerted in order to fulfill her duties. There were about 200 girls to feed, besides the sisters. Often, her best intentions were misinterpreted by the sisters. Because she tried to be more recollected and faithful to God they shunned her. This type of suffering was most painful. In addition, there was one thing she could not understand: Why was it that Jesus ordered her to report everything to her superiors, but her superiors would not believe what she said and treated her with pity as one being deluded or imagining things? (See 38)

Untarnished Chastity

In between reassignments, at the end of April, 1929, Jesus told Sister Faustina that he was giving her eternal love so that her chastity would remain untarnished; and as proof that she would never have temptations of the flesh, He took off His gold belt and tied it around her waist. This happened before Holy Communion just as the sisters were renewing their vows. From then on she had no temptations against chastity in heart or mind. She later understood that this was an exceptional grace, and that she had received it through the intercession of Our Lady because for years she had been begging Her for it. As a result, Sister's devotion to the Mother of God intensified. (See 40)

Assignment to Plock

Sister Faustina was sent to Plock sometime in May or June of 1930. At that time Plock was a quiet, sleepy, middle-sized city. The rich collection of books, preserved in the Zielinski and Seminary Libraries, attests to the fact that in the past it was a powerful and significant city. At the end of Piekarska Street near the Old Market Square stood the congregation's Guardian Angel Home.

At first, Sister Faustina was assigned to work in the kitchen. The work was beyond her strength and after a few months it was evident that she was simply unable to endure the great exertion. She was, therefore, sent to the sisters' rest home in the country at Biala, a village about ten kilometers from Plock. Here she spent the remaining months of the year 1930. As soon as she felt better, she returned to undertake her laborious duties. This time she worked in the bakery and store. Her work was tiring and distracting but she resolved: "I will not allow myself to be so absorbed in the whirlwind of work as to forget about God. I will spend all my free moments at the feet of the Master hidden in the Blessed Sacrament. He has been tutoring me from my most tender years" (82). Now, more than ever, she felt she needed His strength and guidance.

Revelation of the Image of The Divine Mercy

On February 22, 1931, Sister Faustina received the first of many revelations pertaining to her mission in life: to be the confidante, secretary, and messenger of The Divine Mercy to all humankind. She described the event as follows:

> In the evening, when I was in my cell, I saw the Lord Jesus clad in a white garment. One hand [was] raised in the gesture of blessing, the other was touching the garment at the breast. From beneath the garment, slightly drawn aside at the breast, there were emanating two large rays, one red, other the pale. In silence I kept my gaze fixed on the Lord, my soul was struck with awe, but also with great joy. After a while, Jesus said to me, **Paint an image according to the pattern you see, with the signature: Jesus, I Trust in You. I desire that this image be venerated, first in your chapel, and [then] throughout the entire world.**
>
> **I promise that the soul that will venerate this image will not perish. I also promise victory over [its] enemies already here on earth, especially at the hour of death. I Myself will defend it as My own glory.**
>
> When I told this to my confessor, I received this for a reply: "That refers to your soul." He told me, "Certainly, paint God's image in your soul." When I came out of the confessional, I again heard words such as these: **My image already is in your soul. I desire that there to be a Feast of Mercy. I want this image, which you will paint with a brush, to be solemnly blessed on the first Sunday after Easter; that Sunday is to be the Feast of Mercy.**
>
> **I desire that priests proclaim this great mercy of Mine towards souls of sinners. Let the sinner not be afraid to**

approach Me. The flames of Mercy are burning Me—
clamoring to be spent; I want to pour them out upon these
souls.

Jesus complained to me in these words, **Distrust on the
part of souls is tearing at My insides. The distrust of a
chosen soul causes Me even greater pain; despite My
inexhaustible love for them they do not trust Me. Even My
death is not enough for them. Woe to the soul that abuses
these** [gifts].

When I spoke about this to Mother Superior, [Rose,
telling her] that God had asked this of me, she answered that
Jesus should give some sign so that we could recognize Him
more clearly.

When I asked the Lord Jesus for a sign as a proof "that
You are truly my God and Lord and that this request comes
from You," I heard this interior voice, **I will make this all
clear to the Superior by means of the graces which I will
grant through this image.**

When I tried to run away from these interior
inspirations, God said to me that on the day of judgment He
would demand of me a great number of souls. (47-52)

The "Visionary"

It was shortly after the Lord demanded that Sister Faustina
paint His image that the sisters began openly to regard her as an
hysteric and visionary. The rumors grew louder. One sister who
pitied her told her in all sincerity, "I've heard them say that you
are a fantasist, Sister, and that you've been having visions. My
poor Sister, defend yourself in this matter."

She was forced to listen to such things daily; yet she resolved
to bear everything in silence and to give no explanations when
questioned. Some of the sisters were irritated by her silence,
especially those who were more curious. Others, who reflected
more deeply, said, "Sister Faustina must be very close to God if
she has the strength to bear so much suffering." It was as if she
were facing two groups of judges. She strove after interior and
exterior silence. She said nothing about herself, even though she

was questioned directly by some sisters. Her patience annoyed them, but God gave her so much inner strength that she endured it all calmly.

Realizing that no one would help her, Sister Faustina began to beg the Lord for a director. So far, she found no one who was sufficiently sure of himself to give her the assurance she wanted to hear—either, "Be at peace, you are on the right road," or, "Reject all this, for it does not come from God." As her uncertainty continued she resigned herself to whatever God willed and she prayed, "I beg you, Lord, direct my soul yourself and be with me, for of myself, I am nothing." (See 125-127)

For a while the sisters' adverse judgments of Sister Faustina ceased and her tormented soul felt at peace. But this lasted for only a short time. A violent storm of disbelief broke out again. Her sisters now accepted old suspicions as true facts, and she was forced to listen to accusations over again. Strangely enough, she even began to experience exterior failures at her duty and continued to be misunderstood by her sisters. "This brought down on me many sufferings of all sorts, known to God alone," she admitted in her Diary, "but I tried as best I could to do everything with the purest of intentions." (128)

One day she suffered a deep humiliation when one of the mothers said to her, "You queer, hysterical visionary, get out of this room; go on with you, Sister!" As she continued to heap upon her head everything she could think of, Sister Faustina felt this humiliation was too much for her to endure. Outwardly, she concealed everything from the other sisters and behaved as though nothing had happened between the mother and herself. Satan, however, took advantage of this moment and thoughts of discouragement entered her mind: Is this, she found herself asking, the reward for your faithfulness and sincerity? How can one be sincere when one is so misunderstood? "Jesus, Jesus, I cannot go on any longer," she cried when she got to her cell and fell on her face before the crucifix. She broke out in a sweat and was overcome by fear. She had no one to lean on interiorly. Suddenly Sister Faustina heard a voice within her soul: **Do not fear; I am with you.** An unusual light illumined her mind and she understood she should not give in to such sorrow. Filled with strength, she left her cell with new courage to accept all suffering. (See 129)

Because she did not want to fall prey to possible illusions, Sister Faustina would at times try to distract herself from the interior inspirations she encountered in her soul. The Lord, however, kept pursuing her with His gifts of visions and graces, so that she experienced alternate moments of anguish and joy throughout her two and one-half years in Plock. But when the various sufferings came to a peak one day, Sister Faustina resolved to put an end to all her doubts before her profession of perpetual vows. (See 130-131)

THIRD PROBATION AND
PERPETUAL VOWS (1932-1933)

Blessed Assurances

"Sister, you will not be going for the third probation. I myself
will see to it that you will not be permitted to make your vows,"
one of the sisters informed Sister Faustina. Although Faustina
said nothing, these words gave her great pain which she tried to
conceal as best she could.

Later when she was in the chapel, Jesus said to Sister
Faustina, **At this very moment the superiors are deciding which
sisters will be permitted to take perpetual vows. Not all of them
will be granted this grace, but this is their own fault. He who does
not take advantage of small graces will not receive great ones. But
to you, my child, this grace is being given.** (165)

This was a joyful surprise to Sister Faustina because it was
contrary to what the sister had told her to expect. A few weeks
later, she was informed that indeed she would be accepted to the
probation. Her heart was ecstatic at the thought of such an
immense grace, that of perpetual vows. Going before the Blessed
Sacrament she immersed herself in a prayer of thanksgiving and
heard these words in her soul:

> **My child, you are My delight. You are the comfort of My
> Heart. I grant you as many graces as you can hold. As often
> as you want to make Me happy, speak to the world about
> My great and unfathomable mercy.** (164)

Sister Faustina arrived in Warsaw in November 1932 to
begin her third probation. After a cordial meeting with the
mothers she went into the little chapel for a moment. Suddenly
God's presence filled her soul and she heard the words: **My**

daughter, I desire that your heart be formed after the model of My merciful Heart. You must be completely imbued with My mercy. (167)

As Sister had not as yet made a retreat that year, Mother Directress Margaret arranged that she should first have a three-day retreat. There was an eight-day retreat in progress in Walendow and she was to take advantage of it. But because a certain sister was very much against her going, Sister Faustina was not supposed to leave for Walendow. After dinner during her five-minute adoration, Jesus told her, **My daughter, I am preparing many graces for you which you will receive during this retreat which you will begin tomorrow.**

When she told Jesus that the retreat had already begun and she was not to go, Jesus replied, **Get ready for it, because you will begin the retreat tomorrow. And as for your departure, I will arrange that with your superiors.** Sister began to wonder how this was going to happen, but quickly rejected all such thoughts and devoted the time to prayer to the Holy Spirit.

She returned to her duties. Soon Mother General Michael called her and said, "Sister, you will go to Walendow today with Mother Valeria so that you can start the retreat tomorrow. Fortunately, Mother Valeria happens to be here and you can go together." (167)

In less than two hours they arrived at Walendow. It was a town about 20 kilometers from Warsaw, where a house of the congregation was located. When the sister who so strongly opposed her participation in the retreat saw her there, she did not hide her surprise and dissatisfaction. But Sister Faustina just bowed to her warmly and went to the chapel to ask Jesus for directions on how to conduct herself during this retreat. (168)

During their conversation, the Lord Jesus told her that this retreat would be a little different from the others:

> **You shall strive to maintain a profound peace in respect to your communings with Me. I will remove all doubts in this regard. I know that you are at peace now as I speak to you, but the moment I stop talking you will start looking for doubts. But I want you to know that I will affirm your soul to such a degree that even if you wanted to be troubled, it will not be within your power. And as a proof that it is I who am speaking to you, you will go to confession on the second day of the retreat to the priest who is preaching the retreat;**

you will go to him as soon as he has finished his conference and will present to him all your doubts concerning Me. I will answer you through his lips, and then your fears will end. During this retreat, observe such strict silence that it will be as though nothing exists around you. You will speak only to Me and to your confessor; you will ask your superiors only for penances. (169)

The Reverend Edmund Elter, S.J., the priest giving the retreat, was a very learned man. He was a professor of ethics at the Gregorian University in Rome, but was then residing in Warsaw and giving retreats to religious. Sister Faustina described him as a person from whom a deep spirituality shone forth. "His bearing testified to the greatness of his spirit. Mortification and recollection characterized this priest," she wrote in her Diary. (172)

But despite these great virtues of the priest, Sister experienced great difficulties in revealing her soul to him with respect to the graces—for it was always easy for her to do so with respect to sins, but with graces she had to make an extra effort and even then she would not say everything.

Satan, knowing he had much to lose, monopolized on Sister's difficulty to reveal herself. During her meditation before the conference, Satan began his temptations. He tried to persuade her to believe that if her superiors told her that her inner life is a delusion she should accept it:

> Didn't Mother X. [probably Mother Jane] tell you that the Lord Jesus does not commune with souls as miserable as yours? This confessor is going to tell you the same thing. Why speak to him about all this? These are not sins, and Mother X. told you that all this communing with the Lord Jesus was daydreaming and pure hysteria. So why tell it to this confessor? You would do better do dismiss all this as illusions. Look how many humiliations you have suffered because of them, and how many more are still awaiting you, and all the sisters know that you are a hysteric. (173)

In response she cried within her soul, "Jesus!" At that moment the priest entered and began the conference. He spoke only for a short time, as if he were in a hurry. Then he entered the confessional. Seeing that no sister made a move toward the confessional, Sister Faustina sprang from her kneeler and in an instant was in the confessional box. She had no time to deliberate. And instead of revealing her former doubts, she began to speak about the temptations she had just been experiencing. (174)

The confessor immediately understood the entire situation and said to her:

> "Sister, you distrust the Lord Jesus because He treats you so kindly. Well, Sister, be completely at peace. Jesus is your Master, and your communing with Him is neither daydreaming nor hysteria nor illusion. Know that you are on the right path. Please try to be faithful to these graces; you are not free to shun them. You do not need at all, Sister, to tell your superiors about these interior graces, unless the Lord Jesus instructs you clearly to do so, and even then you should first consult with your confessor. But if the Lord Jesus demands something external, in this case, after consulting your confessor, you should carry out what He asks of you, even if this costs you greatly. On the other hand, you must tell your confessor everything. There is absolutely no other course for you to take, Sister. Pray that you may find a spiritual director, or else you will waste these great gifts of God. I repeat once again, be at peace; you are following the right path. Take no heed of anything, but always be faithful to the Lord Jesus, no matter what anyone says about you. It is with just such miserable souls that the Lord Jesus communes in this intimate way. And the more you humble yourself, the more the Lord Jesus will unite Himself with you." (174)

When she left the confessional, such indescribable joy filled her soul that she withdrew to a secluded spot in the garden to be away from the sisters while she allowed her heart to pour itself out to God. She was pervaded by God's presence and in an instant all her nothingness was drowned in God and at the same moment she felt, or rather discerned, the Three Divine Persons dwelling within her. As Jesus predicted, she had such great peace in her soul that she was surprised that she could have had so many misgivings. She made two resolutions at the end of that retreat: to be faithful to inner inspirations, even though she would have no idea how much it would cost her; and to do nothing on her own, without first consulting the confessor. (175)

On the last day of the retreat, from the moment she awoke, Sister Faustina's spirit was immersed in God. During Holy Mass her love for him reached its peak. After renewing her vows and receiving Holy Communion, she saw the Lord Jesus who said to her kindly, **My daughter, look at My merciful Heart.** She wrote:

> As I fixed my gaze on the Most Sacred Heart, the same rays of light, as are represented in the image as blood and water, came forth from it, and I understood how great is the Lord's mercy. And again Jesus said to me with kindness, **My daughter, speak to priests about this inconceivable mercy of Mine. The flames of mercy are burning Me—clamoring to be spent; I want to keep pouring them out upon souls; souls just don't want to believe in My goodness.** (177)

In an instant Jesus disappeared, but throughout that day her spirit remained immersed in God's tangible presence despite the buzz and chatter that usually follow a retreat. Nothing disturbed her. Her spirit was lost in God, although externally she took part in the conversations, and even visited their home for girls at Derdy, which was just one kilometer from Walendow. (177)

"Victim Soul"

The Third Probation began officially on December 1, 1932. While Sister Faustina and two other sisters met in Warsaw with Mother Margaret Gimbutt their Directress, two other sisters from her group were meeting in Cracow with the Directress of Novices. Mother Margaret began the first session with a prayer, explained what the Third Probation entailed, and then spoke of the greatness of the grace of perpetual vows. Suddenly Sister Faustina began to cry aloud. All of God's graces and her own ingratitude to the Lord flashed before her eyes. The sisters rebuked her for her outburst but Mother Directress defended her by commenting that she understood her feelings.

After the conference, Sister Faustina went before the Blessed Sacrament to beg God's mercy. The Lord told her, **My daughter, all your miseries have been consumed in the flame of My love, like**

a little twig thrown into a roaring fire. By humbling yourself in this way, you draw upon yourself and upon other souls an entire sea of My mercy. She replied, "Jesus, mold my poor heart according to Your divine delight." (178)

During the probation period Sister Faustina's duty was to help another sister in the vestiary. Their task was to check the clothing and linen that came back from the laundry, mend those things that needed mending or sew new ones, and distribute them to the sisters. The characters of these two sisters were incompatible and friction often resulted. When Sister Faustina took ill and went to bed she was labeled "lazy" by her companion. This duty provided both of them with many opportunities for practicing virtue. (See 179)

Throughout this time Sister Faustina prayed fervently that God enlighten the priest to whom she was to reveal what was in her soul. She asked the Lord to grant her the grace to express the innermost secrets that existed between the Lord and herself. She was disposed to accept the priest's decision as if it were from Jesus himself. From this time she also began to conceal all the graces within her soul and to wait for the director the Lord would send her.

It was at this time also that Jesus was preparing her to become a victim soul, that is, a sacrifice for souls, especially for sinners. It is no wonder that she prayed:

> O my Jesus, You are the life of my life. You know only too well that I long for nothing but the glory of Your Name and that souls come to know Your goodness. Why do souls avoid You, Jesus?—I don't understand that. Oh, if I could only cut my heart into tiny pieces and in this way offer to You, O Jesus, each piece as a heart whole and entire, to make up in part for the hearts that do not love You! I love You, Jesus, with every drop of my blood, and I would gladly shed my blood for You to give You a proof of the sincerity of my love....
>
> My desires are mad and unattainable. I wish to conceal from You that I suffer. I want never to be rewarded for my efforts and my good actions. You yourself, Jesus, are my only reward; You are enough, O Treasure of my heart! I want to share compassionately in the sufferings of my

neighbors and to conceal my own sufferings, not only from them, but also from You, Jesus.

Suffering is a great grace; through suffering the soul becomes like the Savior; in suffering love becomes crystallized; the greater the suffering, the purer the love. (57)

During a particular hour of adoration, Sister Faustina was granted a vision of what becoming a "victim soul" would encompass. All that she might be called on to suffer passed before her eyes: false suspicions, loss of a good name, and so much more. When the vision ended, a cold sweat bathed her forehead. Jesus made it known to her that even if she did not give her consent to this she could still be saved and He would not lessen His graces and would still continue to have the same intimate relationship with her. Even if she did not consent to make this sacrifice, God's generosity would not lessen thereby. She knew clearly that the whole mystery depended on her, on her free consent to the sacrifice, with full use of her faculties. What then transpired she thus recorded in her Diary:

Suddenly, when I had consented to the sacrifice with all my heart and all my will, God's presence pervaded me. My soul became immersed in God and was inundated with such happiness that I cannot put in writing even the smallest part of it. I felt that His Majesty was enveloping me. I was extraordinarily fused with God. I saw that God was well pleased with me and, reciprocally, my spirit drowned itself in Him. Aware of this union with God, I felt I was especially loved and, in turn, I loved with all my soul. A great mystery took place during that adoration, a mystery between the Lord and myself. It seemed to me that I would die of love [at the sight of] His glance. I spoke much with the Lord, without uttering a single word. And the Lord said to me, **You are the delight of My Heart; from today on, every one of your acts, even the very smallest, will be a delight to My eyes, whatever you do.** At that moment I felt trans-consecrated. My earthly body was the same, but my soul was different; God was now living in it with the totality of His delight. This is not a feeling, but a conscious reality that nothing can obscure. A great mystery has been accomplished between God and me. (See 136-137)

Immediately upon leaving the chapel, Sister Faustina experienced a great suffering and humiliation from a certain person. From now on, no trifle passed unnoticed as every word of hers was analyzed, every step watched. Even the Directress was surprised at all she was forced to endure. "But as for me," wrote Sister Faustina, "I rejoiced at this in the depths of my soul and had been ready for it for a long time.... I see now that a soul cannot do much of itself, but with God it can do all things. Behold what God's grace can do." (See 138)

It was now the Advent Season. A great longing for God was awakened in Sister's soul. Her spirit sought God's will with all its might and the Lord enlightened her with the profound knowledge of his divine attributes: holiness, justice, love and mercy. She learned that the greatest attribute of God is love and mercy. It unites the creature with the Creator and is especially evident in the mystery of the Incarnation and Redemption.

On the day before Christmas, Sister Faustina felt closely united to Our Lady and relived with her the interior sentiments that were hers that First Christmas. Before "sharing the wafer" with her sisters, a Christmas Eve custom, she entered the chapel and in spirit shared the wafer with her loved ones, asking Our Lady to grace them. Her spirit was totally immersed in God, even during the meal and chores that followed. Then, during Midnight Mass, she saw the Child Jesus in the Host, a vision that continued to appear to her quite often. (See 182)

While trying to meditate on the Lord's Passion, one day, the Child Jesus appeared and filled her soul with joy. His majesty pervaded her and she said to him, "Jesus, you are so little, and yet I know that you are my Creator and Lord."

And Jesus answered her, **I am, and I keep company with you as a child to teach you humility and simplicity.** (184)

The Christmas season ended and the Lenten season was fast approaching. Sister Faustina began to gather all her sufferings and troubles to make a bouquet for Jesus on the day of their perpetual betrothal. Above all, she tried to keep the great silence for the Lord's sake, even though she encountered much suffering because of this resolution.

One day Jesus said to her:

I desire that you know more profoundly the love that burns in My Heart for souls, and you will understand this when you meditate upon My Passion. Call upon My mercy on behalf of sinners; I desire their salvation. When you say this prayer, with a contrite heart and with faith on behalf of some sinner, I will give him the grace of conversion. This the the prayer:

O Blood and Water, which gushed forth from the Heart of Jesus as a fount of Mercy for us, I trust in You. (186-187)

To help her enter more fully into the spirit of prayer, penance and suffering that characterizes the Lenten season, Sister Faustina was granted a vision of the scourging of Jesus and an understanding of the greatness of His suffering during that event. This happened during a Holy Hour on Shrove Tuesday, the day before Ash Wednesday. (See 188)

In addition to her usual sufferings, she often took upon herself, with the permission of Jesus and her confessor, the torments of the girls. At one time she took upon herself the terrible temptation of suicide suffered by one of them at the house in Warsaw. The suffering lasted seven days after which Jesus granted Faustina the grace for which she asked and her suffering ceased. She admitted that it was a great torment. (See 192)

When her younger sister Wanda came to visit her in March, Sister Faustina learned from her that she was suffering from a great depression. Greatly concerned, Sister Faustina asked and received permission from her superior to minister to her sister for two weeks. For no other soul did she bring so many sacrifices and prayers before the throne of God as she did for the soul of her sister. She felt that she had forced God to grant her sister the grace of recovery. "When I reflect on all this, I see that it was truly a miracle," she wrote. "Now I can see how much power intercessory prayer has before God." (202)

During Lent, Faustina was given to experience often the Passion of the Lord Jesus in her own heart and body (the stigmata) but no exterior signs betrayed these sufferings. Only her confessor knew about them.

Once during the third probation, Sister Faustina sought Mother Margaret's advice concerning ways to make progress in the spiritual life. Mother answered all her questions with great clarity and then added, "If you continue cooperating with God's grace in this way, Sister, you will be only one step away from close union with God.... You understand what I mean by this. This means that your characteristic trait should be faithfulness to the grace of the Lord. God does not lead all souls along such a path." (204)

Encouraged by these kind words of her Mother Directress, Sister Faustina continued in her heroic efforts to please the Lord. During the Mass of the Resurrection, in the midst of a great light Jesus approached His faithful daughter, and said, **You have taken a great part in My Passion; therefore I now give you a great share in My joy and glory.** She was filled with wondrous recollection throughout this entire festal season. (205)

Soon, however, a terrible darkness again enveloped her soul. The words of a confessor, "I cannot discern what power is at work in you, Sister; perhaps it is God and perhaps it is the evil spirit," only increased the doubts that recurred and troubled her so much. At another time she went to confession again and was told, "It would be better if you did not come to me for confession." Leaving the confessional, oppressed and tormented, she went before the Blessed Sacrament and said, "Jesus, save me; You see how weak I am!"

She then heard the words, **I will give you help during the retreat before the vows.** With a strange impatience Sister Faustina awaited the retreat and continued to ask God to give light to the priest who would hear her confession. (See 211-213)

This priest would be Father Joseph Andrasz, a Jesuit, who had been appointed in 1932 to be the quarterly confessor to the sisters in the Novitiate at Lagiewniki. He would perform this duty satisfactorily for many years.

Return to Cracow

On April 17, 1933, the three probationers had everything ready for the next day's journey to Cracow, where at St. Joseph's in Lagiewniki they would make their retreat. When she entered the chapel to thank Jesus for the blessings of the past five months, Sister Faustina heard him say, **My daughter, be at peace; I am taking all these matters upon Myself. I will arrange all things with your superiors and with the confessor. Speak to Father Andrasz with the same simplicity and confidence with which you speak to Me.** (214-215)

It was a great joy for the sisters to be back in Cracow where they took the first steps in the spiritual life. Sister Faustina found the Mother Directress, Mary Joseph Brzoza, as cheerful and full of charity as ever. Joy filled Sister's heart when she entered the chapel and recalled the ocean of graces she had received there as a novice.

Mother Directress gave them the program of the retreat. As she was speaking, Sister Faustina saw before her eyes all the good things this Mother had done for them. She felt profound gratitude and at the same time heartfelt sorrow, realizing these were her last days in the novitiate under her guidance. She thought:

> Now I must battle together with Jesus, work with Jesus, suffer with Jesus; in a word, live and die with Jesus. Mother Directress will no longer be at my heels to teach me here, warn me there, or to admonish, encourage or reproach me. I am so afraid of being on my own. Jesus, do something about this. I will always have a superior, that's true; but now a person is left more on her own. (217)

The retreat began on April 21, 1933. That evening Jesus told Sister Faustina not to let anything frighten or confuse her and to be at peace because all things are in his hands and because He would help her to understand everything through Father Andrasz. **Be like a child towards him,** He advised. (219)

During a short conference with Mother Directress, Sister Faustina already was set at peace about her spiritual life and reassured that she was on the right path. She thanked the Lord for this great favor; namely, that Mother Joseph was the first of the superiors who did not cause her to have any doubts in regard to God's dealings with her.

On the fourth day of the retreat, Sister Faustina approached the confessional and recounted everything to the confessor with such great ease that it astounded her as well. When she asked Father Andrasz to release her from all those inner inspirations she was receiving and from the duty of painting the image, he told her:

> I will dispense you from nothing, Sister; it is not right for you to turn away from these interior inspirations, but you must absolutely—and I say, absolutely—speak about them to your confessor; otherwise, you will go astray despite the great graces you are receiving from God.
>
> For the present you are coming to me for confession, but understand, Sister, that you must have a permanent confessor, that is to say, a spiritual director. (52-53)

Sister Faustina was very upset by this. She expected to be freed from everything, and just the opposite happened. Now she had an explicit command to follow the requests of Jesus, but, as yet, no regular spiritual director to guide her. Father Andrasz concluded, "You say to me that God demands great trust from souls; well then, you be the first to show this trust. And one more word—accept all this with serenity." (See 55)

After confession, Sister remained deeply immersed in prayer for three hours. To her it seemed like just a few minutes. While absorbed in prayer, she was given a vision of her future spiritual director. It was the same vision she had seen while in Warsaw during her third probation. Encouraged by these two visions and by the assurance she received from Father Andrasz that it was not an illusion but God's grace working in her, Sister resolved to do her best to be faithful to God in everything. The following excerpts from a much longer list of resolutions indicate with what intensity she intended to do this:

> To suffer without complaining, to bring comfort to others and to drown my own sufferings in the most Sacred Heart of Jesus!
>
> I will spend all my free moments at the feet of [Our Lord in] the Blessed Sacrament. At the feet of Jesus I will seek light, comfort and strength. I will show my gratitude unceasingly to God for His great mercy towards me, never forgetting the favors He has bestowed on me, especially the grace of a vocation.

I will hide myself among the sisters like a little violet among lilies. I want to blossom for my Lord and Maker, to forget about myself, to empty myself totally for the sake of immortal souls—this is my delight. (224)

I must pay little attention as to who is for me and who is against me. I must not tell others about those things I have had to put up with... I must maintain peace and equanimity during times of suffering. In difficult moments I must take refuge in the wounds of Jesus; I must seek consolation, comfort, light and affirmation in the wounds of Jesus. (226)

In the midst of trials I will try to see the loving hand of God. Nothing is as constant as suffering—it always faithfully keeps the soul company. O Jesus, I will let no one surpass me in loving You!... (227)

O Jesus, I long for the salvation of immortal souls. It is in sacrifice that my heart will find free expression, in sacrifice which no one will suspect. I will burn and be consumed unseen in the holy flames of the love of God. The presence of God will help my sacrifice to be perfect and pure. (235)

During a holy hour of adoration before the Blessed Sacrament, Sister Faustina reflected on her misery and prayed, "...whatever there is of good in me is Yours, O Lord. But because I am so small and wretched, I have a right to count on Your boundless mercy." (237)

On the eve of perpetual vows, while calling on heaven, earth and all creation to give thanks for God's enormous and incomprehensible favor of perpetual vows, Sister heard the words: **My daughter, your heart is My heaven.** After a few more minutes of prayer Sister Faustina was hurried off to bed by the sisters who were preparing the chapel, dining room, the hall and the kitchen for the great day. But there was no sleep. Joy drove sleep away. She thought, "What is it going to be like in heaven, if already here in exile God so fills my soul." (See 238)

Perpetual Vows

May 1, 1933 dawned. The day of perpetual vows. During Holy Mass Sister Faustina placed her heart on the paten with the

Heart of Jesus and sacrificed herself together with Jesus to God, Father of them both, as an offering of love and adoration, asking the Father of Mercy to look upon the sacrifice of her heart through the wound of Christ's Heart. On this day Jesus became her only treasure. Nothing could now prevent her from proving her love to the Beloved. Jesus told her, **My spouse, our hearts are joined forever. Remember to Whom you have vowed.** We shall never know the depth of her spiritual experience on this memorable day because she herself admitted, "Everything cannot be put into words." (239)

According to the Congregation's custom, just before pronouncing perpetual vows the sisters prostrate themselves before the altar and are covered with a pall (a large piece of black cloth, with a white cross in the middle, used to drape a coffin) as a symbol of being "dead to the world and its enticements." In the meantime the bells toll as at a funeral and the rest of the community recites Psalm 129, the *De Profundis,* which was also recited at funerals. While under the pall, the sisters pray for special favors for themselves and others. Sister Faustina recorded that she asked for the grace never to offend God consciously and willingly, by even the smallest sin or imperfection. She then made certain requests for the Church, for the Congregation, for the girls in their charge, for her family, for the dying; and she asked that all the souls in purgatory be freed that day. She did not forget to pray for the people closest to her, among them Father Andrasz and her future spiritual director. In conclusion she prayed:

> For myself I ask, Lord, transform me completely into Yourself, maintain in me a holy zeal for Your glory, give me the grace and spiritual strength to do Your holy will in all things.... In times of struggle and suffering, of darkness and storm, of yearning and sorrow, in times of difficult trials, in times when no one will understand me, when I will even be condemned and scorned by everyone, I will remember the day of my perpetual vows, the day of God's incomprehensible grace. (See 240)

Bishop Stanislaus Rospond, the chief celebrant, sprinkled the prostrate sisters with holy water and then said, "Rise, you who are dead to the world, and Jesus Christ will give you light."

The church was filled to capacity with sisters, students, invited guests and relatives of the sisters making the profession of vows. Sister Faustina had no guests. Her family could not afford the expense. She told a sister that she was happy that she could spend this day alone with Jesus. The words of the Bishop as he gave her the ring impressed her so much that she recorded them:

> I betroth you to Jesus Christ, the Son of the Father Most High; may He keep you unblemished. Take this ring as a sign of the eternal covenant you are making with Christ, the Spouse of Virgins. May it be for you the ring of faith and the sign of the Holy Spirit, that you may be called the bride of Christ and, if you serve Him faithfully, be crowned [as such] for all eternity. (248)

What she wrote a few days later sheds light on why she was so impressed:

> The moments I lived through when I was taking my perpetual vows are better left unsaid.
> I am in Him, and He in me. As the Bishop was putting the ring on my finger, God pervaded my whole being, and since I cannot express that moment, I will be silent about it. My relationship with God, since perpetual vows, has been more intimate than it had ever been before. I sense that I love God and that He loves me. Having once tasted God, my soul could not live without Him. One hour spent at the foot of the altar in the greatest dryness of spirit is dearer to me than a hundred years of wordly pleasures. I prefer to be a lowly drudge in the convent than a queen in the world. (254)

The seriousness with which Sister Faustina regarded this final step, attaining the goal of becoming a perpetually professed sister in the Congregation of the Sisters of Our Lady of Mercy, is revealed in the following excerpt:

> This year, 1933, is for me an especially solemn year, because in this Jubilee Year of the Lord's Passion, I have taken my perpetual vows. I have joined my sacrifice in a special way to the sacrifice of the crucified Jesus, in order to thus become more pleasing to God. I do all things with Jesus, through Jesus, in Jesus. (250)

As stated earlier, Sister feared leaving the novitiate and the visible help of the Mother Directress, so she thought up the following plan, which would allow her to remain in the novitiate forever. She wrote:

+ O Jesus, hidden in the Blessed Sacrament,
You see that in pronouncing my perpetual vows I am leaving the novitiate today. Jesus, You know how weak and little I am, and so from today on, I am entering Your novitiate in a very special way. I continue to be a novice, but Your novice, Jesus, and You will be my Master to the last day. Daily I will attend lectures at Your feet. I will not do the least thing by myself, without consulting You first as my Master. Jesus, how happy I am that You yourself have drawn me and taken me into Your novitiate; that is to say, into the tabernacle. In making my perpetual vows, I have by no means become a perfect nun. No, no! I am still a weak little novice of Jesus, and I must strive to acquire perfection as I did in the first days of the novitiate, and I will make every effort to keep the same disposition of soul which I had on that first day the convent gate opened to admit me.

With the trust and simplicity of a small child, I give myself to You today, O Lord Jesus, my Master. I leave You complete freedom in directing my soul. Guide me along the paths You wish. I won't question them. I will follow You trustingly. Your merciful Heart can do all things!

The little novice of Jesus, Sister Faustina (228)

THE VILNIUS YEARS (1933-1936)

Between Assignments

After perpetual profession, Sister Faustina was the only one of her group to remain in Cracow without an assignment. Her Mother General noticed how quietly Sister Faustina was taking this delay. When she commented about her patience, the young sister answered, "I want to do God's pure will; wherever you bid me to go, dear Mother, I will know God's pure will for me will be there, without any admixture on my part." Mother General replied to this, "Very well!"

The next day Mother summoned her and told her that since she wanted to do God's pure will, she would be sent to Vilnius to take over the duties of the gardener. While awaiting the day of her departure, Sister Faustina volunteered to help out in the garden; and, because she could do that kind of work by herself and on her own time, she also decided to make a Jesuit Retreat of thirty days. She received much insight from God through this spiritual exercise. (See 251)

On the day before her departure, Sister Faustina went to confession to Father Andrasz. His words reassured her: "No harm will come to you if, in the future, you continue to keep this same simplicity and obedience. Have confidence in God; you are on the right path and in good hands, in God's hands." (257)

But was she? At prayer that evening she told the Lord that here she had found someone who understood her, and now she must leave him behind. What will she do in Vilnius? She knew no one there. Even the language is foreign to her. Again the Lord reassured her, **Do not fear, I will not leave you alone.**

As she continued to pray, this time in thanksgiving for all the graces the Lord had granted her through Father Andrasz, she suddenly remembered the vision in which she had seen that priest between the confessional and the altar—the one whom she would meet some day. The words that she heard then came back vividly: **He will help you to fulfill My will here on earth.** The recollection of the Lord's words gave her great comfort. (See 258)

On the following day Sister Faustina set out, happy that she had permission to stop at Czestochowa where for the first time she would see the icon of Our Lady of Jasna Gora. There she attended the ceremony of unveiling of the icon at five o'clock in the morning and then continued to pray without interruption until eleven. It seemed to her that she had just arrived there when a sister came to fetch her for breakfast. The superior was worried that she might miss her train. This must have been a special encounter for Sister but all she recorded was:

> The Mother of God told me many things. I entrusted my perpetual vows to Her. I felt that I was her child and that she was my Mother. She did not refuse any of my requests. (260)

According to the records of the house in Vilnius, Sister Faustina arrived there on Thursday, May 25, 1933. A few scattered, tiny huts made up the convent complex in Vilnius, a strange contrast to the enormous buildings of St. Joseph's in Cracow. There were only eighteen sisters here, but the community life was more intimate. All the sisters welcomed her very warmly. Even the floor of her cell had been scrubbed in her honor by Sister Justine, a friend from novitiate days. This greatly encouraged Faustina and helped her to endure the hardships which would later beset her. (See 261)

At Benediction that evening, Jesus told her how to conduct herself when dealing with certain persons. In prayer, she clung to His most sweet Heart with all her might, realizing that her new duty as chief gardener would put her in close contact with many lay persons and thus expose her to external distractions. (262)

The Promised Spiritual Director

On the day of confession, Sister Faustina smilingly approached the confessional, a fact well noted and commented upon by her companions. And she had reason to smile! This priest in Vilnius was the same priest she had seen in the two visions! Reverend Michael Sopocko was the man chosen by Jesus to aid Sister in fulfilling God's will.

Father Sopocko was impressed with his new penitent. He took note of her delicate conscience and deep union with God. The sins she confessed were not matter for absolution. From the very beginning she revealed to him the visions she had of him, especially that she knew he was to be her spiritual director so that he would fulfill the Lord's plans. In order to test her sincerity, the priest made light of her account and even put her to a special test. Because of this, Sister Faustina had experienced difficulty in revealing her innermost concerns. She finally decided to look for another confessor.

But her new confessor, Father Dabrowski, S.J., also put her through several trials. She did not go to confession to him again. Instead she made a holy hour before the Blessed Sacrament for his intentions and took on a special mortification to obtain God's light for him so that he would be given the grace of discernment of souls.

After that, Sister Faustina returned to Father Sopocko and announced that she was ready to accept any trial. Never again would she seek out another confessor. When she revealed her soul completely to the priest, Jesus poured an ocean of graces into it. Unknown to her, Father Sopocko had already begun to think seriously about her message.

Meanwhile, everything in the Vilnius house continued according to a convent routine that was unfamiliar to Sister Faustina. This pattern of adjusting to new customs meant that each new assignment became for her a little novitiate. She always seemed to be an inexperienced novice with many new things to learn. What each set of new duties cost her she summarized in her diary thus: "Days of work, of struggle and of suffering have begun." (265)

Faustina's new duty in Vilnius as chief gardener was truly a challenge! She knew nothing about gardening. She believed that because of her obedience God would help her at this task as He had at all previous ones. Immediately after her arrival she zealously went to work. She sought help from a missionary brother who was a professional gardener. Combining his advice with her own native intelligence, Sister Faustina was able to manage very well, and she even began her own greenhouse. The results were excellent. One day guests from the higher offices of government arrived for a tour of the institute. One of the ladies commented to the Superior General, Mother Michael, "My, but you sisters have a gardener here who is a specialist!

However, no one knew what a difficult and exhausting time this frail "specialist" was having. For example, because of heavy rains that year, weeds abounded. Because she and her small number of helpers could not manage to get rid of them, she asked for more help, but in vain. When some of the rows were so overrun with weeds that they had to be cut down, Faustina was accused of being negligent. One sister, however, defended her against this unjust complaint; and both, sisters and girls, marveled at her composure and good humor in the face of such trying circumstances. One sister later remarked, "She did everything as if under God's gaze and in the company of the Lord Jesus." And a student had this to say:

> Sister Faustina eclipsed all the other sisters with her peace, humility, and even temper. She was very obedient and treated her superiors with great respect. I have never known her to murmur or complain. I never saw her impatient though I worked by her side in Vilnius for three years. She was an angel of peace. She never spoke ill of anyone; on the contrary, she would look for, and find, the good side in everyone.

While Sister Faustina worked in the garden, her friend Sister Justine was in charge of the kitchen. Often, it was time for bed and Sister Justine was still washing the supper dishes. Sister Faustina would always go to help her, even though she herself was exhausted after the day's work.

One day when there was much work in the kitchen, Sister Justine was sent to town on business and Sister Faustina was told to take her place. When she returned from town, Sister Justine was surprised to see the work completed and Sister Faustina resting on a nearby bench.

"Sister Faustina," she asked, "how is it that you had so much work and finished so soon? Who helped you?"

With her usual poise and smile Sister answered, "The angels helped me because I never could have done it alone." This was not the only time that Sister spoke of angels. Her Diary contains several entries about her Guardian Angel and other angels who assisted her. (See 419, 474, 490, 630, 1271, 1676)

Two months passed. On August 5, 1933, the Feast of Our Lady of Mercy, Sister Faustina received a great and incomprehensible grace for which, she said, she would be grateful to God in this life, and for all eternity. She made this entry in the diary:

> Jesus told me that I please Him best by meditating on His sorrowful Passion, and by such meditation much light falls upon my soul. He who wants to learn true humility should reflect upon the Passion of Jesus. When I meditate upon the Passion of Jesus, I get a clear understanding of many things I could not comprehend before. "I want to resemble You, O Jesus,—You who were crucified, tortured and humiliated. Jesus, imprint upon my heart and my soul Your own humility. I love you, Jesus, to the point of madness, You who were crushed with suffering, as described by the prophet, [cf. Isaiah 53:2-9], as if he could not see the human form in You because of Your great suffering. It is in this condition, Jesus, that I love You to the point of madness. O eternal and infinite God, what has love done to You?"... (267)

Jesus continued to teach His little novice. At one time, when she had finished a novena to the Holy Spirit for the intentions of her confessor, the Lord said to her: **I made him known to you even before your superiors had sent you here. As you will act towards your confessor, so I will act toward you. If you conceal something from him, even though it be the least of My graces, I too will hide myself from you and you will remain alone.** Sister followed the Lord's wishes and a deep peace filled her soul. She now understood how the Lord defends and protects confessors. (269)

In his counseling, Father Sopocko repeatedly reminded Sister Faustina that without humility we cannot be pleasing to God. Therefore, he told her to practice the third degree of humility. According to the spirituality of St. Ignatius, in this phase one is advised not only to refrain from defending oneself when reproached, but to rejoice in the humiliation. He further prepared her by stating that if all these things that she related to him really came from God, she should prepare her soul for great suffering.

"...You will encounter disapproval and persecution," he told her. "They will look upon you as a hysteric and an eccentric, but the Lord will lavish His graces upon you. True works of God always meet with opposition and are marked by suffering. If God wants to accomplish something, sooner or later He will do so in spite of the difficulties. Your part, in the meantime, is to arm yourself with great patience." (270)

As a prudent director, Father Sopocko meanwhile made inquiries about his unusual penitent. He turned first to Sister Irene Krzyzanowska, Sister Faustina's superior, and requested that Sister be given a physical and psychological evaluation. Though the results of these tests were all favorable, Father still took a waiting stance and sought the advice of learned priests. Everything pointed to the fact that Sister Faustina was a person enriched by God with unusual graces. Father Sopocko became convinced that the gifts of the Holy Spirit were active within her. Unquestionably, she had unusual insight into divine matters.

A Vision Put on Canvas

During her long and frequent confessions Sister Faustina revealed her visions and messages. More and more she referred to conversations with Jesus pertaining to the Divine Mercy. She told Father Sopocko that Jesus demanded the painting of an image that would become a means of grace for an aching world; and, that Jesus was asking that a Feast of Mercy be established in the Church on the first Sunday after Easter. In fact, she had very specific directions as to how the painting of the image should be done.

Not totally convinced, but curious to see what it would look like, Father Sopocko commissioned Eugene Kazimierowski, an artist who lived in the neighborhood, to paint the image. Beginning on January 2, 1934, and continuing every two weeks thereafter, the superior allowed Sister Faustina to work with the artist in order to direct the painting. Father Sopocko w/ other person to hear Sister Faustina's instructions. carefully recorded.

At the request of her spiritual director, Sister Faustina asked the Lord about the meaning of the rays on the image. She heard these words in reply:

> **The two rays denote Blood and Water. The pale ray stands for the Water which makes souls righteous. The red ray stands for the Blood which is the life of souls...**
>
> **These two rays issued forth from the very depths of My tender mercy when My agonized Heart was opened by a lance on the Cross.**
>
> **These rays shield souls from the wrath of My Father. Happy is the one who will dwell in their shelter, for the just hand of God shall not lay hold of him. I desire that the first Sunday after Easter be the Feast of Mercy.**
>
> **Ask of My faithful servant [Father Sopocko] that, on this day, he tell the whole world of My great mercy; that whoever approaches the Fount of Life on this day will be granted complete remission of sins and punishment.**
>
> **Mankind will not have peace until it turns with trust to My mercy.**
>
> **Oh, how much I am hurt by a soul's distrust! Such a soul professes that I am Holy and Just, but does not believe that I am Mercy and does not trust in My goodness. Even the devils glorify My justice but they do not believe in My goodness.**
>
> **My Heart rejoices in this title of Mercy.**
>
> **Proclaim that mercy is the greatest attribute of God. All the works of My hands are crowned with mercy.** (299)

Gift of Knowledge

During her annual retreat, Sister Faustina continued to receive spiritual insights. Chief among these were the following:

> ... True love of God consists in carrying out God's will. To show God our love in what we do, all our actions, even the least, must spring from our love of God...

My child, you please Me most by suffering. In your physical as well as your mental sufferings, My daughter, do not seek sympathy from creatures. I want the fragrance of your suffering to be pure and unadulterated. I want you to detach yourself, not only from creatures, but also from yourself. My daughter, I want to delight in the love of your heart, a pure love, virginal, unblemished, untarnished. The more you will come to love suffering, My daughter, the purer your love for Me will be.... (279)

Approach each of the sisters with the same love with which you approach Me; and whatever you do for them, you do it for Me. (285)

After an adoration which she offered for Poland, a pain pierced Sister's soul and from her heart issued forth this spontaneous prayer which she later recorded:

> Most merciful Jesus, I beseech You through the intercession of Your Saints, and especially the intercession of Your dearest Mother who nurtured You from childhood, bless my native land. I beg You, Jesus, look not on our sins, but on the tears of little children, on the hunger and cold they suffer. Jesus, for the sake of these innocent ones, grant me the grace that I am asking of You for my country. At that moment, I saw the Lord Jesus, His eyes filled with tears, and He said to me, **You see, My daughter, what great compassion I have for them. Know that it is they who uphold the world.** (286)

God continued to fill Sister Faustina's soul with great desires. She wanted to be a priest to constantly remind sinful souls, drowning in despair, of the Divine Mercy. She would like to be a missionary and carry the light of faith to primitive nations so that souls would get to know Him. She desired to empty herself and die a martyr's death for them just as Jesus died for them and for her. She then wrote:

> ...O Jesus, I know only too well that I can be a priest, a missionary, a preacher, and that I can die a martyr's death by completely emptying myself and denying myself for love of You, O Jesus, and of immortal souls.
> Great love can change small things into great ones, and

it is only love which lends value to our actions. And the purer our love becomes, the less there will be within us for the flames of suffering to feed upon and the suffering will cease to be a suffering for us; it will become a delight! By the grace of God, I have received such a disposition of heart that I am never so happy as when I suffer for Jesus whom I love with every beat of my heart. (303)

One day Sister Faustina was suffering so intensely that she left her work and ran to the chapel to ask Jesus for His strength. After a short prayer she returned to her work, filled with enthusiasm and joy. A sister remarked, "You must have many consolations today, Sister; you look so radiant. Surely, God is giving you no suffering but only consolations."

"You are greatly mistaken, Sister," was Sister Faustina's reply, "for it is precisely when I suffer much that my joy is greater; and when I suffer less, my joy also is less."

The sister seemed puzzled so Sister Faustina tried to explain what she meant. "When we suffer much we have a great chance to show God that we love him; but when we suffer little we have less occasion to show God our love; and when we do not suffer at all, our love is then neither great nor pure. By the grace of God, we can attain a point where suffering will become a delight to us, for love can work such things in pure souls." (See 303)

An Act of Oblation

Having thus prepared her for this particular insight, Jesus made it clear to Sister Faustina, during her Holy Thursday prayer time, that He desired her to make an offering of herself for sinners—especialy those who had lost hope in God's mercy.

Sister complied and made the following offering:

God and Souls. An Act of Oblation.

Before heaven and earth, before all the choirs of Angels, before the Most Holy Virgin Mary, before all the Powers of heaven, I declare to the One Triune God that today, in union with Jesus Christ, Redeemer of souls, I make a voluntary offering of myself for the conversion of sinners, especially for those souls who have lost hope in

God's mercy. This offering consists in my accepting, with total submission to God's will, all the sufferings, fears and terrors with which sinners are filled. In return, I give them all the consolations which my soul receives from my communion with God. In a word, I offer everything for them: Holy Masses, Holy Communions, penances, mortifications, prayers. I do not fear the blows, the blows of divine justice, because I am united with Jesus. O my God, in this way I want to make amends to You for the souls that do not trust in Your goodness. I hope against all hope in the ocean of Your mercy. My Lord and my God, my portion— my portion forever, I do not base this act of oblation on my own strength, but on the strength that flows from the merits of Jesus Christ. I will daily repeat this act of self-oblation by pronouncing the following prayer which You Yourself have taught me, Jesus:

O Blood and Water which gushed forth from the Heart of Jesus as a fount of mercy for us, I trust in You!

S.M. Faustina of the Blessed Sacrament
Holy Thursday, during Holy Mass, March 29, 1934. (309)

Jesus ratified this act with the words: **I am giving you a share in the redemption of mankind. You are solace in My dying hour.** (310)

Of course, it was with the confessor's permission that Sister made this act of self-sacrifice. Even though filled with joy because of her privileged closeness to the Lord, she soon learned that there was a reverse dimension to her vocation. As quickly as it was refreshed, her soul became dried out like a stone and filled with torment and unrest. Various blasphemies and curses kept pressing upon her ears. Distrust and despair invaded her heart. She realized that this was the condition of the poor sinners which she had taken upon herself. At first she was greatly frightened by these terrible feelings, but she was set at peace by her confessor.

Jesus commanded Sister Faustina to celebrate the Feast of Mercy on the first Sunday after Easter. On that Sunday, April 8, 1934, Sister spent her time in inward recollection and external mortification—wearing a mortification wire belt for three hours while praying continuously for sinners and for mercy on the whole world. Jesus said to her, **My eyes rest with pleasure upon this house today.** After this, Faustina was inspired to write the following:

> I feel certain that my mission will not come to an end upon my death, but will begin. O doubting souls, I will draw aside for you the veils of heaven to convince you of God's goodness, so that you will no longer continue to wound with your distrust the sweetest Heart of Jesus. God is Love and Mercy. (281)

Her love of Jesus increased her love of neighbor. Sister Faustina desired to become "a mist before the eyes of Jesus" so that He could not see the terrible crimes of earth. The indifference of the world towards Jesus continuously brought tears to her eyes, but the frigid souls of religious persons made her heart bleed.

This growing union with Christ continued amid the daily routine of life. With the coming of spring, work in the garden intensified as did the painting of the Image of the Merciful Christ—a project carefully monitored by Sister Faustina. When she saw that the painting was not as beautiful as the Jesus of her vision, she grew disturbed. At one point she took her disappointment to chapel where she wept for a long while. She said to Jesus, "Who will paint You as beautiful as You are?"

Then she heard the words: **Not in the beauty of the color nor of the brush lies the greatness of this image, but in My grace.** (313) She was consoled.

The painting was completed in June 1934 and placed in the corridor of the convent of the Bernardine Sisters near the church of St. Michael, where Father Michael Sopocko was pastor.

A Predicted Illness

Usually it was the Lord who in His infinite goodness prepared Sister Faustina for what lay ahead. In mid-summer, however, it was the Mother of God who came to tell her that she would be tested by an illness and the subsequent interaction of some doctors. *You will also suffer much because of the Image, but do not be afraid of anything,* Our Lady told her. Almost immediately Sister fell ill, suffering from what was mistakenly diagnosed "a cold." But, in fact, suffering had already become so much a part of her daily experience even before this "cold" that she could write, "Suffering is a constant companion of my life." (316)

It was the custom of the congregation for all the sisters in good health to spend an hour of adoration before the Blessed Sacrament in atonement for sinners. This "Holy Hour" was held each Thursday night from nine to ten o'clock. Before the First Friday of each month, however, the adoration continued throughout the night and the sisters took turns of one hour each. Sister Faustina wrote, under the date of August 9, 1934, that she was able to take her hour of adoration from eleven to twelve o'clock. She offered it for the conversion of impenitent sinners, especially for those who have lost all hope of obtaining God's mercy. She called upon all of heaven to join her in making amends to the Lord for the ingratitude of certain souls.

That night Jesus made known to Sister how very pleasing to Him were prayers of atonement. He said to her, **The prayer of a humble and loving soul disarms the anger of My Father and draws down an ocean of blessings.** (320)

After the adoration, however, when she was halfway to her cell, Sister Faustina found herself surrounded by what she thought to be a pack of huge black dogs who were jumping and howling and trying to tear her to pieces. Instantly she realized they were not dogs but demons. One of them spoke up in a rage, "Because you have snatched so many souls away from us this night, we will tear you to pieces."

Sister Faustina answered, "If that is the will of the most merciful God, tear me to pieces, for I have jusly deserved it, because I am the most miserable of all sinners, and God is ever holy, just, and infinitely merciful."

To these words all the demons answered as one, "Let us flee, for she is not alone; the Almighty is with her!" And they vanished like dust, like the noise of the road, while Sister continued to walk to her cell undisturbed. (320)

Three days later, August 12, Sister Faustina experienced such a sudden weakness, that it seemed to her that she was close to death. She understood that it was not the real death—the transition to real life, as she put it—but a taste of the suffering of death. The episode was frightening: She suddenly felt sick—gasped for breath. It grew dark before her eyes and her limbs went numb. She thought she was suffocating. It was terrible! Even one moment of it seemed extremely long. There was also a strange fear, in spite of trust. She described the experience thus:

> I wanted to receive the last sacraments, but it was extremely difficult to make a confession even though I desired to do so. A person does not know what he is saying; not finishing one thing, he begins another. Oh, may God keep every soul from delaying confession until the last hour! I understood the great power of the priest's words when they are poured out upon the sick person's soul. When I asked my spiritual father whether I was ready to stand before the Lord and whether I could be at peace, I received the reply, "You can be completely at peace, not only right now but after each weekly confession." Great is the divine grace that accompanies these words of the priest. The soul feels power and courage for battle. (321)

It was Father Sopocko who was summoned to her side and who administered the Sacrament of the Anointing of the Sick. There was definite improvement as soon as Sister was anointed. A half hour later, however, she suffered another attack. This one, was less severe, because of medical treatment.

Once again, Sister united her sufferings to those of Jesus, offering them for herself and for the conversion of those souls who do not trust in the goodness of God. Suddenly, her cell was filled with jet black figures who raged in anger and hatred against her. One of them said, "Be damned, you and He who is within you, for you are beginning to torment us even in hell." But Sister calmly said, "And the Word was made flesh and dwelt among us." The figures vanished in a sudden whir. (See 323)

The following day Sister Faustina still felt very weak, but as she experienced no suffering she went to Mass. After Holy Communion she saw the Lord Jesus and said to Him, "Jesus, I thought You were going to take me."

Jesus answered, **My will has not yet been fully accomplished in you; you will still remain on earth but not for long. I am well** pleased with your trust, but your love should be more ardent. Pure love gives the soul strength at the very moment of dying. When I was dying on the cross, I was not thinking about Myself, but about poor sinners, and I prayed for them to my Father. I want your last moments to be completely similar to Mine on the cross. There is but one price at which souls are bought, and that is suffering united to My suffering on the cross. Pure love understands these words; carnal love will never understand them. (324)

On August 15, Feast of the Assumption of Mary into Heaven, the doctor did not allow Sister Faustina to attend Holy Mass. As she prayed fervently in her cell she saw the Virgin, unspeakably beautiful, who said to her, *My daughter, what I demand from you is prayer, prayer, and once again prayer, for the world and especially for your country. For nine days receive Holy Communion in atonement and unite yourself closely to the Holy Sacrifice of the Mass. During these nine days you will stand before God as an offering; always and everywhere, at all times and places, day or night, whenever you wake up, pray in the spirit. In spirit, one can always remain in prayer.* (325)

About this time, Father Sopocko was spending several weeks in the Holy Land. Father Casimir Dabrowski, S.J., the one who had put Sister Faustina through some trials soon after her arrival in Vilnius, was the sisters' substitute confessor. Sister Faustina had no alternative but to go to confession to him. Previously, he had not recognized the depth of her spiritual life. Now, he obliged her to be faithful, saying, "You must not destroy what is going on in your soul, Sister, nor must you change anything on your own. It is not in every soul that the beautiful gift of a higher interior life is manifest as it is in your case, Sister, for it is manifest in an immense degree. Be careful not to waste these great graces of God." (271)

However, Sister Faustina continued to suffer all sorts of persecutions. Humiliations were her daily food. If it were not for the Eucharist, she would not have had enough courage to continue along the way God was leading her. She feared a day without Holy Communion. Perhaps the following notation will partially explain why:

...At those times when I suffer much, I try to remain silent as I do not trust my tongue which, at such moments, is inclined to talk for itself, while its duty is to help me praise God for all the blessings and gifts which He has given me. When I receive Jesus in Holy Communion, I ask Him fervently to deign to heal my tongue so that I would offend neither God nor neighbor by it. I want my tongue to praise God without cease. Great are the faults committed by the tongue. The soul will not attain sanctity if it does not keep watch over its tongue. (92)

A "Troublesome" Vision

On Friday, October 26, 1934, at ten minutes to six, Sister Faustina was visited by Jesus while she and some of the students were leaving the garden on their way to supper. Suddenly she saw the Lord Jesus above the chapel. He appeared just as she saw Him the first time and the same as He is painted in the image. The two rays which came from the Heart of Jesus covered both the chapel and the infirmary, spread out over the whole city, and then over the whole world. The vision lasted about four minutes. Imelda, one of the girls who with Sister Faustina had been walking a little behind the others, also saw the rays. But she did not see Jesus. Thus she did not know their source. Overwhelmed, she began to tell the other girls about them. They laughed and suggested that she must be imagining things or that perhaps she saw the lights of a passing airplane. But she persisted in her conviction, saying that never before had she seen such rays. When the others suggested that it might have been a searchlight, she replied that she knew very well what a searchlight was, but never had she seen rays such as these. After supper Imelda approached Sister Faustina and told her she had been so moved by those rays that she could not keep silent but wanted to tell everyone about them. This placed Sister Faustina in an embarrassing situation because she could not tell the girl of her vision of the Lord Jesus.

The student Imelda was so persistent, however, that a month later, on November 28, 1934, Sister Faustina was compelled by her superior to make a statement regarding the vision. A certain Sister Taida recorded it and it was signed by Sister Faustina,

Sister Taida, and Imelda, and authenticated by Mother Irene Krzyzanowska, the superior of the house in Vilnius.

Concerning this incident that focused attention upon her, Sister Faustina, who wished to remain inconspicuous, noted in her Diary: "My heart rejoiced in the fact that Jesus takes the initiative to make Himself known, even though the occasion of such action on His part causes me annoyance. For the sake of Jesus, one can bear anything." (87)

A Special Feast of Mercy

On November 5, Sister Faustina made a visit to the chapel to renew her intention of the day. She said to the Lord, "Today, Jesus, I offer You all my sufferings, mortifications, and prayers for the intentions of the Holy Father so that he may approve the Feast of Mercy. But, Jesus, I have one more word to say to You: I am very surprised that You bid me to talk about this Feast of Mercy, for they tell me that there is already such a feast and so why should I talk about it?"

Jesus said to her, **And who knows anything about this feast? No one! Even those who should be proclaiming My mercy and teaching people about it often do not know about it themselves. That is why I want the image to be solemnly blessed on the first Sunday after Easter, and I want it to be venerated publicly so that every soul may know about it.**

Make a novena for the Holy Father's intention. It should consist of thirty-three acts; that is, repetition that many times of the short prayer—which I have taught you—to The Divine Mercy. (341)

The prayer Jesus referred to is: "O Blood and Water which gushed forth from the Heart of Jesus as a fount of mercy for us I trust in You." (309)

Advent and Christmas 1934

It was again the Advent season. This year Jesus, with the cooperation of her spiritual director, was teaching Sister Faustina the virtue of simplicity. **Although My greatness is beyond**

understanding, Jesus told her, **I commune only with those who are little. I demand of you a childlike spirit.** Only two weeks ago her confessor told her to reflect upon this spiritual childhood! (332)

Once Sister asked the Lord, "Jesus, why do You now take on the form of a child when You commune with me? In spite of this, I still see in You the infinite God, my Lord and Creator."

Jesus replied, **Until you learn simplicity and humility, I shall commune with you in the form of a little child.** (See 335)

Throughout the season of Advent, Sister Faustina felt the closeness of God more intimately, and often had visions of the Child Jesus.

At this time, Faustina was undergoing interior suffering. In a prayer of thankfulness, which she had written at this time, she revealed the suffering state of her soul—a dryness of spirit, apprehensions, darkness of soul, temptations and various trials—as well as the loving spirit with which she accepted it. Then, under the date of December 20, 1934, she recorded a vision which gave her courage to continue to live out her act of consecration as an oblation:

> One evening as I entered my cell, I saw the Lord Jesus exposed in the monstrance under the open sky as it seemed. At the feet of Jesus I saw my confessor and behind him a great number of the highest ranking ecclesiastics, clothed in vestments the like of which I had never seen except in this vision; and behind them, groups of religious from various orders; and further still I saw enormous crowds of people, which extended far beyond my vision. I saw the two rays coming out from the Host, as in the image, closely united but not intermingled; and they passed through the hands of my confessor, and then through the hands of the clergy and from their hands to the people, and then they returned to the Host... and at that moment I saw myself once again in the cell which I had just entered. (344)

On Christmas Eve, despite all the work she had all day, her spirit was immersed in God. The vigil supper was before six o'clock. There was much joy and excitement during the sharing of the wafer and the exchange of good wishes, but Sister did not for even a moment lose the awareness of God's presence. Having received permission to keep vigil in chapel until the Midnight Mass, she hurried with her chores and arrived there before nine o'clock. From nine to ten o'clock, she offered her adoration for the intentions of her parents and the entire family; from ten to eleven, for the intention of her spiritual director; from eleven to twelve o'clock she prayed for the Holy Church and the clergy, for sinners, for the missions, for the houses of her congregation. The indulgences gained she offered for the souls in purgatory.

During Midnight Mass, Sister Faustina was filled with joy and recollection of spirit. At the Offertory she saw Jesus on the altar in His incomparable beauty. The Infant, with outstretched arms, was gazing at everyone throughout that time. This vision was repeated in all three Masses that day and for the next two days. (See 346)

On the Thursday after Christmas, because of the excitement of the season, Sister Faustina completely forgot what day it was and did not make the Holy Hour of adoration. At nine o'clock she went directly to the dormitory with the other sisters but could not fall asleep. She thought she had forgotten some duty and spent the hour mentally reviewing all her duties but could not recall having omitted any. At ten o'clock she saw the Sorrowful Face of Jesus who said to her, **I have been waiting to share My suffering with you, for who can understand My suffering better than My spouse?** Sister apologized for her coldness and with a contrite heart asked Jesus to give her one thorn from His crown. He answered that He would grant her that favor but not until the next day, and immediately the vision disappeared. (See 348)

The following morning during meditation, Sister Faustina felt a painful thorn in the left side of her head. The suffering remained with her all day. Her constant meditation was wondering how Jesus was able to endure the pain of the many thorns which made up His crown. She joined her suffering to the sufferings of Jesus and offered it for sinners. That afternoon she wrote:

> At four o'clock when I came for adoration, I saw one of our wards offending God greatly by sins of impure thoughts. I also saw a certain person who was the cause of her sin. My soul was pierced with fear, and I asked God, for the sake of Jesus' pain, to snatch her from this terrible misery. Jesus

answered that He would grant that favor, not for her sake, but for the sake of my request. Now I understood how much we ought to pray for sinners... (349-350)

On New Year's Eve, 1934, Sister Faustina asked permission to spend the evening in chapel. The first hour of prayer she offered up for one of the sisters who had asked her to offer an hour of adoration for her intentions. During that adoration God made it known to Sister how pleasing that sister's soul was to Him. The second hour she offered for the conversion of sinners and in atonement to God, especially for the insults that were being committed against Him at that present moment. The third hour of adoration she offered for her spiritual director, that he be enlightened in a particular matter. Finally the clock struck twelve. Sister Faustina offered the last hour of the year in the name of the Holy Trinity and also began the first hour of the New Year 1935 in the name of the Holy Trinity. She asked each of the Three Persons of the Trinity for a blessing and looked with great trust to the New Year which was certain to abound in suffering.

During this time of intensive prayer, Sister formulated an extensive litany to the Sacred Host which she later recorded in her Diary. (See 356). "In the Blessed Host," she wrote, "is our only hope and trust in the midst of darkness, failure and despair."

The Lord's Secretary and Apostle

In December, Mother Borgia Tichy replaced Mother Irene as superior of the house in Vilnius. On January 4, 1935, Mother Borgia held the first house chapter. A "chapter" was the coming together of all the sisters of the house to receive from the superior a short exhortation and observations regarding the keeping of the rules. In her exhortation on that day, Mother Borgia stressed the need of a life of faith and fidelity in small things.

When the sisters left the meeting room, Sister Faustina remained to put things in order. She then heard these words: **Tell all the sisters that I demand that they live in the spirit of faith towards the superiors at this present time.** She begged her confessor to release her from this painful duty, but it is presumed that she did as Jesus demanded. (See 352-353)

That same month Sister Faustina began to experience serious doubts regarding the messages she was recording about God's great mercy. "Is not perhaps all this that I am saying about God's great mercy just a lie or an illusion?" As she began to think about this one night during Benediction, she heard a strong and clear inner voice saying: **Everything that you say about My goodness is true; language has no adequate expression to extol My goodness.** She wrote:

> These words were so filled with power and so clear that I would give my life in declaring they came from God. I can tell this by the profound peace that accompanied them at that time and that still remains with me. This peace gives me such great strength and power that all difficulties, adversities, sufferings, and death itself are as nothing. This light gave me a glimpse of the truth that all my efforts to bring souls to know the mercy of the Lord are very pleasing to God. And from this springs such great joy in my soul that I doubt whether it could be any greater in heaven. Oh, if souls would only be willing to listen, at least a little, to the voice of conscience and the voice—that is, the inspirations—of the Holy Spirit! I say, "at least a little," because once we open ourselves to the influence of the Holy Spirit, He himself will fulfill what is lacking in us. (359)

Because she was open to the influence of the Holy Spirit, Sister Faustina continued to receive messages which at times revealed the inmost feelings of the Heart of Jesus—both His great love and His great disappointment. These she faithfully recorded:

> On one occasion Jesus gave me to know that when I pray for intentions which people are wont to entrust to me, He is always ready to grant His graces, but souls do not always want to accept them: **My Heart overflows with great mercy for souls and especially for poor sinners. If only they could understand that I am the best of Fathers to them and that it is for them that the Blood and Water flowed from My Heart as from a fount overflowing with mercy. For them I dwell in the tabernacle as King of Mercy. I desire to bestow My graces upon souls, but they do not want to accept them. You, at least, come to Me as often as possible and take these**

graces which they do not want to accept. In this way you will console My Heart. Oh, how indifferent are souls to so much goodness, to so many proofs of love! My Heart drinks only of the ingratitude and forgetfulness of souls living in the world. They have time for everything, but they have no time to come to Me for graces.

So I turn to you, you chosen souls, will you also fail to understand the love of My Heart? Here, too, My Heart finds disappointment; I do not find complete surrender to My love. So many reservations, so much distrust, so much caution. To comfort you, let Me tell you that there are souls living in the world who love Me dearly. I dwell in their hearts with delight. But they are few. In religious houses, too, there are souls that fill My Heart with joy. They bear My features; therefore the Heavenly Father looks upon them with special pleasure. They will be a marvel to Angels and men. Their number is very small. They are a defense for the world before the justice of the Heavenly Father and a means of obtaining mercy for the world. The love and sacrifice of these souls sustains the world in existence. The infidelity of a soul specially chosen by Me wounds My Heart most painfully. Such infidelities are swords which pierce My Heart. (367)

The gift of inner knowledge was one of the spiritual gifts granted to Sister Faustina. On January 29, 1935, she recorded the following inner vision:

This Tuesday morning during meditation I had an inner vision of the Holy Father saying Mass. After the Pater Noster, he talked to Jesus about that matter which Jesus had ordered me to tell him. Although I have not spoken to the Holy Father personally, this matter was taken care of by someone else [Father Sopocko]; at that moment, however, I knew by interior knowledge that the Holy Father was considering this matter which will soon come to pass in accordance with the desires of Jesus. (368)

This was confirmed two years later by Father Sopocko when, in a letter to Sister Faustina, he mentioned that he had spoken to the Papal Nuncio Archbishop Cortesim about the establishment of The Feast of The Divine Mercy and depended on him to relate the message to the Holy Father.

An Eight-Day Retreat, 1935

Before she was to begin her annual retreat, Sister Faustina went to ask her spiritual director if she could practice certain mortifications during that time. To her disappointment, Father Sopocko gave his consent only to some of her requests.

When she returned home, she went to the chapel for a moment and there she heard in her soul:

> **There is more merit to one hour of meditation on My sorrowful Passion than there is to a whole year of bloody scourging; the contemplation of My painful wounds is of great profit to you, and it brings Me great joy. I am surprised that you still have not completely renounced your self-will, but I rejoice exceedingly that this change will be accomplished during the retreat. (369)**

The retreat began on February 4, 1935. It was directed by Father Macewicz, S.J. After the first conference Sister Faustina heard these words:

> **I am with you. During this retreat, I will strengthen you in peace and in courage so that your strength does not fail in carrying out My designs. Therefore you will cancel out your will absolutely in this retreat and, instead, My complete will shall be accomplished in you. Know that it will cost you much, so write these words on a clean sheet of paper: "From today on, my own will does not exist," and then cross out the page. And on the other side write these words: "From today on, I do the Will of God everywhere, always, and in everything." Be afraid of nothing; love will give you strength and make the realization of this easy. (372)**

Sister Faustina did as Jesus directed. Self-denial became her constant practice. She recorded her specific resolutions. (See 375). During this retreat she also received many other graces, most notably during the hours of adoration before the Blessed Sacrament. At one point Jesus made her this great promise:

With the souls that will have recourse to My mercy and with those who will glorify and proclaim My great mercy to others, I will deal according to My infinite mercy at the hour of their death. (379)

The Lord also allowed her to experience how particularly painful to Him was the ingratitude of those souls who were especially chosen by God. Each time she thought of God's great mercy and of the ingratitude of souls, pain stabbed her heart and she understood how painfully the Heart of Jesus was wounded. With a burning heart she renewed her act of self-oblation on behalf of sinners. During the renewal of the vows, God permitted Sister Faustina to see, in a vision, the scales of justice. On one scale she saw Jesus put a sword. On the other scale the Angels placed the sacrifices of the sisters' vowed lives. She learned that the sacrifices of the sisters were so pleasing to God that they outweighed the sword of punishment that was ready to fall upon the world. (See 394)

A Visit to the Family

Immediately after the retreat, Sister Faustina was handed a letter from home. She learned that her mother who was seriously ill and at the point of death was asking to see her once more. She had last been at home thirteen years before, in the autumn of 1922. She was deeply moved by the news. How she longed to see her beloved mother. But she left the matter in God's hands, resigning herself completely to His will.

On her feast day, February 15, Mother Superior handed her a second letter from her family and gave her permission to go home and fulfill her dying mother's wish. Sister Faustina left Vilnius that evening and she offered the entire night for the intention that God would grant His grace to her seriously ill mother and that her sufferings would lose none of their merit.

By eight p.m. the following day, she arrived in Glogowiec. She greeted her mother with the customary "Praised be Jesus Christ," knelt by her bed and said, "Mother, you will be up and about yet. I want to talk to you." The mother sat up in bed.

One of the daughters, who was busy at the stove, noticed this and cried out, "Mother, are you well already?"

"Yes," she replied. "As soon as I saw her, I got well." Up to this time her health had improved only slightly, and the doctor claimed there was no hope of a complete recovery without an operation.

It is difficult to describe the mutual joy they all felt as they greeted one another. After exchanging greetings they all fell to their knees and thanked the Lord for the grace of being together again. When Sister Faustina saw how her father prayed, she was very much ashamed to admit that after so many years in the convent she was not able to pray as sincerely and as ardently as he. For this reason she continually thanked God for such exemplary parents.

In her Diary, Sister left a simple and candid account of this visit:

> O, how everything had changed beyond recognition during those ten years! The garden had been so small, and now I could not recognize it. My brothers and sisters had still been children, and now they were all grown up. I was surprised that I did not find them as they had been when we parted. [Sister did not mention that the following day was a Sunday and they all went to church, including the mother who only the day before had been close to death.] (399)
>
> The days at home passed in much company, as everybody wanted to see me and talk with me. Often I could count as many as twenty-five people there. They listened with great interest to my accounts of the lives of the saints. It seemed to me that our house was truly the house of God, as each evening we talked about nothing but God. When, tired from these talks and yearning for solitude and silence, I quietly slipped out into the garden in the evening so I could converse with God alone, even in this I was unsuccessful; immediately my brothers and sisters came and took me back into the house and, once again, I had to talk with all those eyes fixed on me. But I struck on one way of getting some respite; I asked my brothers to sing for me, inasmuch as they had lovely voices; and besides, one played the violin and another, the mandolin. And during this time I was able to devote myself to interior prayer without shunning their

company.

What also cost me a lot was that I had to kiss the children. The women I knew came with their children and asked me to take them in my arms, at least for a moment, and kiss them. They regarded this as a great favor, and for me it was a chance to practice virtue, since many of the children were quite dirty. But in order to overcome my feelings and show no repugnance, I would kiss such a dirty child twice. One of these friends came with a child whose eyes were diseased and filled with pus, and she said to me, "Sister, take it in your arms for a moment, please." My nature recoiled, but not paying attention to anything, I took the child and kissed it twice, right on the infection, asking God to heal it.

I had many opportunities to practice virtue. I listened to people pour out their grievances, and I saw that no heart was joyful, because no heart truly loved God; and this did not surprise me at all. I was very sorry not to have seen two of my sisters. I felt interiorly that their souls were in great danger. Pain gripped my heart at the thought of them. Once when I felt very close to God, I fervently asked the Lord to grant them grace, and the Lord answered me, **I am granting them not only necessary graces, but special graces as well.** I understood that the Lord would call them to a greater union with Him. I rejoice immensely that such great love reigns in our family.

Stanley accompanied me to church every day. I felt that he was very pleasing to God. On the last day, when everyone had left the church, I went before the Blessed Sacrament with him, and together we recited the *Te Deum*. After a moment of silence, I offered his soul to the Sweetest Heart of Jesus. How easy it was to pray in that little church! I remembered all the graces that I had received there, and which I had not understood at the time and had so often abused. I wondered how I could have been so blind. And as I was thus regretting my blindness, I suddenly saw the Lord Jesus, radiant with unspeakable beauty, and He said to me with kindness, **My chosen one, I will give you even greater graces that you may be the witness of My infinite mercy throughout all eternity.**

As I was taking leave of my parents and asking for their blessing, I felt the power of the grace of God being poured out upon my soul. My father, my mother and my godmother blessed me with tears in their eyes, wished me the greatest faithfulness to God's graces, and begged me never to forget how many graces God had granted me in calling me to the religious life. They asked me to pray for them. Although everyone was crying, I did not shed a single tear. I tried to be brave and comforted them as best I could, reminding them of heaven where there would be no more parting.

Stanley walked with me to the car. I told him how much God loves pure souls and assured him that God was satisfied with him. When I was telling him about the goodness of God and of how He thinks of us, he burst out crying like a little child, and I was not surprised for his was a pure soul and, as such, more capable of recognizing God.

Once I was in the car, I let my heart have its way and I, too, cried like a baby, for joy that God was granting our family so many graces, and I became steeped in a prayer of thanksgiving. [Note: Sister Faustina never saw her parents again. The mother lived to be ninety. Her father died at the age of seventy-eight. Both outlived their daughter.]

By evening I was already in Warsaw. Firstly I greeted the Lord of the house [Jesus in the Eucharist], and then I went to greet the whole community. When I entered the chapel to say goodnight to the Lord before retiring, and apologized for having talked so little to Him when I was at home, I heard a voice within my soul, **I am very pleased that you had not been talking with Me, but were making My goodness known to souls and rousing them to love Me.** (400-404)

In the morning Mother Superior Mary Joseph took Sister Faustina to Jozefinek to see Mother General Michael. After spending a pleasant afternoon with her, Sister Faustina left for Vilnius, arriving there the next day. "Oh, how happy I felt to be back in our convent!" she wrote. "I felt as though I were entering the convent for the second time. I took unending delight in the silence and peace in which the soul can so easily immerse itself in God, helped by everyone and disturbed by no one." (407)

Lent and Easter, 1935

The lenten season became another opportunity for Sister Faustina to deepen her intimacy with the Lord. As she meditated on the Lord's Passion, Sister Faustina was allowed to see more clearly and feel more deeply the sufferings Jesus had endured for sin:

> ... When I become immersed in the Lord's Passion, I often see the Lord Jesus, during [my time for] adoration, in this manner: after the scourging, the torturers took the Lord and stripped Him of His own garment, which had already adhered to the wounds; as they took it off, His wounds reopened; then they threw a dirty and tattered scarlet cloak over the fresh wounds of the Lord. The cloak, in some places, barely reached His knees. They made Him sit on a piece of beam. And then they wove a crown of thorns, which they put on His sacred head. They put a reed in His hand and made fun of Him, bowing to Him as to a king. Some spat in His face, while others took the reed and struck Him on the head with it. Others caused Him pain by slapping Him; still others covered His face and struck Him with their fists. Jesus bore all this with meekness. Who can comprehend Him—comprehend His suffering? Jesus' eyes were downcast. I sensed what was happening in the most sweet Heart of Jesus at that time. Let every soul reflect on what Jesus was suffering at that moment. They tried to outdo each other in insulting the Lord. I reflected: Where does such malice in man come from? It is caused by sin. Love and sin have met. (408)

Sister Faustina's union with God grew more pervasive and enduring. She could sense God's greatness and majesty permeating every church she visited. This awe of God prompted her to write, "Oh, if only all souls knew who is living in our churches, there would not be so many outrages and so much disrespect in these holy places." (409)

During Mass she often saw God within her soul and felt His presence pervade her being. Without words, she talked at length with Him. She loved Him to distraction and felt that she was loved by God. Such moments were short, however, because a soul could not bear the ecstasy for long; separation from the body would be inevitable. But the power which is transmitted to the soul remained with her for a very long time. Without the least effort, Sister continued to experience the profound recollection which enveloped her during Mass; and it did not diminish when she talked to people, nor did it interfere with the performance of her duties. "I know that I am united with Him as closely as a drop of water is united with the bottomless ocean," she wrote. (411)

One day, after Sister entered the chapel for a moment, the power of grace enveloped her heart. As she continued in a state of recollection, Satan took a flowerpot and angrily hurled it to the ground with all his might. She saw all his rage and jealousy. Before she could pick up the pieces and repot the flower, Mother Superior, sister sacristan, and several other sisters came in. Mother Superior was surprised that Sister had been touching something on the altar and thus caused the flowerpot to fall. Sister sacristan showed her displeasure and Sister Faustina tried her best not to exonerate herself.

That evening she felt so exhausted that she was not able to make a holy hour. She asked Mother Superior to allow her to go to bed early. As soon as she lay down, she fell asleep. But at about eleven o'clock she felt her bed shaking. She awoke instantly and peacefully began to pray to her Guardian Angel. Then she saw souls who were doing penance in purgatory. They appeared like shadows and among them she saw many demons. One of these tried to vex her. Taking the form of a cat, he kept throwing himself onto her bed and on her feet. It seemed to her that he weighed a ton.

Sister Faustina continued to pray the rosary and toward dawn those beings vanished and she was able to get some sleep. When she entered the chapel in the morning she heard a voice in her soul, **You are united to Me; fear nothing. But know, My child, that Satan hates you; he hates every soul, but he burns with a particular hatred for you, because you have snatched so many souls from his dominion.** (412)

On Holy Thursday, April 18, Jesus told Sister Faustina that she would not feel His presence until the Mass of the Resurrection on Easter morning and immediately her soul was filled with a great yearning. The separation she felt from her beloved Jesus was more than her heart could bear. When it was time for Holy Communion she saw the Sorrowful Face of Jesus in every Host reposed in the ciborium. At this sight an even more intense longing flooded her heart.

At three o'clock on Good Friday, she entered the chapel and heard the words: **I desire that the image be publicly honored.** Then she saw the Lord Jesus dying on the Cross in great agony, and the same two rays, as shown in the image, were issuing from His Heart. (See 414)

First Exposition of the Image of The Divine Mercy

As soon as she possibly could, Sister Faustina made known Jesus' request to her spiritual director. She told him he was to place the Image for three days in Ostra Brama [Eastern Gate to the city of Vilnius] where a three-day celebration for the closing of the Jubilee Year of the Redemption of the World was to be held, coinciding with the projected Feast of Mercy which Our Lord desired to be observed on the first Sunday after Easter.

To Father Sopocko the whole project seemed impossible! "How could anyone think of introducing another devotion at the shrine of Our Lady?" he thought to himself. "Surely, such a request will be denied. And is it true that such a three-day celebration will be held as Sister said?"

He soon learned that there would indeed be a triduum held at Ostra Brama from April 26 to 28. The pastor, Reverend Canon Stanislaus Zawadzki invited him to preach the sermons! Father Sopocko, truly amazed and thoroughly convinced of the truth of Sister's message, agreed to preach, provided the Image of The Divine Mercy be placed "as a decoration" in the window of the church near the icon of Our Lady. At first, the permission was denied, but finally granted by the Archbishop. Sister Faustina asked to be present when the image was being hung in place. The following is Sister Faustina's account of the three-day celebration:

On the eve of the exposition of the image, I went with our Mother Superior to visit our confessor [Father

Sopocko]. When the conversation touched upon the image, the confessor asked for one of the sisters to help make some wreaths. Mother Superior replied, "Sister Faustina will help." I was delighted at this, and when we returned home, I immediately set about preparing some greens, and with the help of one of our wards brought them over. Another person, who works at the church, also helped. Everything was ready by seven o'clock that evening, and the image was already hanging in its place. However, some ladies saw me standing around there, for I was more a bother than a help, and on the next day they asked the sisters what this beautiful image was and what was its significance. Surely these sisters would know, [they thought] as one of them had helped adorn it the day before. The sisters were very surprised for they knew nothing about it; they all wanted to see it and immediately began to suspect me. They said, "Sister Faustina must certainly know all about it."

When they began asking me, I was silent since I could not tell the truth. My silence increased their curiosity, and I was even more on my guard not to tell a lie and not to tell the truth, since I had no permission [to do so]. Then they started to show their displeasure and reproached me openly, saying, "How is it that outsiders know about this and we, nothing?" Various judgments were being made about me. I suffered much for three days, but a special power took over in my soul. I was happy to suffer for God and for the souls that have been granted His mercy during these days. Seeing that so many souls have been granted divine mercy these days, I regard as nothing even the greatest suffering and toil, even if they were to continue until the end of the world; for they will come to an end, while these souls have been saved from torments that are without end. It was a great joy for me to see others returning to the source of happiness, the bosom of The Divine Mercy. (421)

When the image was displayed on Thursday evening, Sister Faustina saw Jesus' hand come alive and He made a large sign of the cross. That night when she went to bed, she saw the painted image walking above the town which seemed to be covered with a mesh and nets. As Jesus passed, He cut throught the nets, made a large sign of the cross and disappeared. She then saw herself surrounded by a multitude of malicious figures burning with hatred against her. They hurled all sorts of threats against her, but none of them touched her. The apparition vanished after a while, but for a long time she could not fall asleep. (See 416)

On Friday, April 26, Sister Faustina attended the ceremonies and heard a sermon on The Divine Mercy preached by her confessor. It was the fulfillment of the first request that Jesus had made a long time ago. When Father Sopocko began to speak about the great mercy of the Lord, to her the image came alive and the rays pierced the hearts of those present, but not all the people in the same degree: some more, some less. Great joy filled her heart and she heard the words: **You are a witness to My mercy. You shall stand before My throne forever as a living witness to My mercy.** (417)

She hurried back to the convent as soon as the sermon was over and did not wait for the end of the service. She had walked only a few steps when a whole multitude of demons blocked her way. They threatened her with terrible tortures and she heard voices saying, "She has snatched away everything we have worked for over so many years!"

She asked them, "Where have you come from in such great numbers?"

The wicked forms answered, "Out of human hearts; stop tormenting us!"

Sensing their great hatred towards her, Sister Faustina immediately invoked the help of her Guardian Angel. At once the bright and radiant figure appeared and he said to her, "Do not fear, spouse of my Lord; without His permission these spirits will do you no harm." Immediately the evil spirits vanished, and the faithful Guardian Angel accompanied her, in a visible manner, right to the doorstep. His look was modest and peaceful and a flame of fire sparkled from his forehead.

Faustina wrote, "O Jesus, I would like to toil and labor and suffer all my life for that one moment in which I saw Your glory, O Lord, and profit for souls." (419)

On Sunday, April 28, 1935, Sister Faustina made this entry in her diary:

Low Sunday, that is, the Feast of The Divine Mercy, the conclusion of the Jubilee of Redemption. When we went to take part in the celebrations, my heart leapt with joy that the two solemnities were so closely united. I asked God for mercy on the souls of sinners. Toward the end of the service, when the priest took the Blessed Sacrament to bless the people, I saw the Lord Jesus as He is represented in the image. The Lord gave His blessing and the rays extended over the whole world. Suddenly, I saw an impenetrable brightness in the form of a crystal dwelling place, woven together from waves of a brilliance unapproachable to both creatures and spirits. Three doors led to this resplendence. At that moment, Jesus, as He is represented in the image, entered this resplendence through the second door to the Unity within. It is a triple Unity, which is incomprehensible—which is infinity. I heard a voice, **This Feast emerged from the very depths of My mercy, and it is confirmed in the vast depths of My tender mercies. Every soul believing and trusting in My mercy will obtain it.** I was overjoyed at the immense goodnes and greatness of my God. (420)

Father Sopocko also shared in the bitter-sweetness of this great weekend. Seeing his sacrifice and efforts to accomplish this work, Sister Faustina admired his patience and humility. All this cost a great deal not only in terms of trouble and sorrow but also, of money. Father paid for all. She could see that Divine Providence had prepared him to carry out this work of mercy, even before she had asked God for help to accomplish His requests. (See 422) Her soul burst forth in praise of mercy:

Praise the Lord, my soul, for everything, and glorify His mercy, for His goodness is without end. Everything will pass, but His mercy is without limit or end. And although evil will attain its measure, in mercy there is no measure.

O my God, even in the punishments You send down upon the earth I see the abyss of Your mercy, for by punishing us here on earth You free us from eternal punishment. Rejoice, all you creatures, for you are closer to God in His infinite mercy than a baby to its mother's heart.

O God, You are compassion itself for the greatest sinners who sincerely repent. The greater the sinner, the greater his right to God's mercy. (423)

After the celebrations, the Image of The Divine Mercy was returned to the dark corridor of the Bernardine Sisters' convent.

Urgencies and Apparent Obstacles

Although Sister Faustina was receiving many extraordinary graces and revelations, she also continued to have inner conflicts to surmount. When she sensed God's great plans for her, she was frightened at their immensity and felt herself quite incapable of fulfilling them. She therefore began to avoid conversations with Jesus, preferring to recite prayers instead. She said she did this out of humility. Soon, however, she recognized that this was really the temptation of the devil. One day when she decided to read rather than meditate, she heard these forceful and distinct words: **You will prepare the world for My final coming.** The words moved her deeply. Yet, even though she understood what she had heard, she pretended not to.

When Sister revealed to Father Sopocko the state of her soul and especially the fact that she was avoiding interior conversations with God, he advised her to listen intently to the words God was speaking to her. The next time the Lord appeared to her, Sister Faustina fell at His feet and with a grief-stricken heart apologized for her behavior. Jesus lifted her up from the ground, sat her beside Himself and allowed her to rest her head on His bosom. He said to her, **My daughter, have fear of nothing; I am always with you. All your adversaries will harm you only to the degree that I permit them to do so. You are My dwelling place and My constant repose. For your sake I will withhold the hand which punishes; for your sake I bless the earth.** (429-4321)

At that very moment, Sister Faustina experienced an ecstasy she could not adequately explain:

> ...I felt some kind of fire in my heart. I feel my senses deadening and have no idea of what is going on around me... An extraordinary suffering pervades my soul together with a joy I cannot compare with anything. I feel powerless in the

embrace of God. I feel that I am in Him and that I am dissolved in Him like a drop of water in the ocean... after such interior prayer, I feel strength and power to practice the most difficult virtues. I feel a dislike for all things that the world holds in esteem. With all my soul I desire silence and solitude. (432)

Union with the Lord seemed to become more tangible and enduring. After Holy Communion, she could see in her heart the year-old Child Jesus whom she often saw during Holy Mass, and all day long she could feel Him physically within her heart. Deep recollection unconsciously gained such mastery over her that she could not even exchange a word with anyone. In fact, Sister Faustina began to avoid people as much as she could. She would always answer questions regarding her duties, but beyond that, not a word more. Evidently, the Lord was preparing her for something more. (See 434)

A New Congregation?

It was on Pentecost, June 9, 1935, that Sister Faustina for the first time heard a message which suggested to her that a significant change would soon occur. That evening, as she was walking in the garden, she heard the words: **By your entreaties, you and your companions shall obtain mercy for yourselves and for the world.** Somehow she understood that she was not to remain in the present congregation and that this was clearly God's will for her. The thought of beginning something new overwhelmed her. All she could think of was her own incompetence and inability to carry out God's intentions. When she heard the words, **Do not fear; I Myself will make up for everything that is lacking in you,** they pierced her deeply and made her even more aware of her misery. She understood that God was demanding a more perfect way of life from her; excuses like incompetence would no longer be enough. (See 435)

Later that month, Sister Faustina told her director in confession about the various matters the Lord wanted accomplished through her. She was sure that he would tell her that the Lord Jesus did not use miserable souls like hers for the works He wanted done. On the contrary, she heard him say that it was precisely such souls that God chose most frequently to carry out His plans. Moreover, much to her amazement, Father Sopocko revealed to her the secret of her soul—which she had not disclosed to anyone—namely, the secret that God wanted the establishment of a congregation that would proclaim His Mercy to the world and by prayer obtain that mercy for the world. When she tried to excuse herself, saying that she had no definite order from the Lord, she suddenly saw the same Jesus as He is painted in the image, standing in the doorway and telling her, **I desire that there be such a congregation.** She did not speak about this vision to her confessor immediately because she was in a hurry to return to the convent. As she hurried home, she kept repeating, "But I am not capable of fulfilling Your demands, Lord; I am not capable." (437)

At the very beginning of Holy Mass the next day, Sister Faustina saw Jesus in all His unspeakable beauty. He told her He wanted the congregation to be founded as soon as possible,

> **... and you shall live in it together with your companions. My Spirit shall be the rule of your life. Your life is to be modeled on Mine, from the crib to My death on the Cross. Penetrate My mysteries, and you will know the abyss of My mercy towards creatures and My unfathomable goodness— and this you shall make known to the world. Through your prayers, you shall mediate between heaven and earth.** (438)

It was time to receive Holy Communion. Jesus disappeared and Sister saw a great brightness. Then she heard these words: **We give Our blessing,** and at that moment a bright ray issued from that light and pierced her heart; an extraordinary fire was enkindled in her soul—she thought she would die of joy and happiness. She felt the separation of her spirit from her body. She felt totally immersed in God, snatched up by the Almighty like a particle of dust into unknown expanses.

When Sister recovered her senses, she felt she had the strength and courage needed to do God's will. Nothing seemed difficult to her now and she said to the Lord, "I am ready for every beck and call of Your will!" She had undergone interiorly all that would be her lot in the future. (439)

On July 30, the feast of St. Ignatius, patron of the congregation, Sister Faustina prayed to the saint fervently and almost reproachingly for not coming to her aid in carrying out God's plan. During Mass she saw him at the left side of the altar, holding a large book in his hand. And he said to her, "My daughter, I am not indifferent to your cause. This rule can be adapted, and it can be adapted to this congregation." And gesturing with his hand toward the big book, he disappeared. She rejoiced at the fact of how much the saints think of us and of how closely we are united with them. "Oh, the goodness of God!" she wrote. "How beautiful is the spiritual world, that already here on earth we commune with the saints!" All that day Sister could feel the presence of this dear patron saint. (448)

The inner struggle concerning the leaving of her beloved community to begin a new community, which she felt God was asking her to found, remained constantly with Sister Faustina until only a few months before her death. On the Feast of Our Lady of Mercy, August 5, 1935, her meditation and first Mass passed in that very struggle. During the second Mass, she turned to Our Lady saying it was difficult for her to separate from a community which enjoyed such special protection from Her. Then she saw the Blessed Virgin, unspeakably beautiful. She came down from the altar to her kneeler, held her close and said to her, *I am Mother to you all, thanks to the unfathomable mercy of God. Most pleasing to Me is that soul which faithfully carries out the will of God.* Sister Faustina was given to understand that she had faithfully fulfilled the will of God and had thus found favor in His eyes. *Be courageous. Do not fear apparent obstacles, but fix your gaze upon the Passion of My Son, and in this way you will be victorious,* the Mother of God told her. (449)

God and Souls

At these words of the Mother of God, Sister Faustina recalled the vision granted her on Thursday night, August 1, 1935, during her adoration of the Blessed Sacrament before the First Friday. She had recorded it thus:

When I came for adoration, an inner recollection took

hold of me immediately, and I saw the Lord Jesus tied to a pillar, stripped of His clothes, and the scourging began immediately. I saw four men who took turns at striking the Lord with scourges. My heart almost stopped at the sight of these tortures. The Lord said to me, **I suffer even greater pain than that which you see.** And Jesus geve me to know for what sins He subjected Himself to the scourging; these are sins of impurity. Oh, how dreadful was Jesus' moral suffering during the scourging! Then Jesus said to me, **Look and see the human race in its present condition.** In an instant, I saw horrible things: the executioners left Jesus and other people started scourging Him; they seized the scourges and struck the Lord mercilessly. These were priests, religious men and women, and high dignitaries of the Church, which surprised me greatly. There were lay people of all ages and walks of life. All vented their malice on the innocent Jesus. Seeing this, my heart fell as if into a mortal agony. And while the executioners had been scourging Him, Jesus had been silent and looking into the distance; but when those other souls I mentioned scourged Him, Jesus closed His eyes, and a soft, but most painful moan escaped from His Heart. And Jesus gave me to know in detail the gravity of the malice of these ungrateful souls: **You see, this is a torture greater than My death.** Then my lips too fell silent and I began to experience the agony of death, and I felt that no one would comfort me or snatch me from that state but the One who had put me into it. Then the Lord said to me, **I see the sincere pain of your heart which brought great solace to My Heart. See and take comfort.**

Then I saw the Lord Jesus nailed to the cross. When He had hung on it for a while, I saw a multitude of souls crucified like Him. Then I saw a second multitude of souls, and a third. The second multitude were not nailed to [their] crosses, but were holding them firmly in their hands. The third were neither nailed to [their] crosses nor holding them firmly in their hands, but were dragging [their] crosses behind them and were discontent. Jesus then said to me, **Do you see these souls? Those who are like Me in the pain and contempt they suffer will be like Me also in glory. And those**

who resemble Me less in pain and contempt will also bear less resemblance to Me in glory.

Among the crucified souls, the most numerous were souls of the clergy. I also saw some crucified souls whom I knew, and this gave me great joy. Then Jesus said to me, **In your meditation tomorrow, you shall think about what you have seen today.** And immediately Jesus disappeared from me. (445-446)

The next morning, Sister was too ill to attend Mass. Yet somehow, during that hour for Mass, from her bed she could see her confessor saying Mass in St. Michael's Church. During this time she saw the Child Jesus. Towards the end of the Mass the vision disappeared and she found herself back in the cell as before. She recorded, "Indescribable joy took hold of me because, although I could not go to Mass in our own chapel, I had assisted at it in a church which was far distant. Jesus has a remedy for everything." (See 447)

A week later, Sister was feeling so sick that she collapsed in her cell. Ignoring the pain because of her devotion to the Passion of Jesus, she was determined to make her Thursday evening adoration. When she reached the chapel she received an inner understanding of the great reward that God is preparing for us not only for our good deeds, but also for our sincere desire to perform them. "What a great grace of God this is!" she noted, and went on to reflect:

Oh, how sweet it is to toil for God and souls! I want no respite in this battle, but I shall fight to the last breath for the glory of my King and Lord. I shall not lay the sword aside until He calls me before His throne; I fear no blows, because God is my shield. It is the enemy who should fear us, and not we him. Satan defeats only the proud and the cowardly, because the humble are strong. Nothing will confuse or frighten a humble soul. I have directed my flight at the very center of the sun's heat and nothing can lower its course. Love will not allow itself to be taken prisoner; it is free like a queen. Love attains God. (450)

Special Graces

After Holy Communion, on another day, Sister Faustina heard these words: **You are Our dwelling place.** At that moment she felt the presence of the Holy Trinity—the Father, the Son and the Holy Spirit—in her soul. She felt she was God's temple, a child of the Father. She had no words to explain all of this, but her spirit understood it well. She then reflected, "O Infinite Goodness, how low You stoop to Your miserable creature! If only souls would want to be recollected, God would speak to them at once, for dissipation drowns out the word of the Lord." (451-452)

Union with the Holy Trinity became more frequent. Sister cooperated more faithfully with His graces. At one time the Lord said to her: **My daughter, take the graces that others spurn, take as many as you can carry.** At that moment, her soul was inundated with the love of God. She wrote:

I look for no happiness beyond my own interior where God dwells. I rejoice that God dwells within me; here I abide with Him unendingly; it is here that my greatest intimacy with Him exists; here I dwell with Him in safety; here is a place not probed by the human eye. (454)

The Blessed Virgin encouraged her to commune with God in this way. Enjoying full happiness within her soul, Sister Faustina was no longer filled with bitterness when suffering afflicted her, nor was she carried away by great consolation. Peace and equanimity were becoming the hallmarks of her life.

To further encourage her, Jesus told Sister Faustina at the beginning of a three-day retreat, which took place August 12 to 16, 1935, under the direction of Fr. Rzyczkowski, S.J.:

...During this retreat I will speak to you through the mouth of this priest to strengthen you and assure you of the truth of the words which I address to you in the depths of your soul. Although this is a retreat for all the sisters, I have you especially in mind, as I want to strengthen you and make you fearless in the midst of all the adversities which lie ahead. Therefore, listen intently to his words and meditate upon them in the depths of your soul. (456)

To Sister Faustina's astonishment, everything the priest was saying about union with God and obstacles to that union she had experienced literally in her soul and heard of it from Jesus; all that he said about God's mercy and goodness was exactly what Jesus had said to her concerning the Feast of Mercy. She now understood clearly all that the Lord had promised, and she had no doubt about anything. In her diary she wrote:

> Throughout that entire meditation I saw the Lord Jesus on the altar, in a white garment, His hand holding the notebook in which I write these things. Throughout the entire meditation Jesus kept turning the pages of the notebook and remained silent; however, my heart could not bear the fire that was enkindled in my soul. Despite the great effort of my will to take control of myself and not let others see what was going on in my soul, toward the end of the meditation I felt that I was completely beyond my own control. Then Jesus said to me, **You have not written everything in the notebook about My goodness towards mankind; I desire that you omit nothing; I desire that your heart be firmly grounded in total peace.** (459)

To Sister Faustina, this retreat was indeed very special. She saw that Jesus will not leave in doubt any soul that loves Him sincerely. Now she understood clearly that what unites the soul most closely with God is self-denial, that is, joining our will to the will of God. This is what makes the soul truly free, contributes to profound recollection of the spirit and makes all life's burdens light and death sweet.

At the renewal of vows on August 15, Sister Faustina saw Jesus bless the sisters and enter the tabernacle. Suddenly, the Mother of God in a white garment and blue cloak, with Her head uncovered, approached Sister from the altar, touched her and covered her with Her mantle, saying, *Offer these vows for Poland. Pray for her.* (468)

Throughout the entire retreat Sister Faustina had been in uninterrupted communion with Jesus. After such sweet intimacy with the Lord, she experienced a great yearning for God, for now she could no longer see Him with the eyes of the body as before. She now realized in what close intimacy her heart had been with Love Eternal!

One day at adoration, when her spirit seemed to be dying for Jesus' visible presence and she could not hold back the tears, she saw a spirit of great beauty who said to her, "Don't cry—says the Lord." When she asked who he was, he answered, "I am one of the seven spirits who stand before the throne of God day and night and give Him ceaseless praise." Instead of soothing her yearning for God, this spirit aroused in her an even greater longing for Him. The spirit did not leave her for a moment but accompanied her everywhere. On the following day during Mass, after the elevation of the Host, this same spirit began to sing the words, "Holy, Holy, Holy" in a voice that sounded like a thousand voices. It was indescribable! Her spirit became united to God, and in that instant she saw the grandeur and the inconceivable holiness of God and, at the same time, she realized the nothingness that she was of herself. A greater knowledge of the Holy Trinity was also revealed to her in a purely interior manner, independent of the senses. Such revelations began to occur more often now, and not only in chapel, but also at work and at such times when she would least expect them. (See 471-472)

The Chaplet of The Divine Mercy

On Friday, September 13, 1935, the Lord revealed to Sister Faustina a powerful means by which to obtain God's mercy for the world. She recorded it as follows:

> In the evening, when I was in my cell, I saw an Angel, the executor of divine wrath. He was clothed in a dazzling robe, his face gloriously bright, a cloud beneath his feet. From the cloud bolts of thunder and flashes of lightning were springing into his hands; and from his hand they were going forth, and only then were they striking the earth. When I saw this sign of divine wrath which was about to strike the earth, and in particular a certain place, which for good reasons I cannot name, I began to implore the Angel to hold off for a few moments, the world would do penance. But my plea was a mere nothing in the face of the divine anger. Just then I saw the Most Holy Trinity. The greatness of Its majesty pierced me deeply, and I did not dare to repeat

my entreaties. At that very moment I felt in my soul the power of Jesus' grace, which dwells in my soul. When I became conscious of this grace, I was instantly snatched up before the Throne of God. Oh, how great is our Lord and God and how incomprehensible His holiness! I will make no attempt to describe this greatness, because before long we shall all see Him as He is. I found myself pleading with God for the world with words I heard interiorly.

As I was praying in this manner, I saw the Angel's helplessness: he could not carry out the just punishment which was rightly due for sins. Never before had I prayed with such inner power as I did then....

The next morning when I entered the chapel, I heard these words interiorly: **Every time you enter the chapel, immediately recite the prayer which I taught you yesterday.** When I had said the prayer, in my soul I heard these words: **This prayer will serve to appease My wrath. You will recite it for nine days, on the beads of the rosary, in the following manner. First of all, you will say one OUR FATHER and HAIL MARY and the I BELIEVE IN GOD. Then on the OUR FATHER beads you will say the following words: "Eternal Father, I offer You the Body and Blood, Soul and Divinity of Your dearly beloved Son, Our Lord Jesus Christ, in atonement for our sins and those of the whole world." On the HAIL MARY beads, you will say the following words: "For the sake of His sorrowful Passion, have mercy on us and on the whole world." In conclusion, three times you will recite these words: "Holy God, Holy Mighty One, Holy Immortal One, have mercy on us and on the whole world."** (474-476)

It is this Chaplet that Jesus asked Sister Faustina to introduce to her community and to the world. In 1936, Father Michael Sopocko had the Cebulski Publishing House in Cracow print it on the reverse side of a prayer card, a copy of The Divine Mercy Image which Eugene Kazimierowski painted in Vilnius.

On the last day of September, Faustina was definite about her life mission. She wrote:

O my God, I am conscious of my mission in the Holy Church. It is my constant endeavor to plead for mercy for the world. I unite myself closely with Jesus and stand before Him as an atoning sacrifice on behalf of the world. God will refuse me nothing when I entreat Him with the voice of His Son. My sacrifice is nothing in itself, but when I join it to the sacrifice of Jesus Christ, it becomes all-powerful and has the power to appease divine wrath. God loves us in His Son; the painful Passion of the Son of God constantly turns aside the wrath of God.

O God, I desire that souls come to know You and to see that You have created them because of Your unfathomable love. O my Creator and Lord, I feel that I am going to remove the veil of heaven so that earth will not doubt Your goodness.

Make of me, Jesus, a pure and agreeable offering before the Face of Your Father. Jesus, transform me, miserable and sinful as I am, into Your own self (for You can do all things), and give me to Your Eternal Father. I want to become a sacrificial host before You, but an ordinary wafer to people. I want the fragrance of my sacrifice to be known to You alone. O Eternal God, an unquenchable fire of supplication for Your mercy burns within me. I know and understand that this is my task, here and in eternity. You yourself have told me to speak about this great mercy and about Your goodness. (482-483)

Eight-day Retreat and More on the New Congregation

Sister Faustina was preparing to go to Cracow to make an eight-day retreat and at the same time to carry out Father Sopocko's request. He, not certain about Sister Faustina's inspirations regarding the founding of a new community, wanted to refer the matter to yet another priest. For this reason, he told Sister to give an account of all the commands Jesus gave her concerning the new community to her former confessor, Father Joseph Andrasz, S.J.

On October 19, Sister and her companion Sister Antonina left Vilnius by train. Their first stop was the convent in Warsaw.

Sister Faustina's Guardian Angel, visible only to her, accompanied them on the journey. At the convent gate he disappeared only to appear again as they boarded the train from Warsaw to Cracow. Sister saw him sitting beside her, absorbed in prayer, contemplating God; her thoughts followed his. Again, when they reached the convent gate, he disappeared.

From the beginning of this retreat to its termination, Sister Faustina experienced a great desire to do God's will, but she was not without moments of temptation and inner turmoil which at one point left her weakened and exhausted. Two things were the cause of her unrest: firstly, the realization that of herself she can do nothing; and secondly, the fact that, because of Jesus' request, she must soon leave this community she loved, to found another.

On the second day of retreat, the superior arranged a meeting with Father Andrasz in the parlor. God gave Sister the grace of complete confidence, and after the conversation, the grace of deep peace and light concerning these matters. Father Andrasz advised Sister to do nothing without the consent of her superiors. Because she had taken perpetual vows in this congregation, he felt that was evidence of God's will for her and that she should remain where she was. If she continues in simplicity and in this spirit of obedience, God will not allow her to fall into error. Father Andrasz added, however, that it would indeed be good if there were a group of souls pleading with God for the world. Sister Faustina accepted his advice and made it part of her retreat resolutions. (See 489-506)

The Feast of Christ the King was celebrated on the last Sunday of October. On that day Sister ardently prayed that Jesus would be the King of all hearts and that His divine grace would shine in every soul. Jesus told her, **My daughter, you give Me the greatest glory by faithfully fulfilling My desires.** (500)

On the last day of retreat Sister saw Jesus during Mass. He told her, **You are My great joy; your love and your humility make Me leave the heavenly throne and unite Myself with you. Love fills up the abyss that exists between My greatness and your nothingness.** (512)

Immersed in an ocean of love and lost in Jesus, Sister Faustina nevertheless thought of others: "Jesus, make my heart like unto Yours, or rather transform it into Your own Heart that I may sense the needs of other hearts, especially of those who are sad and suffering. May the rays of mercy rest in my heart." (514)

On Saturday, November 2, Sister Faustina and her companion began their return trip, making a stop at Czestochowa to pray before the miraculous icon of Our Lady. On the evening of November 4 they were back in Vilnius.

Thoughts of the new congregation filled her mind more and more with an urgency to act. On November 14, during the nocturnal adoration, Sister found herself unable to pray or meditate on Jesus' Sorrowful Passion so she lay prostrate and offered the Most Sorrowful Passion of Jesus to the Heavenly Father in reparation for the sins of all the world. After the prayer she got to her feet and walked to the kneeler. Suddenly she saw Jesus next to her. The Lord appeared as He was during the scourging. In His hands he was holding a white garment and cincture (cord). He clothed her with the garment and girded her with the cord. Then Jesus covered her with a red cloak like the one He was covered with during His Passion, and on her head He put a veil of the same color as He said: **This is how you and your companions will be clothed. My life, from birth to death on the cross, will be the rule for you. Fix your eyes upon Me and live according to what you see. I desire that you penetrate into My spirit more deeply and understand that I am meek and humble of heart.** (526)

Sister felt an urge to set to work and fulfill the Lord's demands. For about a month she worked on the rules and regulations that were meant to govern the new community. While writing one evening, Sister Faustina heard a voice in her cell. It said, "Do not leave this Congregation; have mercy upon yourself, such great sufferings are in store for you." When she looked in the direction of the voice she saw nothing and continued to write. Suddenly she heard a noise and the words, "When you leave, we will destroy you. Do not torture us." She glanced around and saw many ugly monsters. Mentally she made the sign of the cross and they immediately disappeared. "How terribly ugly Satan is!" she wrote. "The poor damned souls that have to keep him company! Just the sight of him is more disgusting than all the torments of hell." Jesus again reassured her that nothing would happen to her against His will and a wondrous strength entered her soul after these words of the Lord. (See 540)

On one occasion, when Sister entered the chapel, she had a vision of a building in a state of disrepair and she heard the words, **This is where the convent will be.** She was somewhat disappointed that these ruins were to be the convent. (559)

In the middle of December Jesus appeared to Sister Faustina in the greenhouse and said to her:

> **Write what I say to you. My delight is to be united with you. With great desire, I wait and long for the time when I shall take up My residence sacramentally in your convent. My spirit will rest in that convent and I will bless its neighborhood in a special way. Out of love for you all, I will avert any punishments which are rightly meted out by My Father's justice. My daughter, I have inclined My Heart to your requests. Your assignment and duty here on earth is to beg mercy for the whole world. No soul will be justified until it turns with confidence to My mercy, and this is why the first Sunday after Easter is to be the Feast of Mercy. On that day, priests are to tell everyone about My great and unfathomable mercy. I am making you the administrator of My mercy. Tell the confessor that the image is to be on view in the church and not within the enclosure at the convent. By means of this image I shall be granting many graces to souls, so let every soul have access to it.** (570)

On December 21, Father Sopocko asked Sister Faustina to go look at a certain house to see whether it was the same one she had seen in the vision. When she went with him to see the house, or rather those ruins, at a glance she recognized that everything agreed perfectly with what she saw. The confessor then spoke to her about his ideas of the arrangement of the cells and other things. She again recognized everything to be the same as had been told to her by Jesus.

Immediately upon returning home, she went to the chapel to rest a while. Suddenly she heard these words in her soul: **Do not fear anything. I am with you. These matters are in My hands and I will bring them to fruition according to My mercy, for nothing can oppose My will.** (573)

Christmas 1935

The Christmas Season of 1935 was one of great interior joy and happiness for Sister Faustina. She listened to Jesus and entered wholeheartedly into the spirit of Christmas. It was a time of great interior joy and happiness. On Christmas Eve, from early morning, her spirit was immersed in God; His presence pervaded her entire being. On Christmas Day after Holy Communion she heard the words: **I am always in your heart; not only when you receive Me in Holy Communion, but always.**

Her writings reveal a new stage of mystical union:

O Holy Trinity, Eternal God, my spirit is drowned in Your beauty. The ages are as nothing in Your sight. You are always the same. Oh, how great is Your majesty. Jesus, why do You conceal Your majesty, why have You left Your heavenly throne and dwelt among us? The Lord answered me, **My daughter, love has brought Me here, and love keeps Me here. My daughter, if you knew what great merit and reward is earned by one act of pure love for Me, you would die of joy. I am saying this that you may constantly unite yourself with Me through love, for this is the goal of the life of your soul. This act is an act of the will. Know that a pure soul is humble. When you lower and empty yourself before My majesty, I then pursue you with My graces and make use of My omnipotence to exalt you.** (575-576)

And again:

The interior of my soul is like a large and magnificent world in which God and I live. Except for God, no one is allowed there. At the beginning of this life with God, I was dazzled and overcome with awe. His radiance blinded me, and I thought He was not in my heart; and yet those were the moments when God was working in my soul. Love was becoming purer and stronger, and the Lord brought my will into the closest union with His own holy will. No one will understand what I experience in that splendid palace of my soul where I abide constantly with my Beloved. No exterior thing hinders my union with God.... (582)

On onother occasion, Jesus told Sister Faustina:

When you reflect upon what I tell you in the depths of your heart, you profit more than if you had read many books. Oh, if souls would only want to listen to My voice when I am speaking in the depths of their hearts, they would reach the peak of holiness in a short time. (584)

A YEAR OF MANY CHANGES (1936)

The New Congregation Again

Early in January, 1936, Sister Faustina visited the Archbishop of Vilnius, Romuald Jalbrzykowski, to tell him again of Jesus' requests that she pray for God's mercy on the world and that there be a religious community which by its entreaties would obtain Divine Mercy for the world. Last year, when she had asked the archbishop's permission to do all that the Lord Jesus demanded of her, he told her that entertaining thoughts of leaving the present congregation would be a serious interior temptation. "If these things come from God, they will be realized sooner or later," he said. This time, the Archbishop answered her in these words: "As for prayer, I give my permission and even encourage you, Sister, to pray as much as possible for the world and to beg God's mercy, as mercy is what we all need. But as regards this congregation, wait a while, Sister, so that all things may arrange themselves more favorably. This thing is good in itself, but there is no need to hurry. If it is God's will, it will be done, whether it be a little sooner or a little later. Why shouldn't it be? There are so many different kinds of congregations; this one, too, will come to be if God so wills. Be completely at peace. The Lord Jesus can do all things. Strive for a close union with God and do not lose heart." (585)

As she joyfully left the Archbishop she heard these words in her soul:

> **To confirm your spirit, I speak through My representatives in accordance with what I demand of you, but know that this will not always be so. They will oppose you in many things and through this My grace will be manifest in you, and it will be evident that this matter is My doing. But as for**

you, fear nothing; I am always with you. And know this too, My daughter: all creatures, whether they know it or not, and whether they want to or not, always fulfill My will. (586)

This assurance of the Lord gave her some peace for the time being.

An Understanding of The Mystery of Suffering

On January 29, Sister recorded, among other things, a vision concerning her confessor, and an understanding of the mystery of suffering. She saw, partially, the condition of his soul and the ordeals God was sending him. His sufferings were of the mind and in a form so acute that she pitied him and said to the Lord, "Why do You treat him like that?" And the Lord answered that it was for the triple crown meant for him—that of virginity, the priesthood and martyrdom. And the Lord gave her to understand what unfathomable glory awaits the person who resembles the suffering Jesus here on earth. That person will resemble Jesus in His glory. The Heavenly Father will recognize and glorify our soul to the extent that He sees in us a resemblance to His Son. She understood that this assimilation into Jesus is granted to us while we are here on earth. "I see pure and innocent souls upon whom God has exercised His justice; these souls are the victims who sustain the world and who fill up what is lacking in the Passion of Jesus. They are not many in number. I rejoice greatly that God has allowed me to know such souls," she wrote. (See 604)

In another entry, however, Sister confessed that in spite of the many and unusual graces she received, the road to holiness was not an easy one for her:

My Jesus, despite Your graces I see and feel all my misery. I begin my day with battle and end it with battle. As soon as I conquer one obstacle, ten more appear to take its place. But I am not worried because I know that this is a time of struggle, not peace. When the burden of battle becomes too much for me, I throw myself like a child into the arms of the Heavenly Father and trust I will not perish. O my Jesus, how prone I am to evil, and this forces me to be constantly vigilant. But I do not lose heart. I trust in God's grace, which abounds in the worst misery. (606)

On February 2, after Holy Communion, Sister pleaded with Jesus, asking Him to grant Father Sopocko the grace to fight and to take from him a particular trial he was suffering. The answer was, **As you ask, so shall it be, but his merit will not be lessened.** Joy filled her soul because God was so good and merciful. "God grants everything that we ask of Him with trust," she wrote. (609)

A Time of Trial and of Graces

On March 1, 1936, Sister Faustina entered a struggle that lasted several days. She clearly realized that God was demanding the founding of a new congregation but something in her resisted. The struggle that ensued seemed to her to be as great as the Lord's was in Gethsemane. She felt an extraordinary force urging her to action. One thing alone held her back. It was holy obedience. "O my Jesus," she cried, "You urge me on the one hand and hold me back and restrain me on the other." (615) This spiritual turmoil aggravated her physical weakness. Although she spoke to no one about it, Mother Superior noticed her changed and pale condition and told her to get to bed earlier and to sleep longer. She even had someone bring a cup of hot milk to her in the evening. However, these material things could not bring relief.

By March 18, nothing was yet resolved. Sister Faustina asked Jesus to initiate the first step by some external event, even that of having her expelled from the congregation, because of herself she could not leave. It was a day of agony for her. The next day, Mother Superior told her that Mother General was taking her to Warsaw. Sister thought this was the external sign and even told Mother Superior that she regarded it as such; so she felt she need not go to Warsaw but leave the community right then and there. At first Mother Superior had nothing to say but after a while she called her again and suggested that Sister Faustina go anyway and not worry about wasting the trip, even if she were to return immediately. Faustina was distressed because the trip would again delay matters; but she decided to go. She always tried to be obedient.

That evening during prayer, the Mother of God, referring to the New Congregation, told her: *Your lives must be like Mine— quiet and hidden, in unceasing union with God, pleading for humanity and preparing the world for the second coming of God.* (625)

While she communed with God the Father during Benediction, she heard the words: **Do not fear anything, My daughter; all the adversaries will be shattered at My feet.** At these words a deep peace and a strange inner calm entered her soul. (626)

On the evening before her departure from Vilnius, an elderly sister approached her, revealed to her a spiritual problem and asked her to ask Jesus for His answer because "I know that the Lord Jesus speaks to you, Sister." To be freed from the hand clutching her, Faustina promised to pray for her. At Benediction that evening she heard the words: **Tell her that her disbelief wounds My Heart more than the sins she committed.** When Sister Faustina related the message, the overjoyed sister cried like a child. (628)

As she was taking leave of the sisters the next day, one of them kept apologizing for having helped her so little in her duties; and not only for having neglected to help her, but also for having tried to make things more difficult for her. In her diary Sister made this comment about the whole affair:

> However, in my own heart, I regarded her as a great benefactress, because she had exercised me in patience to such an extent that one of the older sisters had once said, "Sister Faustina must be either a fool or a saint, for truly, an ordinary person would not tolerate having someone constantly do such things out of spite." However, I had always approached her with good will. That particular sister had tried to make my work more difficult to the point that, despite my efforts, she had sometimes succeeded in spoiling what had been well done, as she herself admitted to me at our parting, and for which she begged my pardon. I had not wanted to probe her intentions, but took it as a trial from God...
>
> I am greatly surprised at how one can be so jealous.

When I see someone else's good, I rejoice at it as if it were mine. The joy of others is my joy, and the suffering of others is my suffering, for otherwise I would not dare to commune with the Lord Jesus. The spirit of Jesus is always simple, meek, sincere; all malice, envy, and unkindness disguised under a smile of good will are clever little devils. A severe word flowing from sincere love does not wound the heart. (632-633)

Sister Faustina must have traveled to Warsaw without a sister companion. But she did not travel alone. One of the seven spirits, radiant as before as a figure of light sat beside her throughout the trip. Sister saw, on every church they passed, an angel of paler light than that of the spirit accompanying her; and each of those spirits guarding the churches bowed his head to the spirit that was with her. When she entered the convent gate at Warsaw, the spirit disappeared. Sister wrote in her Diary:

I thanked God for His goodness, that He gives us angels for companions. Oh, how little people reflect on the fact that they always have beside them such a guest, and at the same time a witness to everything! Remember, sinners, that you likewise have a witness to all your deeds. (630)

And then she added this consoling thought:

O my Jesus, Your goodness surpasses all understanding, and no one will exhaust Your mercy. Damnation is for the soul that wants to be damned; but for the one who desires salvation, there is the inexhaustible ocean of the Lord's mercy to draw from. How can a small vessel contain the unfathomable ocean? (631)

Arriving in Warsaw, on March 22, Sister Faustina first entered the little chapel to thank the Lord for a safe journey and to ask His help and grace for everything that was in store for her. She submitted in all things to His holy will. Then she heard the words: **Fear nothing; all difficulties will serve for the fulfillment of My will.** (634)

Three days later, on the Feast of the Annunciation, Sister Faustina was enveloped by God's presence and saw the greatness of the infinite God and likewise His condescension toward His creatures. Then she saw the Mother of God who gave her the following awesome message:

> *Oh, how pleasing to God is the soul that follows faithfully the inspirations of His grace! I gave the Savior to the world; as for you, you have to speak to the world about His great mercy and prepare the world for the Second Coming of Him who will come, not as a Merciful Savior but, as a Just Judge. Oh, how terrible is that day! Determined is the day of justice, the day of divine wrath. The angels tremble before it. Speak to souls about this great mercy while it is still the time for [granting] mercy. If you keep silent now, you will be answering for a great number of souls on that terrible day. Fear nothing. Be faithful to the end. I sympathize with you.* (635)

New Assignments: Walendow and Derdy

Evidently, Sister Faustina felt this was not the time to leave the community for she accepted yet another assignment, this time in Walendow a country place about 20 kilometers from Warsaw. The sisters there gave her a sincere and joyful welcome. One of the sisters said to her, "Sister, you have come to us so everything will be all right now."

"Why do you say that, sister?" asked Sister Faustina.

"I have such a feeling about it in my soul," she replied.

The truth was that the house was in financial straits. In order to make ends meet, the sisters were compelled to work in the fields from dawn to dusk. Often they were unable to perform their spiritual exercises adequately.

Placed in such a situation, Sister Faustina's health began to deteriorate again; but without complaint, Sister accepted all the opportunities for sacrifice and self-denial as part of her Lenten program. When the superior ordered her to dust the walls, Sister Faustina humbly asked for another duty as she felt too sick to do such work. When the request was refused, she obediently did as she was told. Didn't she once say that she would rather be a cinderella in the convent than a queen in the world? Before Holy Communion on First Friday, Sister Faustina saw a large ciborium filled with hosts. A hand placed the ciborium in front of her and she took it into her own hands. There were a thousand living hosts within. Then she heard a voice: **These are hosts which have been received by souls for whom you have obtained the grace of true conversion during this Lent.** (640)

On first Friday, just a week before Good Friday, Sister spent the day in even greater interior recollection, emptying herself for the sake of souls:

> O, what joy it is to empty myself for the sake of immortal souls! I know that the grain of wheat must be destroyed and ground between millstones in order to become food. In the same way, I must become destroyed in order to be useful to the Church and souls, even though exteriorly no one will notice my sacrifice. O Jesus, outwardly I want to remain hidden, just like this little wafer wherein the eye perceives nothing, and yet I am a host consecrated to You. (641)

On Palm Sunday, Sister Faustina experienced in a unique way the sentiments of the most sweet Heart of Jesus as He rode into Jerusalem, praised by young and old. Everyone around Him was full of joy, but Jesus was very grave and allowed her to know how much He was suffering. At that particular moment she saw only Jesus whose Heart was saturated with the ingratitude of humankind.

On Wednesday of Holy Week the occasional confessor, Father Bukowski came to Walendow to hear the sisters' confessions. Father Aloysius Bukowski, S.J., had been the occasional confessor at the convent on Zytnia Street in Warsaw when Sister Faustina spent her first years there. Sister felt she could no longer put off the matter of the new congregation so in the confessional she told Father everything. Father answered, "Sister, this is an illusion! The Lord Jesus cannot be demanding this. You have made your perpetual vows! You are inventing some sort of heresy!!" He was actually shouting at her, almost at the top of his voice. (See 643)

When Sister asked him what course she should follow, he told her, "Well, Sister, you must not follow any inspiration. You should get your mind off all this. You should pay no attention to what you hear in your soul and just try to carry out your exterior duties well. Give no thought to these things and put them completely out of your mind."

She answered, "Good, up to now, I have been following my conscience, but now that you direct me, Father, to pay no heed to my interior, I will cease to do so."

Father then said, "If the Lord Jesus tells you something again, please let me know, but you must take no action."

She replied, "Very well; I will try to be obedient."

Sister Faustina had no idea why Father was being so severe. A multitude of thoughts began to oppress her when she left the confessional. It was good she no longer needed to heed the inner voice that often cost her so much humiliation; however, a strange pain seized her soul and from the moment of the confessor's prohibition, her soul was enveloped in great darkness.

Her suffering further intensified on Holy Thursday when Satan added his taunts. Her own words best describe what she then experienced:

> ...When I came to make my meditation, I entered into a kind of agony. I did not feel the presence of God, but all the justice of God weighed heavily upon me. I saw myself as if knocked down for the sins of the world. Satan began to mock me, "See, now you will no longer strive to win souls; look how you've been paid! Nobody will believe you that Jesus demands this. See how much you are suffering now, and how much more you are going to suffer! After all, the confessor has now released you from all these things." Now I can live as I like, as long as things are all right outwardly. These dreadful thoughts tormented me throughout the whole hour.
>
> When it was almost the time for Holy Mass, my heart was seized with pain; am I, then, to leave the Congregation? And since Father has told me that this is a kind of heresy, am I to fall away from the Church? I cried out to the Lord with a sorrowful interior cry, "Jesus, save me!" Still, not a single ray of light entered my soul, and I felt my strength failing, as if the body were separating itself from the soul. I submitted to the will of God and repeated, "O God, let whatever You have decided upon happen to me. Nothing in me is any

longer my own." Then, suddenly, God's presence enveloped me and penetrated me through and through. This was just as I was receiving Holy Communion. A moment after Holy Communion, I lost all awareness of everything around me and of my whereabouts.

Then I saw the Lord Jesus, as He is represented in the image, and He said to me, **Tell the confessor that this work is Mine and that I am using you as a lowly instrument.** And I said, "Jesus, I can no longer do anything You command me to do, because my confessor has told me that all this is an illusion, and that I am not allowed to obey any of Your commands. I will do nothing that You will tell me to do now. I am sorry, my Lord, but I am not allowed to do anything, and I must obey my confessor. Jesus, I most earnestly ask Your pardon. You know how much I suffer because of this, but it can't be helped, Jesus. The confessor has forbidden me to follow Your orders." Jesus listened to my arguments and complaints with kindness and satisfaction. I thought the Lord Jesus would be grievously offended but, on the contrary, He was pleased and said to me kindly, **Always tell your confessor about everything I say to you and command you to do, and do only that for which you obtain permission. Do not be upset, and fear nothing; I am with you.** My soul was filled with joy and all those oppressive thoughts vanished. Certitude and courage entered my soul.

But after a short while, I entered into the sufferings which Jesus underwent in the Garden of Olives. This lasted until Friday morning... On that day, Father Bukowski came from Derdy. Some strange power pushed me to go to confession and tell him about everything that had happened to me and about what Jesus had said to me. When I told Father, he was quite different and he said to me, "Sister, don't be afraid of anything; you will come to no harm, for the Lord Jesus will not allow it. If you are obedient and persevere in this disposition, you need not worry about anything. God will find a way to bring about His work. You should always have this simplicity and sincerity and tell everything to Mother General. What I said to you was said as a warning, because illusions may afflict even holy persons, and Satan's insinuations may play a part in this, and sometimes this comes from our own selves, so one has to be careful. And so continue as you have thus far. You can see, Sister, that the Lord is not angered by this. And Sister, you can repeat these things that presently have happened to you to your regular confessor [Father Sopocko]."

From this I came to understand one thing: that I must pray much for each one of my confessors, that he might obtain the light of the Holy Spirit, for when I approach the confessional without first praying fervently, the confessor does not understand me very well. (644-647)

At three o'clock on Good Friday, Sister saw the Lord Jesus on the cross. He looked at her and said, **I thirst.** Then she saw the two rays issue from His side just as in the image, and she felt the desire to save souls and to empty herself for the sake of poor sinners. She offered herself together with the dying Jesus to the Eternal Father for the salvation of the whole world.

On Easter Sunday, April 12, 1936, Sister Faustina's spirit was immersed in the Lord. She wished only that God's will be accomplished in and through her; she praised His inscrutable mercy:

O my Jesus, my Master and Director, strengthen and enlighten me in these difficult moments of my life. I expect no help from people; all my hope is in You. I feel alone in the face of Your demands, O Lord.... Let what You have planned before all ages happen to me. I am ready...

O incomprehensible God, how great is Your mercy! It surpasses the combined understanding of all men and angels. All the angels and all humans have emerged from the very depths of Your tender mercy. Mercy is the flower of love. God is love, and mercy is His deed. In love it is conceived; in mercy it is revealed. Everything I look at speaks to me of God's mercy. Even God's very justice speaks to me about His fathomless mercy, because justice flows from love. (650-651)

Sister Faustina's physical condition grew steadily worse. Two weeks after Easter she was transferred to Derdy, another country home for the girls. It was about one kilometer from

Walendow and administered by the same Mother Superior. This home was in the forest. Sister reveled in its peace and quiet and in the beauty of nature which made God's presence more manifest. Her work here was comparatively easy and she had more time to rest and pray. This was one home that later brought back many pleasant memories. She felt it was like Nazareth. In its peaceful atmosphere her soul was strengthened. She was so happy that she shared her joy with Father Sopocko in a letter she had written him on May 10, 1936.

However, it was now becoming evident that Sister Faustina never fully recovered from her serious illness in Vilnius in 1934. She had been assigned to Walendow and then to Derdy for reasons of health, but difficulties in communication between Warsaw and these country places necessitated still another transfer. This time she was assigned to the house in Cracow, where contact with doctors would be more readily available.

Before she left Derdy on May 11, Sister Faustina said goodby to her friend Sister Justine and told her in the strictest confidence that she would die in the autumn, two years hence, and that they would never see each other again on this earth. "You must tell this to no one while I am still alive," she told her. Sister Justine kept the confidence as directed.

Further Testing

Happiness filled Sister Faustina's heart when she returned to Cracow. She was sure that now, finally, she would be able to do all that Jesus was demanding—referring, of course, to the founding of the new congregation. She confided her inspirations to Father Joseph Andrasz, S.J., who told her to pray and make sacrifices until the Feast of the Sacred Heart, and then he would give her an answer. Sister, however, felt such an urge to leave that, when she went to confession, she told Father that she decided to leave. Father answered, "Sister, since you have made the decision by yourself, then take the responsibility for yourself. Go." She was happy that she had finally made up her mind. But the next day God's presence suddenly left her, and such a great darkness enveloped her soul that she could not pray. Because of this, she decided to postpone the matter of leaving until she had again spoken to Father Andrasz. He explained to her that such changes in souls were frequent and that it was not an obstacle to take action. (See 655)

When she related everything to Mother Michael, Mother General told her, "Sister, I am locking you in the tabernacle with the Lord Jesus; wherever you go from there, that will be the will of God." And so the struggle within her continued. (656)

One day in June, Sister Faustina wrote:

O my Jesus, how immensely I rejoice at the assurance You have given me that the Congregation will come into being. I no longer have the least shadow of a doubt about this, and I see how great is the glory which it will give to God. It will be the reflection of God's greatest attribute; that is, His divine mercy. Unceasingly, they will intercede for divine mercy for themselves and for the whole world. And every act of mercy will flow from God's love, that love with which they will be filled to overflowing. They will strive to make their own this great attribute of God, and to live by it and to bring others to know it and to trust in the goodness of the Lord. This Congregation of Divine Mercy will be in God's Church like a beehive in a magnificent garden, hidden and meek. The sisters will work like bees to feed their neighbors' souls with honey, while the wax will flame for the glory of God. (664)

...I understood that nothing could resist or nullify the will of God. I understood that I must carry out this will of God despite obstacles, persecutions and sufferings of all kinds, and despite natural repugnance and fear. (665)

I understood that all striving for perfection and all sanctity consist in doing God's will. Perfect fulfillment of God's will is maturity in sanctity; there is no room for doubt here. To receive God's light and recognize what God wants of us and yet not do it is a great offense against the majesty of God. Such a soul deserves to be completely forsaken by God. It resembles Lucifer, who had great light, but did not do God's will. An extraordinary peace entered my soul when I reflected on the fact that, despite great difficulties, I had always faithfully followed God's will as I knew it. (666)

Throughout the months of June and July, Sister Faustina encountered many disappointments from those in authority and put up with the reproaches and ironic smiles of those who lived with her. The desire to do God's will, on the one hand, and the lack of confirmation from her confessor and religious authorities, on the other, caused great suffering and sorrow which she bore in silence and unusual composure. In addition, Sister's health was steadily declining. Three years ago she had told the doctor about the pain in her lungs, but after examination, the doctor found no positive evidence of any ailment, and an analysis of the sputum showed no signs of sickness. "And yet it hurts," was Sister Faustina's quiet reply then.

Her difficult days were punctuated with moments of untold happiness. On August 7, 1936, for instance, Sister Faustina was overjoyed when she received a brochure on Divine Mercy written by Father Michael Sopocko and published in Vilnius. On the cover of the brochure was a copy of the Image of The Divine Mercy. She left this note in her Diary:

> When I steeped myself in a prayer of thanksgiving, I suddenly saw the Lord Jesus in a great brightness, just as He is painted, and at His feet I saw Father Andrasz and Father Sopocko. Both were holding pens in their hands, and flashes of light and fire, like lightning, were coming from the tips of their pens and striking a great crowd of people who were hurrying I know not where. Whoever was touched by the ray of light immediately turned his back on the crowd and held out his hands to Jesus. Some returned with great joy, others with great pain and compunction. Jesus was looking at both priests with great kindness. After a while, I was left alone with Jesus, and I said, "Jesus, take me now, for Your will has already been accomplished." And Jesus answered, **My will has not yet been completely accomplished in you; you will still suffer much, but I am with you; do not fear.** (675)

Warning for Poland

It was evening, the First Friday of September, 1936. Sister Faustina had a vision of the Mother of God whose uncovered breast was pierced with a sword. The Blessed Mother was shedding bitter tears and shielding the people against God's terrible punishment. Sister was seized by a horrible fear and kept praying incessantly for Poland, her dear Poland, which was showing so little gratitude for the Mother of God. If it were not for the Mother of God, all efforts would be useless. She multiplied her prayers and sacrifices for her native land, but saw she was but a drop as compared to the wave of prevalent evil. She commented in her diary, "How can a drop stop a wave? O yes! A drop is nothing of itself, but with You, Jesus, I shall stand up bravely to the whole wave of evil and even to the whole of hell. Your omnipotence can do all things."

It seems God accepted the prayers of His Mother and the sacrifices of His servant, and prolonged the time of mercy for Poland. (686)

A few days into September, as Sister Faustina was walking down the corridor to the kitchen, the Lord gave her an important message:

> **Unceasingly say the chaplet that I have taught you. Whoever will recite it will receive great mercy at the hour of death. Priests will recommend it to sinners as their last hope of salvation. Even if there were a sinner most hardened, if he recites this chaplet only once, he will receive grace from My infinite mercy. I desire that the whole world know My infinite mercy. I desire to grant unimaginable graces to those souls who trust in My mercy. (687)**

Opportunities for Trust in Mercy

On September 14, Archbishop Romuald Jalbrzykowski of Vilnius was visiting in Cracow and called upon the sisters in Lagiewniki. Although he stayed for only a short time, Sister Faustina was given the opportunity to speak to him about the work of Divine Mercy. He showed himself favorably disposed and said, "Sister, be completely at peace; if this is within the plans of divine providence, it will come about. In the meantime, Sister, pray for a clearer outward sign. Let the Lord Jesus give you a clearer knowledge of this. I beg you to wait a little while longer.

The Lord Jesus will so arrange the circumstances that everything will turn out all right." (693)

Perhaps the Archbishop noticed Sister's poor physical appearance and brought it to the Mother Superior's attention. At any rate, on September 19, Sister was sent to a lung specialist. He did not hide his concern. In the sanatorium chapel where Sister and her companion stopped for a quick visit, Sister Faustina heard these words in her soul: **My child, just a few more drops in your cup; it won't be long now.** Her soul was filled with joy. That was the first call from her beloved Master. (694)

Five days later, on the night of September 24, Sister Faustina was awakened by severe pains which lasted for about three hours. Her suffering was so great that it prevented her from making the slightest movement; she was unable to swallow her saliva. Sister did not call for help but resigned herself completely to the will of God and thought that surely the day of her death, the day she so much desired, had come. When the pain subsided she broke out in a sweat. Each movement brought on another attack. She dared not move. The next morning she felt no further physical pain but was so very tired that she could not get up to attend Mass. As she lay there she thought, "If after such suffering death does not come, then how great the sufferings of death must be!" Only trust in the unfathomable mercy of God took away her fear. (See 696)

Soon after this painful attack, Sister Faustina recorded in her diary what is now considered the principal message given to her concerning the Feast of The Divine Mercy:

> **My daughter, tell the whole world about My inconceivable mercy. I desire that the Feast of Mercy be a refuge and shelter for all souls, and especially for poor sinners. On that day the very depths of My tender mercy are open. I pour out a whole ocean of graces upon those souls who approach the fount of My mercy. The soul that will go to Confession and receive Holy Communion shall obtain complete forgiveness of sins and punishment. On that day are open all the divine floodgates through which graces flow. Let no soul fear to draw near to Me, even though its sins be as scarlet. My mercy is so great that no mind, be it of man or of angel, will be able to fathom it throughout all eternity. Everything that exists has come forth from the very**

depths of My most tender mercy. Every soul in its relation to Me will contemplate My love and mercy throughout eternity. The Feast of Mercy emerged from My very depths of tenderness. It is My desire that it be solemnly celebrated on the first Sunday after Easter. Mankind will not have peace until it turns to the Fount of My Mercy. (699)

By repeating the above message to Sister Faustina at least fourteen times, the Lord thereby emphasized how important it was to Him. (See 49; 88; 280; 299; 341; 420; 570; 699; 742; 964; 998; 1072; 1082; 1109; 1517)

Meanwhile, to the recipient of this message Jesus gave more opportunity to practice trust in His mercy. Sister Faustina was now experiencing continual tiredness and pain. She mentioned this one day to the Mother Superior. Mother's answer was that she should get used to sufferings. Faustina listened respectfully to what Mother had to say, and then departed. She reasoned that if Mother Superior, who was known for her charity especially towards the sisters who were ill, did not understand her, it must be that the Lord is allowing that she be tested in this way. So on this particular day Sister went to work in the fields, despite the pain. It was such a hot day that even a healthy person who was not working could not endure it. Before noon, Sister straightened up from her work, looked up at the sky and with great trust said to the Lord, "Jesus, cover the sun for I cannot stand this heat any longer." At that very moment a white cloud covered the sun and from then on the heat was less intense. When a little later she began to reproach herself for begging relief from the heat, Jesus himself put her at ease. Thus, as the sufferings increased day by day, so did the graces Sister needed to bear them. In union with God she found inner peace and outward strength. The practice of uniting with the Merciful Christ was still the topic of her daily examination of conscience, for she knew that through this union she gained unusual strength. And thus, no matter what, her actions were regulated by mercy which flowed from love. (See 701)

As was already mentioned, angels served Sister in special ways. On September 29, the Feast of St. Michael the Archangel, Sister saw this great leader by her side. He said to her, "The Lord has ordered me to take special care of you. Know that you are hated by evil; but do not fear—'Who is like God!'" He disappeared but Sister felt his presence and assistance from then on. (See 706)

The interweaving of suffering and grace continued. The doctor, at the sanatorium on Pradnik, who diagnosed her illness as tuberculosis, ordered that Sister Faustina be separated from the other sisters in order to prevent the spread of the disease. She was placed in the infirmary section of the convent, but was not relieved of her daily tasks.

One day Sister Faustina felt that she could not carry on until nine o'clock. She asked the sister on duty in the kitchen for something to eat, explaining that she was going to bed early as she was not feeling well. The sister retorted, "But you are not ill, Sister; they only wanted you to have some rest, so they made up this illness." Sister Faustina accepted this rash judgment in silence and offered it up as she did all other pains and hurts. (710)

Great joy filled Sister's heart when on October 5, she received a letter from Father Sopocko. He intended to publish a holy card of the Merciful Christ and was asking her to send him a certain prayer of hers which would be printed on the reverse side of it, if the Archbishop granted the approbation. On this occasion she noted:

> Oh, what great joy fills my heart that God has let me see this work of His mercy! How great is this work of the Most High God! I am but His instrument. Oh, how ardently I desire to see this Feast of The Divine Mercy which God is demanding through me. But if it is the will of God that it be celebrated solemnly only after my death, even so I rejoice in it already, and I celebrate it interiorly with my confessor's permission. (711)

On October 11, while Sister was writing about the great mercy of God and its great advantage to souls, she suddenly felt the presence of Satan in the room. With great fury and anger he made every attempt to disturb her peace. This frightened her, but she immediately picked up her crucifix and made the sign of the cross. At once the beast settled down and disappeared, and she then peacefully continued to write. The anger and hatred of the evil one was often openly manifest while she was writing about the divine mercy, and the fact that he could not disturb her drove him to greater madness.

It was also one day in October that the Lord said to Sister Faustina, **Go to the Superior and tell her that I want all the sisters and wards to say the chaplet which I have taught you. They are to say it for nine days in the chapel in order to propitiate My Father and to entreat God's mercy for Poland.** (714)

She answered that she must first speak about this to Father Andrasz. However, due to certain circumstances to which she should not have paid attention, she admitted, when Father Andrasz did come, she did not speak to him about it, but decided to do so when he came again. She learned how greatly this action displeased God. Immediately the continuous and distinct presence of God left her, and darkness dominated her soul to such an extent, that she became uncertain as to whether she was in the state of grace; and for four days she did not receive Holy Communion. For her, this omission was a great sacrifice. When she saw Father Andrasz again, she told him everything. He comforted her, saying, "You have not lost the grace of God, but all the same, be true to Him." The moment she left the confessional, God's presence enveloped her as before. She understood that "God's grace must be received just as God sends it, in the way He wants, and one must receive it in that form under which God sends it to us." She then made a resolution to be faithful to even the smallest of God's graces. (See 715)

That night physical suffering kept her awake, so she spent the night preparing herself to receive Jesus in Holy Communion on the following day. The next morning, after receiving Holy Communion, Jesus told her: **Because you are such great misery, I have revealed to you the whole ocean of My mercy. I seek and desire souls like yours, but they are few. Your great trust in Me forces Me to continuously grant you graces. You have great and incomprehensible rights over My Heart for you are a daughter of complete trust.** (718) At another time, soon after this, Jesus told her:

> **The graces I grant you are not for you alone, but for a great number of souls as well.... And your heart is My constant dwelling place, despite the misery that you are. I unite Myself with you, take away your misery and give you My mercy. I perform works of mercy in every soul. The greater the sinner, the greater the right he has to My mercy. My**

mercy is confirmed in every work of My hands. He who trusts in My mercy will not perish, for all his affairs are Mine, and his enemies will be shattered at the base of My footstool. (723)

An Unusual Eight-day Retreat

The eight-day retreat, under the direction of Father Walter Wojton, S.J., was to begin on October 20, 1936. As Sister Faustina prayed "for just a little health so that I could take part in the retreat," she felt a strange dissatisfaction. She interrupted her prayer of supplication and changed it to a prayer of thanksgiving for everything God sends her, submitting herself completely to His Holy will. Profound peace of soul returned immediately. (724)

When she asked the Lord how she should conduct herself during this retreat, she heard in her soul: **I desire that you be entirely transformed into love and that you burn ardently as a pure victim of love…. In this retreat, I shall keep you continually close to My Heart, that you may better know My mercy, that mercy which I have for all people and especially for poor sinners.** (726, 730)

Vision of Hell

During this retreat Sister Faustina was taken to the heights of mystical union. She was also shown the abysses of hell with its various torments. In one moment of union with Jesus, she learned more than she would have after long hours of intellectual inquiry and meditation. At the command of Jesus, she left a description of hell:

> Today I was led by an Angel to the chasms of hell. It is a place of great torture; how awesomely large and extensive it is! The kinds of tortures I saw: the first torture that constitutes hell is the loss of God; the second is perpetual remorse of conscience; the third is that one's condition will never change; the fourth is the fire that will penetrate the soul without destroying it—a terrible suffering, as it is a

purely spiritual fire, lit by God's anger; the fifth torture is continual darkness and a terrible suffocating smell, and, despite the darkness, the devils and the souls of the damned see each other and all the evil, both of others and their own; the sixth torture is the constant company of Satan; the seventh torture is horrible despair, hatred of God, vile words, curses and blasphemies. These are the tortures suffered by all the damned together, but that is not the end of the sufferings. There are special tortures destined for particular souls. These are the torments of the senses. Each soul undergoes terrible and indescribable sufferings, related to the manner in which it has sinned. There are caverns and pits of torture where one form of agony differs from another. I would have died at the very sight of these tortures if the omnipotence of God had not supported me. Let the sinner know that he will be tortured throughout all eternity, in those senses which he made use of to sin. I am writing this at the command of God, so that no soul may find an excuse by saying there is no hell, or that nobody has ever been there, and so no one can say what it is like.

I, Sister Faustina, by the order of God, have visited the abysses of hell so that I might tell souls about it and testify to its existence. I cannot speak about it now; but I have received a command from God to leave it in writing. The devils were full of hatred for me, but they had to obey me at the command of God. What I have written is but a pale shadow of the things I saw. But I noticed one thing: that most of the souls there are those who disbelieved that there is a hell. When I came to, I could hardly recover from the fright. How terribly souls suffer there! Consequently, I pray even more fervently for the conversion of sinners. I incessantly plead God's mercy upon them. O my Jesus, I would rather be in agony until the end of the world, amidst the greatest sufferings, than offend You by the least sin. (741)

True Worship of Divine Mercy

Jesus also gave Sister Faustina at this retreat explicit

directives as to what constitutes true worship of His mercy:

> **My daughter, if I demand through you that people worship My mercy, you should be the first to distinguish yourself by this confidence in My mercy. I demand of you deeds of mercy, which are to arise out of love for Me. You are to show mercy to your neighbors always and everywhere. You must not shrink from this or try to excuse or absolve yourself from it.**

> **I am giving you three ways of exercising mercy toward your neighbor: the first—by deed, the second—by word, the third—by prayer. In these three degrees is contained the fullness of mercy, and it is an unquestionable proof of love for Me. By this means a soul glorifies and pays reverence to My mercy. Yes, the First Sunday after Easter is the Feast of Mercy, but there must also be acts of mercy, and I demand the worship of My mercy through the solemn celebration of the Feast and through the veneration of the image which is painted. By means of this image, I shall grant many graces to souls. It is to be a reminder of the demands of My mercy, because even the strongest faith is of no avail without works."** (742)

The words Jesus spoke to Sister Faustina at the beginning of retreat had begun to take effect. On the Feast of Christ the King, celebrated on October 25, in 1936, Sister wrote in her diary:

> During Holy Mass I was so enveloped in the great interior fire of God's love and the desire to save souls that I do not know how to express it. I feel I am all aflame. I shall fight all evil with the weapon of mercy. I am being burned up by the desire to save souls. I traverse the world's length and breadth and venture as far as its ultimate limits and its wildest lands to save souls. I do this through prayer and sacrifice. I want every soul to glorify the mercy of God, for each one experiences the effects of that mercy on himself. The saints in heaven worship the mercy of the Lord. I want to worship it even now, here on earth, and to spread devotion to it in the way that God demands of me. (745)

Sister realized that in her great desire to save souls, she must become a pure victim of love; she must walk the path marked out by the footprints of Jesus. The path of suffering, contempt, ridicule, persecution and humiliation would be her constant lot. She accepted all of this because she knew that Jesus would be with her. "My Jesus, my strength and my only hope, in You alone is all my hope. My trust will not be frustrated," she wrote. (See 746)

In her talk with Father Andrasz after the retreat, Sister Faustina noticed that he answered clearly and decidedly all of her questions concerning the matters the Lord demanded of her. It was as if he, too, were experiencing it all. She thanked God for the grace of enlightened directors and for the Church that nurtures them.

But the question of leaving the order was still unanswered; and on October 31, after the retreat, Sister spoke of it again to Mother General. They both agreed that Sister Faustina should stay in the Congregation until the Lord would let Mother know by some sign that it was His will that she leave. Sister was told to pray for such a sign. Thus the matter was again postponed. But, despite the great urgings within her to begin the new congregation, Sister Faustina was at peace. It was up to Jesus, now. She told Him: "I want to love You at every moment of my life. If you tell me to leave, O Jesus, in order to carry out Your will, I will leave. If You tell me to stay, I will stay. It matters not what I will suffer in the one instance or the other." (751)

One day, in accordance with the Lord's bidding, Sister Faustina related to Mother General His desire that the community say the chaplet to appease God's anger. Mother answered that she could not introduce such new, unapproved prayers; but she asked for the chaplet, commenting that perhaps it could be said some day during the adoration of the Blessed Sacrament. "It would be good if Father Sopocko could publish a pamphlet with the chaplet; then it would be better and easier to recite it in the Congregation, for it is a bit difficult to do so now," she said. (752) Soon after this meeting Sister recorded the following entry in the diary and underlined it to emphasize its importance:

The Lord's promise: **The souls that will say this chaplet will be embraced by My mercy during their lifetime and especially at the hour of their death.** (754)

The Invisible Stigmata

It was on Friday, November 20, 1936, that Sister Faustina revealed another source of secret suffering; namely, the stigmata:

> When I experienced these suffering for the first time, it was like this: after the annual vows [April 30, 1928], on a certain day, during prayer, I saw a great brilliance and, issuing from the brilliance, rays which completely enveloped me. Then suddenly, I felt a terrible pain in my hands, my feet and my side, and the thorns of the crown of thorns. I experienced these sufferings during Holy Mass on Friday, but this was only for a brief moment. This was repeated for several Fridays, and later on I did not experience any sufferings up to the present time; that is, until the end of September of this year. In the course of the present illness [tuberculosis], during Holy Mass one Friday, I felt myself pierced by the same sufferings, and this has been repeated on every Friday and sometimes when I meet a soul that is not in the state of grace. Although this is infrequent, and the suffering lasts a very short time, still it is terrible, and I would not be able to bear it without a special grace from God. There is no outward indication of these sufferings. What will come later, I do not know. All this, for the sake of souls.... (759)

It seems that the Lord allowed Sister Faustina's superiors to be a source of trial for her also. "I see that even the superiors do not always understand the road along which God is leading me, and I am not surprised at this," she wrote on November 21, 1936. The next day during her confession, the Lord spoke to Sister through the lips of the priest without his realizing it. The priest did not know her soul; she only accused herself of her sins. Yet, he spoke to her words of consolation very important for her to hear that day: "Accomplish faithfully everything that Jesus asks of you, despite the difficulties. Know that, although people may be angry with you, Jesus is not angry and never will be angry with you. Pay no attention to human opinion." Her joyful interior reaction was: "O holy mystery, what great treasures are contained in you! O holy faith, you are my guidepost!" (See 761-763)

Meanwhile, from a letter received on November 24 from Father Sopocko, Sister Faustina learned some details regarding the spreading of the devotion to The Divine Mercy and the founding of the new congregation. After reading it, she entered this comment in the diary:

> I learned from it that God himself is conducting this whole affair. And as the Lord has begun it, so will He continue to carry it along. And the greater the difficulties which I see, the more am I at peace. Oh, if in this whole matter the glory of God and the profit to souls were not greatly served, Satan would not be opposing it so much. But he senses what he is going to lose because of it. I have now learned that Satan hates mercy more than anything else. It is his greatest torment. Still, the word of God will not pass away; God's utterance is living; difficulties will not suppress the works of God, but will reveal that they are God's.... (764)

Vision of Heaven

Previously, Sister Faustina had been granted visions of purgatory and hell. On November 27, when weakness confined her to bed, she recorded the following vision of heaven:

> Today, I was in heaven in spirit, and I saw its inconceivable beauties and the happiness that awaits us after death. I saw how all creatures give ceaseless praise and glory to God. I saw how great is this happiness in God, which spreads to all creatures, making them happy; and then all the glory and praise which springs from this happiness returns to its source; and they enter into the depths of God, contemplating the inner life of God, the Father, the Son, and the Holy Spirit, whom they will never comprehend nor fathom.
>
> This source of happiness is unchanging in its essence, but it is always new, gushing forth happiness for all creatures. Now I understand Saint Paul, who said, "Eye has not seen, nor has ear heard, nor has it entered into the heart of man what God has prepared for those who love Him."
>
> And God has given me to understand that there is but

one thing that is of infinite value in His eyes, and that is love of God; love, love and once again, love; and nothing can compare with a single act of pure love of God. Oh, with what inconceivable favors God gifts a soul that loves Him sincerely! Oh, how happy is the soul who already here on earth enjoys His special favors! And of such are the little and humble souls.

The sight of this great majesty of God, which I came to understand more profoundly and which is worshiped by the heavenly spirits according to their degrees of grace and the hierarchies into which they are divided, did not cause my soul to be stricken with terror or fear; no, no, not at all! My soul was filled with peace and love; and the more I come to know the greatness of God, the more joyful I become that He is as He is. And I rejoice immensely in His greatness and am delighted that I am so little because, since I am little, He carries me in His arms and holds me close to His Heart.

O my God, how I pity those people who do not believe in eternal life; how I pray for them that a ray of mercy would envelop them too, and that God would clasp them to His Fatherly bosom. (777-780)

As her strength continued to fail, Sister Faustina noticed that she was becoming over-sensitive to everything, and saw the need to be more vigilant. "Things I would not pay any attention to when I am healthy bother me today," she wrote, and she prayed for strength to emerge victorious in battle this day. At the same time, she thanked God for the illness and physical discomfort because she now had time to spend long hours at the feet of the hidden God, hours that passed like minutes. She had lost track of time. (See 783-784)

A Lesson from the Mother of God

This year the Mother of God herself taught her how to prepare for Christmas. On November 29, Our Lady appeared to her with the Infant Jesus and told her:

My daughter, strive after silence and humility, so that Jesus, who dwells in your heart continuously, may be able to rest. Adore Him in your heart; do not go out from your inmost being. My daughter, I shall obtain for you the grace of an interior life which will be such that, without ever leaving that interior life, you will be able to carry out all your external duties with even greater care. Dwell with Him continuously in your own heart. He will be your strength. Communicate with creatures only in so far as is necessary and is required by your duties. You are a dwelling place pleasing to the living God; in you He dwells continuously with love and delight.... Try to act in this way until Christmas Day, and then He himself will make known to you in what way you will be communing and uniting yourself with Him. (785)

During Vespers the next day, an unusual pain pierced Sister's soul. She felt that God's great graces have become a burden too difficult for her to carry. Her superiors' disbelief and doubts have resulted in a distrustful relationship with her. She recorded in her diary:

My Jesus, I see that even such great graces can be a [source of] suffering. And yet, it is so; not only may they be a cause of suffering, but they must be such, as a sign of God's action.... As I continued Vespers, meditating on this mixture of suffering and grace, I heard the voice of Our Lady: *Know, My daughter, that although I was raised to the dignity of the Mother of God, seven swords of pain pierced My heart. Don't do anything to defend yourself; bear everything with humility; God himself will defend you.* (786)

Sister Faustina's main concern during her one-day retreat on December 1, 1936, was that she do the will of God as she had come to know it. The Lord gave her to understand that she should not be spending so much time reflecting and building up fear of the difficulties she might encounter. He told her: **Know that I am with you; I bring about the difficulties, and I overcome them; in one instant, I can change a hostile disposition to one which is favorable to this cause.** (788)

Renewed and strengthened in spirit, Faustina made her resolutions for the month. Her rule of conduct would be: Never to speak of her own experiences; ...always have an open heart to the sufferings of others, but drown her own sufferings in the Divine Heart so that they would remain unnoticed outwardly, in so far as possible; and spend this Advent season in meekness and humility as Our Lady directed. (See 792)

With great longing Sister Faustina awaited the Lord's coming. She prayed,

> I would like to prepare all nations for the coming of the Word Incarnate. O Jesus, make the fount of Your mercy gush forth more abundantly, for humankind is seriously ill and has more need than ever of Your compassion. You are a bottomless sea of mercy for us sinners; and the greater our misery, the more right we have to Your mercy. You are a fount which makes all creatures happy by Your infinite mercy... (793)

The Sanatorium

On December 9, 1936, Sister Faustina was told that this very day she was going to the sanatorium on Pradnik. The treatment she needed would take about three months. She gratefully accepted the solicitude of her superiors, especially that of Mother General, Michael Moraczewska, but a Diary entry reveals that a return to health was not more desirable to her than death. Her only desire was to fulfill God's will. (See 795)

The sanatorium, situated about ten kilometers from Cracow, was directed by Dr. Adam Silberg, a recent convert to Catholicism, and staffed by Sisters of the Congregation of the Servants of the Sacred Heart of Jesus. It was this doctor who first correctly diagnosed her case a few months ago.

When Sister Faustina became a little fearful of being away from the community for such a long time by herself, Jesus told her:

> **You will not be alone, because I am with you always and everywhere... I myself am the cause of your departure.... I am bringing you into seclusion so that I myself may form your heart according to My future plans.... Speak to Me about everything in a completely simple and human way; by this you will give Me great joy.... This simple language of**

your heart is more pleasing to Me than the hymns composed in My honor. Know, My daughter, that the simpler your speech is, the more you attract Me to yourself. And now, be at peace close to My Heart. Lay your pen aside and get ready to leave. (797)

Sister Chrysostom drove her to the sanatorium. Because she was given a private room, Sister Faustina felt much like a cloistered Carmelite. As soon as Sister Chrysostom left, Sister began to pray, placing herself under the special protection of the Mother of God, who told her She was watching over all her trials and efforts. Jesus came and filled her with peace and strength. Before retiring, Sister made a short visit to the Blessed Sacrament, in the chapel located some distance from her building. Jesus directed her how to behave toward those around her. Her last note for that day was, "The doctor is taking good care of me; all those around me are very kind to me." (See 801)

The next morning Sister Faustina rose early and made her meditation before the 6:00 a.m Mass. When she returned to her room she became so ill that she had to lie down at once. Sister David, her nurse, brought some medication but it did not make her feel any better. That evening she was too ill to make her Thursday Holy Hour. All she could do was to unite herself with the suffering Jesus.

Sick as she was, she already noted the following observation:

My room is next to the men's ward. I didn't know that men were such chatterboxes. From morning till late at night, there is talk on various subjects. The women's ward is much quieter. It is women who are always blamed for this; but I have had occasion to be convinced that the opposite is true. It is very difficult for me to concentrate on my prayer in the midst of these jokes and this laughter. They do not disturb me when the grace of God takes complete possession of me, because then I do not know what is going on around me.

My Jesus, how little these people talk about You. They talk about everything but You, Jesus. And if they talk so little [about You], it is quite probable that they do not think about You at all. The whole world interests them; but about

You, their Creator, there is silence. Jesus, I am sad to see this great indifference and ingratitude of creatures. O my Jesus, I want to love You for them and to make atonement to You, by my love. (803-804)

A Time of Intercession

The next day was Friday. Sister attended Mass, but immediately after Holy Communion she returned to her room. God's presence took hold of her and for a brief moment she felt the Lord's Passion, during which she was given a more profound knowledge of the work of mercy. That night Sister was suddenly awakened and knew that some needy soul was asking her for prayer. Briefly, but most heartily, Sister asked Jesus to grant that soul His grace.

The following afternoon, when she entered the ward, Sister saw a dying person and was told the agony began during the night. After some inquiry, she was certain that it was precisely the time she had been asked for prayers. Suddenly Sister Faustina heard a voice in her soul: **Say the chaplet which I taught you.** She ran to get her rosary and knelt down by the dying person and ardently began to pray the chaplet. Suddenly the dying person opened her eyes and looked at her. Before Sister finished praying the chaplet, the woman died peacefully. The Lord let Sister know that she had been granted the grace He promised. "That was the first soul to receive the benefit of the Lord's promise," she wrote. When she entered her own room, Sister heard these words:

> **At the hour of their death, I defend as My own glory every soul that will say this chaplet; or when others say it for a dying person, the indulgence is the same. When this chaplet is being said by the bedside of a dying person, God's anger is placated, and unfathomable mercy envelops the soul, and the very depths of My tender mercy will be moved for the sake of the sorrowful Passion of My Son.** (808-811)

For about three weeks Sister Faustina was unable to go to confession for a variety of reasons: illness, a visit to the doctor, and another visit to the hospital. All these took place on the days assigned for confession. She began to cry, for she really felt the need to go to confession. That afternoon, Father Andrasz entered her room and immediately sat down to hear her confession. She recorded:

> I was delighted because I was extremely anxious to go to confession. As usual, I unveiled my whole soul. Father gave a reply to each little detail. I felt unusually happy to be able to say everything as I did. For penance, he gave me the Litany of the Holy Name of Jesus. When I wanted to tell him of the difficulty I have in saying this litany, he rose and began to give me absolution. Suddenly his figure became diffused with a great light, and I saw that it was not Father A., but Jesus. His garments were bright as snow, and He disappeared immediately. At first, I was a little uneasy, but after a while a kind of peace entered my soul; and I took note of the fact that Jesus heard the confession in the same way that confessors do; and yet something was strangely transpiring in my heart during this confession; I couldn't at first understand what it signified. (817)

On December 16, Sister Faustina offered her whole day—all her prayers and sufferings—for Russia. After Holy Communion Jesus said to her: **I cannot suffer that country any longer. Do not tie my hands, My daughter.** She understood that if it had not been for the prayers of souls pleasing to God, that whole nation would have already been reduced to nothingness. "Oh, how I suffer for that nation which has banished God from its borders!" she commented. (818)

She offered the next day for priests. Her entry that evening was: "I have suffered more today than ever before, both interiorly and exteriorly. I did not know it was possible to suffer so much in one day. I tried to make a Holy Hour, in the course of which my spirit had a taste of the bitterness of the Garden of Gethsemane." (823)

Her Work and Mission

In the seclusion to which He brought her, Jesus continued to educate His beloved daughter and allowed her to penetrate incomprehensible mysteries "There is one mystery," she wrote, "which unites me with the Lord, of which no one—not even angels—may know. And even if I wanted to tell of it, I would not know how to express it. And yet, I live by it and will live by it forever. This mystery distinguishes me from every other soul here on earth or in eternity." (824)

She then wrote ecstatically of the day of her death:

> O bright and clear day on which all my dreams will be fulfilled; O day so eagerly desired, the last day of my life! I look forward with joy to the last stroke the Divine Artist will trace on my soul, which will give my soul a unique beauty that will distinguish me from the beauty of other souls. O great day, on which divine love will be confirmed in me. On that day, for the first time, I shall sing before heaven and earth the song of the Lord's fathomless mercy. This is my work and the mission which the Lord has destined for me from the beginning of the world. That the song of my soul may be pleasing to the Holy Trinity, do You, O Spirit of God, direct and form my soul Yourself! I arm myself with patience and await Your coming, O merciful God, and as to the terrible pains and fear of death, at that moment more than at any other time, I trust in the abyss of Your mercy and am reminding You, O merciful Jesus, sweet Savior, of all the promises You have made to me. (825)

Although Faustina was attaining such great heights in heroic virtue and in prayer, she was still very much human. On December 18, she felt sad and lonely because a week had gone by and no one had come to visit her. When she complained of this to the Lord, He answered, **Isn't it enough for you that I visit you every day?** She apologized to the Lord and the hurt vanished. (See 827)

It was especially during her hospital stay that Sister was given the special grace of becoming aware of a dying person's need for prayer, and of the efficacy of the Chaplet of Mercy, as noted earlier. She would then pray until she felt peace in her soul. This was not always for the same amount of time, but depended on the length of the soul's final agony. God had given her an extraordinary bond with the dying, whether they were near or as far away as several hundred kilometers; whether they were known to her or complete strangers. Gratitude for this extraordinary grace is shown in the following prayer which Sister recorded:

> O God of fathomless mercy, who allow me to give relief and help to the dying by my unworthy prayer, be blessed as many thousand times as there are stars in the sky and drops of water in all the oceans! Let Your mercy resound throughout the orb of the earth and let it rise to the foot of Your throne, giving praise to the greatest of Your attributes; that is, Your incomprehensible mercy... (835)

> O most sweet Jesus, who have deigned to allow miserable me to gain knowledge of Your unfathomable mercy; O most sweet Jesus, who have graciously demanded that I tell the whole world of Your incomprehensible mercy, this day I take into my hands the two rays that spring from Your merciful Heart; that is, the Blood and Water; and I scatter them all over the globe so that each soul may receive Your mercy and, having received it, may glorify it for endless ages.... (836)

Thus, during her first two weeks in the hospital, Sister Faustina suffered, interceded, and prayed. Since it was the Advent season, she was likewise preparing herself for the solemn moment of Jesus' coming. The Mother of God herself instructed her how to live the interior life of the soul with Jesus, especially during the time of Holy Communion. She wrote on December 23, 1936: "It is only in eternity that we shall know the great mystery effected in us by Holy Communion. O, most precious moments of my life!" (840)

Sister Chrysostom visited Faustina on December 23, and brought her some apples and lemons and a tiny Christmas tree. She informed the doctor of Mother Superior's request that Sister be allowed to go home for Christmas, and he readily agreed to let her go. Sister Faustina was so happy she burst into tears like a little child. Sister Chrysostom was surprised at the change she saw in Sister. "You know, Little Faustina," she said, "probably you will die. You must be suffering a great deal, Sister." Faustina modestly replied that she was suffering more that day than she had on other days, but that it was nothing. For the salvation of souls it was not too much. (See 842)

The next afternoon, Sister Cajetan came to take her back to the convent for the holidays. Even the ride back home did not disrupt her contemplative spirit. As they were riding through the city, Sister Faustina imagined it was the town of Bethlehem. As she watched the people hurrying about she wondered: "Who is meditating today, in recollection and silence, on this inconceivable mystery? O pure Virgin, You are traveling today, and so am I. I feel that today's journey has its symbolism. O radiant Virgin, pure as crystal, all immersed in God, I offer You my spiritual life; arrange everything that it may be pleasing to Your Son." (844)

Christmas—1936

As was her custom, Sister Faustina first went to the chapel, before the vigil supper, to share the wafer spiritually with those dearest to her heart, presenting them all by name to the Lord. She also commended all those who were being persecuted, those who were suffering, those who did not know His Name, especially the poor sinners, and asked Him to enclose them all in the ocean of His incomprehensible mercy.

Because she was tired and in much pain, Sister Faustina was forced to lie down after supper; but she kept vigil with the Most Holy Mother, awaiting the arrival of the Little Child.

At Midnight Mass, a moment before the elevation of the Host, Sister saw the Mother of God, the Infant Jesus, and St. Joseph. Our Lady said to her, *My daughter, Faustina, take this most precious Treasure,* and She gave her the Infant Jesus. Sister's joy was indescribable! (846)

On the second day of the feast, Father Andrasz heard her confession in the afternoon. She questioned him about the work Jesus entrusted to her, namely, the founding of a congregation. Father did not give an answer to some of her questions, but he counseled her to get well first, and, in the meantime, to try to make good use of the graces God was giving her. Her penance was to say the chaplet Jesus taught her. While saying it she heard a voice which said:

Oh, what graces I will grant to souls who say this chaplet; the very depths of My tender mercy are stirred for

the sake of those who say the chaplet. Write down these words, My daughter. Speak to the world about My mercy; let all mankind recognize My unfathomable mercy. It is a sign for the end times; after it will come the day of justice. While there is still time, let them have recourse to the fount of My mercy; let them profit from the Blood and Water which gushed forth for them. (848)

To what she just wrote, Sister Faustina added:

O human souls, where are you going to hide on the day of God's anger? Take refuge now in the fount of God's mercy. O what a great multitude of souls I see! They worshiped the Divine Mercy and will be singing the hymn of praise for all eternity. (848)

The Glory of The Work of Mercy

On December 27, Sister Damian drove Sister Faustina back to the sanatorium. The yearning for God, which grew during the holidays, was not stilled, but rather increased. At the very mention of the Name of Jesus, her spirit leaped out to God.

The next day Sister began a novena to The Divine Mercy for the intentions of the Archbishop of Vilnius and Father Sopocko, earnestly asking the Lord to inspire the Archbishop to approve the chaplet and image soon. The novena consisted of the chaplet that the Lord taught her. As she recited it, she placed herself in spirit before the Image of The Divine Mercy.

On the second day of the novena she saw the Image, as it were, come alive. It was adorned with numberless votive lamps, and she saw great crowds of people going to it and many of them being filled with happiness.

After Holy Communion Sister heard a voice in her soul: **My daughter, stand ready for I will come unexpectedly.**

"Jesus," she said, "You do not want to tell me the hour I am looking forward to with such longing?"

My daughter, it is for your own good. You will learn it, but not now; keep watch.

"O Jesus," she exclaimed, "do with me as You please. I know You are the merciful Savior and You will not change towards me at the hour of my death. If at this time You are showing me so much special love, and are condescending to unite Yourself with me in such an intimate way and with such great kindness, I expect even more at the hour of my death.... So come as You like and when You like. Father of infinite mercy, I, Your child, wait longingly for Your coming." (See 854)

During her one-day retreat on December 30, Sister contemplated the benefits God had lavished upon her throughout the year 1936. For a whole hour she remained immersed in adoration and thanksgiving. "All that this year contained has gone into the abyss of eternity," she thought. "Nothing is lost. I am glad that nothing gets lost." (855)

On the evening of New Year's Eve, December 31, 1936, Sister Faustina devoted her prayer to petitions on behalf of her parents and relatives, her Mother General, the entire Congregation, for the girls in their care, and for the three priests to whom she owed very much. Then she offered up the length and breadth of the whole world, thanking the unfathomable mercy of God for all the graces granted to people and begging pardon for everything by which they have offended Him.

At midnight, Sister bid good-by to the old year. In the first hour of the New Year 1937, with fear and trembling, she anticipated the new period of time awaiting her. She prayed: "Merciful Jesus, with You I will go boldly and courageously into conflicts and battles. In Your Name, I will accomplish everything and overcome everything. My God, Infinite Goodness, I beg of You, let Your infinite mercy accompany me always and in all things." (859)

Jesus brought her out of her fear during this time of prayer and gave her to know what great glory the work of mercy will bring Him. This experience prompted her to write: "There are times in life when the soul finds comfort only in profound prayer. Would that souls knew how to persevere in prayer at such times. This is very important." (860)

INTERCESSORY SUFFERING AND CONSUMING LOVE (1937)

For the New Year 1937, Sister Faustina again resolved to unite with the Merciful Christ; that is, to act as Jesus would in such and such an instance; and in spirit to envelop the whole world, especially Russia and Spain. She recorded thirteen resolutions for the New Year. (See 861) These manifested her determination to continue steadfastly on the road to perfection. She would not allow sickness to excuse her from striving to fulfill them.

A particularly important day for Sister was January 2, Feast of the Holy Name of Jesus, because it reminded her of many special graces received on that day. For example, in 1934, she made her first visit on that day to the artist who painted the image and thus, for the first time, the Divine Mercy received special honor in the form requested by the Lord.

Longing to be united with God became a new source of suffering for Sister Faustina as she advanced on the road to perfection. "O Jesus," she wrote, "what a dreadful jungle this life seems to me!... You have left me the Sacred Host, O Lord, but it enkindles in my soul an even greater longing for You...." (867)

Then, on January 6, an entry in the diary revealed God's touches of grace which were leading Sister into greater love of God and neighbor:

> Today during Holy Mass I was unwittingly absorbed in the infinite majesty of God. The whole immensity of God's love flooded my soul.... Taking advantage of the intimacy to which the Lord was admitting me, I interceded before Him for the whole world. At such moments I have the feeling that the whole world is depending on me. (870)

My Master, cause my heart never to expect help from anyone, but I will always strive to bring assistance, consolation and all manner of relief to others. My heart is always open to the sufferings of others; and I will not close my heart to the sufferings of others, even though because of this I have been scornfully nicknamed "dump"; that is [because] everyone dumps his pain into my heart.... Taunts regarding the law of love will not narrow my heart. My soul is always sensitive on this point, and Jesus alone is the motive for my love of neighbor. (871)

Sister Faustina's love of neighbor increased to include the dying sinners. For them she offered the day of January 8. After Holy Communion she looked at the Lord with trust and said to Him, "Jesus, I so much desire to tell You something."

The Lord looked at her with love and said, **And what is it that you desire to tell Me?**

"Jesus, I beg You, by the inconceivable power of Your mercy, let all the souls who will die today escape the fire of hell, even if they have been the greatest sinners. Today is Friday, the memorial of Your bitter agony on the Cross; because Your mercy is inconceivable, the Angels will not be surprised at this."

Jesus pressed her to His heart' and said, **My beloved daughter, you have come to know well the depths of My mercy. I will do what you ask, but unite yourself continually with My agonizing Heart to make reparation to My justice. Know that you have asked Me for a great thing, but I see that this was dictated by your pure love for Me; that is why I am complying with your requests.** (873)

That same day Sister felt called to make reparation by offering up the great suffering she experienced from the visit of her fellow sisters:

I learned of something that hurt me terribly, but I controlled myself so that the sisters did not notice anything. For some time, the pain was tearing my heart apart, but all that is for the sake of poor sinners.... O Jesus, for poor sinners.... Jesus, my strength, stay close to me, help me.... (See 875)

What Sister learned will never be known, but the pain it

caused must have aggravated her physical condition. She became weak, faint, and feverish. When she thought this condition may prevent her from receiving Holy Communion, she bargained with the Lord:

> ... My Master, I ask You with all my thirsting heart to give me, if this is according to Your holy will, any suffering and weakness that You like—I want to suffer all day and all night—but please, I fervently beg You, strengthen me for the one moment when I am to receive Holy Communion. You see very well, Jesus, that here they do not bring Holy Communion to the sick; so if You do not strengthen me for that moment so that I can go down to the chapel, how can I receive You in the Mystery of Love? And You know how much my heart longs for You. O my sweet Spouse, what's the good of all these reasonings? You know how ardently I desire You, and if You so choose You can do this for me.... (876)

On the following morning Sister felt healed. Yet, as soon as she returned from the chapel, all the sufferings and weaknesses returned immediately, as if they had been waiting for her. "But," she wrote, "I had no fear of them at all, because I had been nourished by the Bread of the Strong. I boldly look at everything; even death itself I look straight in the eye." (876)

When the doctor made his rounds that day (January 12), Sister's temperature had risen considerably. He decided she should not go to Holy Communion until her temperature dropped to normal. After some discussion they came to a mutual agreement. If the weather was fine and it wasn't raining and she felt all right, then, she could go. But she would have to weigh these matters in her conscience. It made her very happy that the doctor was being so considerate for her sake. She told Jesus, "You see, Jesus, that I have already done whatever was up to me; now I am counting on You and am quite at peace." (878)

As Sister Faustina's level of spirituality deepened, her days and nights were intermingled with the joy of intimate union with God, and the affliction of heart that comes from feeling the whole misery of exile from heaven.

The Value of Obedience

On January 22, the doctor decided that Sister was not to go to Mass, but only to Holy Communion. She spoke of this to her confessor. He was in agreement with the doctor and told her, "It is God's will, Sister, that you should get well, and you must not undertake mortifications of any kind. Be obedient and the Lord will reward you for it."

Faustina felt that the confessor's words were Jesus' words. And although it made her sad to miss Holy Mass because God had been granting her the grace of seeing the Infant Jesus, she nevertheless placed obedience above everything else. While absorbed in prayer after the confession, she suddenly saw the Lord who said to her, **My daughter, know that you give Me greater glory by a single act of obedience than by long prayers and mortifications.** (894)

On January 23, Sister did not feel like writing, perhaps because of her increased sufferings of the past few days. Then she heard a voice in her soul saying:

> **My daughter, you do not live for yourself but for souls; write for their benefit. You know that My will as to your writing has been confirmed many times by your confessors. You know what is pleasing to Me, and if you have any doubts about what I am saying, you also know whom you are to ask. I grant him light to pronounce judgment on My case. My eye watches over him.... Put his judgment above all My demands. He will guide you according to My will. If he doesn't allow you to carry out My demands, be at peace; I will not judge you, but the matter will remain between Me and him. You are to be obedient.** (895)

Two days later she was still steeped in suffering and bitterness. "O Jesus, O my Jesus, today everyone can add to my cup of bitterness," she wrote. "It makes no difference whether they be friend or foe, they can all inflict suffering on me.... O Blessed Host, support me and seal my lips against all murmuring and complaint." (See 896)

After two more days, her health improved so that she felt almost completely well. "Jesus is bringing me from the gates of death to life because there was so little left but for me to die, and lo, the Lord grants me the fullness of life," she wrote. She realized she had not yet fulfilled all that the Lord had planned for her. "He will not leave me in exile any longer, for heaven is my home," she added. "But before we go to our Homeland, we must fulfill the will of God on earth; that is, trials and struggles must run their full course in us.... I have desired death so much! I do not know whether I shall ever again in my life experience such great longing for God.... Oh, how ugly the earth when one knows heaven! I must do violence to myself in order to live. O will of God, you are my nourishment." (See 897-899)

A Sacrifice for Sinners

On January 29, the snow was knee-deep. That morning Sister overslept and had to hurry to get to Communion on time because the chapel was a good way from her ward. She went out. And before it occurred to her that Dr. Silberg would not have allowed her to go out into so much snow, she had already arrived at the chapel. She received Holy Communion and was back in her room in no time. She heard in her soul, **My daughter, rest close to My heart. Known to Me are Your efforts.** (902)

The next day, Sister made her usual monthly one-day retreat, during which time she renewed the offering of herself for sinners:

O Jesus, how sorry I feel for poor sinners. Jesus, grant them contrition and repentance. Remember Your own sorrowful Passion. I know Your infinite mercy and cannot bear it that a soul that has cost You so much should perish. Jesus, give me the souls of sinners; let Your mercy rest upon them. Take everything away from me, but give me souls. I want to become a sacrificial host for sinners. Let the shell of my body conceal my offering, for Your Most Sacred Heart is also hidden in a Host, and certainly You are a living sacrifice.

Transform me into Yourself, O Jesus, that I may be a living sacrifice and pleasing to You. I desire to atone at each moment for poor sinners. The sacrifice of my spirit is hidden under the veil of the body; the human eye does not perceive it, and for that reason it is pure and pleasing to You. O my Creator and Father of great mercy, I trust in You, for You are Goodness Itself. Souls, do not be afraid of God, but trust in Him, for He is good, and His mercy is everlasting. (908)

Sister Faustina gave herself completely to God. Not to be outdone in generosity, He desired to give Himself completely to her. Two special spiritual graces were conferred on her at this time: a deeper knowledge of the oneness of the Three Divine Persons in the Most Holy Trinity and The Divine Espousals (Spiritual Marriage). She had come to the point where she could say, "...I don't know how to live without Him. I would rather be with Him in afflictions and suffering than without Him in the greatest heavenly delights." (See 911-912)

Although her suffering was great on February 2, her soul overflowed with joy, and this for two reasons: The great value of the Sacrifice of the Mass was revealed to Sister, and a great grace was granted her when she prayed before the Image of The Divine Mercy. During Mass that morning, Sister saw the Crucified Jesus in great agony. His suffering pierced her soul and body, invisibly, but nonetheless most painfully. She noted:

Oh, what awesome mysteries take place during Mass!... With what great devotion should we listen to and take part in this death of Jesus. One day we will know what God is doing for us in each Mass, and what sort of gift He is preparing in it for us. Only His Divine Love could permit that such a gift be provided for us. O Jesus, my Jesus, with what great pain is my soul pierced when I see this fountain of life gushing forth with such sweetness and power for each soul, while at the same time I see souls withering away and drying up through their own fault. O Jesus, grant that the power of mercy embrace these souls. (914)

This same day Sister was inspired to pray before the image which Jesus had instructed that she have painted. She took the leaflet which had the image on the cover and said to the Lord, "Jesus, You yourself told me that You would grant many graces through this image. I ask You, then, for the grace of Holy Baptism for this Jewish lady [in the private room next to mine]...." The next day, just before the lady's agony began, the Lord arranged for favorable conditions for the baptism to be performed, and Sister Faustina was elated when, shortly after the woman's death, she saw her soul ascending to heaven in wondrous beauty. "Joy flooded my heart," she wrote, "that before this image I had received so great a grace for this soul.... This is the second great grace which I have received here for souls before this image." Jesus was honoring His word and her trust in it. (See 916-917)

Life on earth was now an exile for Sister Faustina. Though she desired the bliss of heaven, she was willing to let God's Will be the rapture of her soul. "But, if it is Your will that I still go on living and suffering, then I desire what You have destined for me. Keep me here on earth for as long as You wish, even though this be till the end of the world." (918)

On February 7, 1937, Jesus told her:

I demand of you a perfect and whole-burnt offering; an offering of the will. No other sacrifice can compare with this one. I myself am directing your life and arranging things in such a way that you will be for Me a constinual sacrifice and will always do My will. And for the accomplishment of this offering, you will unite yourself with Me on the Cross. I know what you can do. I myself will give you many orders directly, but I will delay the possibility of their being carried out and make it depend on others. But what the superiors will not manage to do, I myself will accomplish directly in your soul. And in the most hidden depths of your soul, a perfect holocaust will be carried out, not just for a while, but, know My daughter, that this offering will last until your death. But, there is time, so that I the Lord will fulfill all your wishes. I delight in you as in a living host; let nothing terrify you; I am with you. (923)

That very day Sister Faustina's obedience was tested. She received a note from her Mother Superior with explicit orders not to go any more to the bedside of the dying. She decided to send obedience to Mother Superior in her place. It would be a source of grace for them. Such was God's will and that was enough for her. What she could not understand now, she would know later, she reasoned.

Lent and Easter 1937

During the days before Ash Wednesday, 1937, God allowed Sister Faustina to know, in one instant, all the sins being committed throughout the entire world during those carnival days before Lent. It made her faint from fright. Even though she knew the depth of God's mercy, she was surprised that God allowed humankind to exist. The Lord gave her to know that it is the chosen souls that uphold the existence of mankind. When the number of the chosen ones is complete, the world will cease to exist. As an act of reparation, on these two days, Sister offered her Holy Communions and everything she did, for sinners. "Let the blows of Your justice fall on me, and the sea of Your mercy engulf the poor sinners," she asked the Lord. And the Lord heard her prayer. Many souls returned to the Lord, but she remained in agony under the yoke of God's justice. She felt she was the object of the anger of the Most High God. She reached such a stage of interior desolation that moans welled up involuntarily from her breast. In her locked room she began a Holy Hour. But, even then, moans and weeping were her only prayer. Then, suddenly, she saw the Lord who clasped her to His Heart and said to her, **My daughter, do not weep, for I cannot bear your tears. I will grant you everything you ask for, but stop crying.** (927-928)

The next day was Shrove Tuesday. Encouraged by His kindness, Sister Faustina talked to Jesus at greater length, enumerating the pains of her heart and her great concern for all humankind. Jesus listened to all those outpourings of her heart and said to her, **My daughter, those words of your heart are pleasing to Me, and by the saying of this chaplet you are bringing humanity closer to Me.** (929) Her love of God and neighbor had attained new heights.

The Lenten Season began the next day, February 10, Ash Wednesday. During Holy Mass Sister felt for a short time the Passion of Jesus in her members. "Lent is a very special time for the work of priests," she wrote. "We should assist them in rescuing souls." Although she desired to practice great mortifications as before, she could no longer do so because of her illness. She therefore received permission to carry out small practices of mortification, such as: to sleep without a pillow; keep herself a little hungry; every day with her arms outstretched in the form of a cross to say the chaplet which the Lord taught her; and occasionally to pray for an indefinite period of time with arms outstretched. These were simple things, but she was taking Jesus at His word: **Know this, My daughter, and act accordingly: anything, no matter how small it be, that has the seal of obedience of My representative is pleasing to Me and great in My eyes.** Her intention in all this was to beg Divine Mercy upon poor sinners and to obtain for priests the power to bring sinful hearts to repentance. (See 931-934.)

During Mass on Friday, Sister Faustina suffered pain in her hands, feet and side. She offered it all for sinners. The sensation of those few minutes of suffering lasted a long time and remained very vivid. In addition to this, she would suffer desolation of soul, such as a heart wounded by love would feel. Then she would say, "O souls of sinners, you have taken the Lord away from me, but all right, all right; you get to know how sweet the Lord is, and let the whole sea of bitterness flood my heart. I have given all my divine comforts to you." (See 943)

About this time Sister Faustina was inspired to write a litany of praises to the Divine Mercy so that doubting souls would "read these considerations on Divine Mercy and become trusting." At a later date Father Sopocko had this litany published. (See 949-951.)

The next day God filled her with His consolation. She recorded:

> Today, the presence of God is piercing me through and through, like a ray from the sun. My soul is longing for God so intensely that I fall into a swoon every now and then. I feel Eternal Love touching my heart, and my littleness cannot bear it, and this causes me to swoon.... How unfathomable are the mysteries of the soul and God! Sometimes there are whole hours when my soul is lost in wonder at seeing the infinite majesty of God abasing Itself to the level of my soul.... (See 946-947)

On Sunday, during the singing of the "Bitter Lamentations" at the Passion Service, Sister Faustina saw Jesus being tortured, crowned with thorns and holding a reed in His hand. She wrote,

Jesus said nothing, but just looked at me, and in that gaze I felt His pain, so terrible that we have not the faintest idea of how much He suffered for us before He was crucified.... When I see Jesus tormented, my heart is torn to pieces, and I think: what will become of sinners if they do not take advantage of the Passion of Jesus? In His Passion I discern a whole sea of mercy. (948)

On her feast day, February 15, Sister happily received feast day greetings from Father Sopocko; but the news of his poor health saddened her. It confirmed for her that the interior knowledge she had concerning him, even the matters he did not write about, were true.

Father Sopocko also must have had some interior knowledge concerning Sister, because he again requested that she underline in her notebooks all that she was sure did not come from her but was heard in her soul. On several previous occasions he had asked her to do this, but she had been in no hurry to do so. "But how does he know that I have not done this?" she wondered, and she earnestly set out to do what he requested.

Intercession for sinners was uppermost on Sister's mind. She did this not only through her sufferings and prayers, but also through whatever else she was given to do. On February 16, after completing her spiritual exercises, she immediately took up her crochet hook. The deep and sweet consciousness of God's presence in the silence of her heart inspired her to say to the Lord, "O Most Holy Trinity dwelling in my heart, please grant the grace of conversion to as many souls as the number of stitches I make today with this hook."

Then she heard these words in her soul: **My daughter, you are asking too much.**

"Jesus, You know that for You it is easier to grant much, rather than a little," she replied.

That is so, it is less difficult for Me to grant a soul much rather than a little, but every conversion of a sinful soul demands sacrifice, He said.

"Well, Jesus," she answered, "I offer You this whole-hearted work of mine; this offering does not seem to me to be too small for such a large number of souls; You know, Jesus, that for thirty years You were saving souls by just this kind of work. And since holy obedience forbids me to perform great penances and mortifications, therefore I ask You, Lord: accept these mere nothings stamped with the seal of obedience as great things."

Then she heard a voice in her soul: **My dear daughter, I will comply with your request.** (961)

That same day Sister recorded this precious thought on suffering:

> Oh, if only the suffering soul knew how it is loved by God, it would die of joy and excess of happiness! Some day, we will know the value of suffering, but then we will no longer be able to suffer. The present moment is ours. (963)

During Holy Mass the next day, Sister again saw the suffering Jesus; and His Passion was imprinted on her body invisibly but no less painfully. Jesus looked at her and said:

Souls perish in spite of My bitter passion. I am giving them the last hope of salvation; that is, the Feast of My Mercy. If they will not adore My mercy, they will perish for all eternity. Secretary of My mercy, write, tell souls about this great mercy of Mine, because the awful day, the day of My justice, is near. (965)

Later that day Sister heard these words in her soul: **My daughter, it is time for you to take action; I am with you. Great persecutions and sufferings are in store for you, but be comforted by the thought that many souls will be saved and sanctified by this work** [the entire message of Divine Mercy]. (966)

That same day, as Sister meditated before the Blessed Sacrament, she was told, **Know this, My daughter, that you are already tasting now what other souls will obtain only in eternity.** All of a sudden her soul was flooded with the light of the knowledge of God. She could not put into words even a little of what her soul experienced when resting near the Heart of the incomprehensible Majesty! Only a soul who had at least once experienced a similar grace will know what it was like. (See 969-970.)

When Sister was told, on February 19, that she must remain in the sanatorium until April, she accepted the decision as God's will, although she did want to return to the company of the sisters.

That day she also received the news that one of the sisters died in Plock. But this was no surprise to her. The soul of that sister had already paid her a visit. (See 972-973)

Also, during this Lenten Season, Sister Faustina prayed more ardently for priests, especially after Jesus said to her, **My loving host, pray for priests, especially during this time of harvest [of souls]. My Heart is pleased with you, and for your sake I am blessing the earth.** (980)

A retreat for the hospital attendants began on February 22, 1937, and anyone wishing to do so could take part in it. The daily conference was given by Father Bonaventure who usually spoke for an hour. He had the grace of speaking directly to souls. On February 28 Sister was happy to be able to take advantage of this time to make her monthly one-day retreat. During the last conference, the priest was speaking about the world's great need of God's mercy, and that this seems to be a very special time when mankind finds itself in such dire need of God's mercy and prayer. Then she heard a voice in her soul:

> **These words are for you. Do all you possibly can for this work of My mercy. I desire that My mercy be worshiped, and I am giving mankind the last hope of salvation; that is, recourse to My mercy. My Heart rejoices in this feast.** (998)

After those words Sister understood that nothing can dispense her from the obligation that the Lord is demanding from her. She wrote that day:

> Today I was undergoing the Passion of Jesus for a longer time, and thus I saw that many souls were in need of prayer. I feel that I am being completely transformed into prayer in order to beg God's mercy for every soul. O my Jesus, I am receiving You into my heart as a pledge of mercy for souls. (996)

Also that same day, Sister Faustina included the following incident which would repeat itself again some time later (See 1276):

> Last night I was in such pain that I thought it was the end. The doctors could not diagnose what the sickness was. I

felt as if my entrails had been torn to shreds, but after a few hours of such sufferings I am all right. All this is for sinners. Let Your mercy descend upon them, O Lord. (999)

According to Sister's diary, it was Our Lord's desire that the heart of the "Apostle of My Mercy," as He called her, be imbued with that divine attribute—mercy. He drew her heart more strongly to those works of mercy which not only brought temporal relief, but which also benefited the soul for all eternity. The following excerpts from her notes reveal Sister's primary and intense concern with saving sinners, helping the dying, and bringing relief to the souls in purgatory:

March 5, 1937. Today I experienced the Passion of the Lord Jesus in my own body for a long while. The pain is very great, but all this is for the sake of immortal souls. (1010)

March 8, 1937. Today, as I was praying for the intention of Father Andrasz, I suddenly understood how intimately this soul communed with God and how pleasing he was to the Lord. It gave me immense joy, because I desire intensely that all souls be united with God as closely as possible. (1012)

March 12, 1937. I felt today how greatly a certain dying soul desired prayers. I prayed until I felt she had died. Oh, dying souls are in such great need of prayer! O Jesus, inspire souls to pray often for the dying. (1015)

March 15, 1937. Today, I entered into the bitterness of the Passion of the Lord Jesus. I suffered in a purely spiritual way. I learned how horrible sin was. God gave me to know the whole hideousness of sin. I learned in the depths of my soul how horrible sin was, even the smallest sin, and how much it tormented the soul of Jesus. I would rather suffer a thousand hells than commit even the smallest venial sin. (1016)

The Lord said to me, **I want to give myself to souls and to fill them with My love, but few there are who want to accept all the graces My love has intended for them. My grace is not lost; if the soul for whom it was intended does not accept it, another soul takes it.** (1017)

During Mass on Palm Sunday, March 21, Sister Faustina's

soul was drowned in the bitterness and sufferings of Jesus. He allowed her to know how much He had suffered in that triumphal procession. She felt in a special way the "Hosanna" reverberating in Jesus' heart as an echo of "Crucify." (See 1028)

The doctor did not allow Sister to go that afternoon to the Passion Service, so she prayed in her room. Suddenly she heard the bell in the room next to hers. She went in and rendered a service to a seriously sick person. When she returned to her room she saw the Lord Jesus who said: **My daughter, you gave Me greater pleasure by rendering Me that service than if you had prayed for a long time.**

She answered, "But it was not to You, Jesus, but to that patient that I rendered this service."

And the Lord replied, **Yes, My daughter, but whatever you do for your neighbor, you do for Me.** (1029)

During Holy Mass the next day Sister saw the crucified Jesus in great torments. A silent moan issued from His heart. After a while He said, **I thirst. I thirst for the salvation of souls. Help me, My daughter, to save souls. Join your sufferings to My passion and offer them to the heavenly Father for sinners.** (1032) That same day she was given the opportunity to do so:

> This evening, a certain young man was dying; he was suffering terribly. For his intention, I began to say the chaplet which the Lord had taught me. I said it all, but the agony continued. I wanted to start the Litany of the Saints, but suddenly I heard the words, **Say the chaplet.** I understood that the soul needed the special help of prayers and great mercy. And so I locked myself in my room and fell prostrate before God and begged for mercy upon that soul. Then I felt the great majesty of God and His great justice. I trembled with fear, but did not stop begging the Lord's mercy for that soul. Then I took the cross off my breast, the crucifix I had received when making my vows, and put it on the chest of the dying man and said to the Lord, "Jesus, look on this soul with the same love with which You looked on my holocaust on the day of my perpetual vows, and by the power of the promise which You made to me in respect to the dying and those who would invoke Your mercy on them, [grant this man the grace of a happy death]." His suffering

then ceased, and he died peacefully. Oh, how much we should pray for the dying! Let us take advantage of mercy while there is still time for mercy. (1035)

I realize more and more how much every soul needs God's mercy throughout life and particularly at the hour of death. This chaplet mitigates God's anger, as He himself told me. (1036)

The Feast of The Divine Mercy

Again and again the Lord reminded Sister Faustina of His desire for the **Feast of Mercy** to be established. This desire began to burn up her soul. She found some relief in fervent prayer for the hastening of this Feast, and had already begun a novena for the intention of certain priests that God grant them the light and inspiration to seek the establishment of this Feast, and that the Spirit of God inspire the Holy Father regarding the entire matter. The novena consisted of an hour's adoration before the Blessed Sacrament. It would end on Holy Thursday.

On March 23, Tuesday of Holy Week, and the seventh day of the novena, Sister Faustina was granted this vision:

Suddenly God's presence took hold of me, and at once I saw myself in Rome, in the Holy Father's chapel and at the same time I was in our chapel. And the celebration of the Holy Father and the entire Church was closely connected with our chapel and, in a very special way, with our Congregation. And I took part in the solemn celebration simultaneously here and in Rome, for the celebration was so closely connected with Rome that, even as I write, I cannot distinguish the two but I am writing it down as I saw it. I saw the Lord Jesus in our chapel, exposed in the monstrance on the high altar. The chapel was adorned as for a feast, and on that day anyone who wanted was allowed in. The crowd was so enormous that the eye could not take it all in. Everyone was participating in the celebrations with great joy, and many of them obtained what they desired. The same celebration was held in Rome, in a beautiful church, and the Holy Father, with all the clergy, was celebrating this Feast, and then suddenly I saw Saint Peter, who stood between the altar and the Holy Father. I could not hear what Saint Peter said but I saw that the Holy Father understood his words....

Then some clergymen whom I did not know began to examine me and to humiliate me, or rather, what I had written; but I saw how Jesus himself was defending me and giving them to understand what they did not know.

Then suddenly I saw how the two rays, as painted in the image, issued from the Host and spread over the whole world. This lasted only a moment, but it seemed as though it had lasted all day, and our chapel was overcrowded all day long, and the whole day abounded in joy.

Then, suddenly I saw on our altar the living Lord Jesus, just as He is depicted in the image. Yet I felt that the sisters and all the people did not see the Lord Jesus as I saw Him. Jesus looked with great kindness and joy at the Holy Father, at certain priests, at the entire clergy, at the people, and at our Congregation.

Then, in an instant I was caught up to stand near Jesus, and I stood on the altar next to the Lord Jesus, and my spirit was filled with a happiness so great that I am unable to comprehend it or write about it. A profound peace as well as repose filled my soul. Jesus bent toward me and said with great kindness, **What is it you desire, My daughter?** And I answered, "I desire that worship and glory be given to Your mercy." **I already am receiving worship by the institution and celebration of this Feast; what else do you desire?** I then looked at the immense crowd worshiping The Divine Mercy and I said to the Lord, "Jesus, bless all those who are gathered to give glory to You and to venerate Your infinite mercy." Jesus made a sign of the cross with His hand, and this blessing was reflected in the souls like a flash of light. My spirit was engulfed in His love. I felt as if I had dissolved and disappeared completely in God. When I came to myself, a profound peace was flooding my soul, and an extraordinary understanding of many things was communicated to my intellect, an understanding that had not been granted me previously.

I am immensely happy, although I am the least of all;

and I would not change anything of what God has given me. I would not want to change places even with a Seraph, as regards the interior knowledge of God, which He himself has given me. The intimate knowledge I have of the Lord is such as no creature can comprehend, particularly, the depth of His mercy that envelops me.... (1044-1049)

Compassionate Suffering

On Wednesday, Sister continued to yearn for God, wishing to be united with Him, while in her body she felt such terrible suffering that, without the Lord's support, she would have been unable to bear it. In her agony she prayed for the entire Church, especially for priests.

During Mass on Holy Thursday, March 25, the Lord told Sister Faustina: **I shall give you a small portion of My Passion, but do not be afraid, be brave; do not seek relief, but accept everything with submission to My will.** The following is a record of her experience:

When Jesus was taking leave of me, such great pain filled my soul that it is impossible to express it. Physical strength left me; I left the chapel quickly and went to bed. I was oblivious of what was going on around me. My soul was filled with longing for the Lord, and all the bitterness of His Divine Heart was imparted to me. This lasted for about three hours. I asked the Lord to protect me from the eyes of those around me. Although I wanted to, I could not take any food all day, until evening.

I earnestly desired to spend the whole night with Jesus in the dark prison cell. I prayed until eleven o'clock. At eleven, the Lord said to me, **Lie down and take your rest. I have let you experience in three hours what I suffered during the whole night.** And immediately I went to bed.

I had no physical strength left; the suffering had deprived me of it completely. Throughout all this time, I had been in a sort of swoon. Every beat of Jesus' Heart was reflected in my heart and pierced my soul. If these tortures had concerned me only, I would have suffered less; but as I looked at the One whom my heart has loved with all its might and saw that He was suffering, and that I could not bring Him any relief, my heart dissolved in love and bitterness. I was dying with Him, and yet I could not die. But I would not have exchanged that martyrdom for all the pleasures in the whole world. In the course of this suffering, my love grew immeasurably. I know that the Lord was supporting me with His omnipotence, for otherwise I would not have been able to endure it for even a moment. Together with Him, I underwent, in a special way, all the various tortures. The world still has no idea of all that Jesus suffered. I accompanied Him to the Garden of Gethsemane; I stayed with Him in the prison; I went with Him before the judges; I underwent with Him each of the tortures. Not a single one of His movements or looks escaped my notice. I came to know all the omnipotence of His love and of His mercy toward souls. (1054)

Upon awakening on the morning of Good Friday, Sister Faustina felt the pain of His five wounds in her body. This suffering continued until three o'clock. Although there were no visible signs of these wounds, the torture was no less painful. At eleven o'clock Jesus said to her, **My host, you are refreshment for My tormented heart,** and a new mystical experience was granted her. She wrote:

I thought, after these words, that my heart would burn up. And He brought me into such close intimacy with Himself that my heart was espoused to His Heart in a loving union, and I could feel the faintest stir of His Heart and He, of mine. The fire of my created love was joined to the ardor of His eternal love. This one grace surpasses all others in its immensity. His Trinitarian Being enveloped me entirely, and I am totally immersed in Him. My littleness is, as it were, wrestling with this Immortal Mighty One. I am immersed in incomprehensible love and incomprehensible torture because of His Passion. All that concerns His Being is imparted to me also.

Up to now, Jesus had been bringing me to know about, and to have a presentiment of this grace, but today He granted it to me. I would not even dare to dream about it. My heart is in ceaseless ecstasy, as it were, although outwardly nothing disturbs my contacts with my neighbor or my attending to various matters. Nothing is capable of interrupting my ecstasy, nor can anyone suspect it, because I have asked God to protect me from detection by people. And, together with this grace, there entered my soul a whole ocean of light, enabling me to understand God and myself. Amazement overwhelms me entirely and leads me as if into a new ecstasy [aroused by the fact] that God has deigned to descend to me, who am so little. (1056-1057)

At three o'clock, prostrated in the form of a cross, Sister Faustina prayed for the whole world. She heard Jesus' seven last words and then these: **Beloved daughter of My Heart, you are My solace amidst terrible torments.** (1058)

Jesus then ordered Sister to make a novena before the Feast of Mercy, and to begin it that very day for the conversion of the whole world, and that The Divine Mercy become known, so that every soul would praise God's goodness. He further told her these consoling words for sinners:

> **...I desire trust from My creatures. Encourage souls to place great trust in My fathomless mercy. Let the weak, sinful soul have no fear to approach Me, for even if it had more sins than there are grains of sand in the world, all will be drowned in the unmeasurable depths of My mercy.** (1059)

As Jesus requested, Sister made this novena but she did not record it in her Diary until after the tenth of August of that year. Father Sopocko used that entry as the basis for the Novena which he published later that same year together with the Litany and Chaplet to The Divine Mercy.

At the moment that Jesus expired, Sister felt as if her soul dissolved from pain, and for a long time she was unable to come to herself. She did find a bit of relief in tears. Her Beloved died. Anyone who had lost a loved one can surely understand her grief. Later in the day, when she heard some priests singing psalms on the radio, she burst into tears and all the pain was renewed in her soul. She wept sorrowfully, unable to calm herself because of her pain. Then she heard the voice in her soul, **Do not cry; I am not suffering any more. And for the faithfulness with which you accompanied Me in My sufferings and death, your own death will be a solemn one, and I will accompany you in that last hour. Beloved pearl of My Heart, I see your love so pure, purer than that of the angels, and all the more so because you keep fighting. For your sake I bless the world. I see your efforts to please Me, and they delight My Heart.** (1061)

Consoled by these words, Sister wept no more but instead thanked the Heavenly Father for having sent us His Son and for the work of Redemption. That evening she spent an hour of adoration in thanksgiving for the graces granted her and for the four months of illness which, to her, were also a great grace. "All has been for God and souls," she recorded. (See 1062)

Return to Joseph's Place

On Holy Saturday, March 27, Sister Faustina was well enough to return to the convent in Lagiewniki. When she stepped into the chapel for a moment, she again was given to know how much she would have to suffer and struggle in connection with the mission of spreading the devotion to The Divine Mercy and the founding of the new congregation. In Jesus, she sought the strength and fortitude which He alone could provide. (See 1066)

On Easter Sunday during the Resurrection Mass, Sister Faustina saw Jesus in His beauty and splendor, and He said to her, **My daughter, peace to you.** He blessed her and disappeared, but her soul was filled with gladness and joy beyond words. Her heart was fortified for the struggle ahead. When later that day she told Father Andrasz that Jesus had suddenly appeared to her that morning, Father told her to be careful because these sudden appearances arouse suspicion. And even though he did not see anything wrong or contrary to faith in this matter, he again cautioned her to be careful and to speak about these things to Mother General when she arrives. (See 1067-1068)

The next day, the Lord suddenly appeared to her during meditation and said, **Peace be to you, My daughter.** Her entire being trembled with love for Him and she said, "O Lord, although I love You with all my heart, please do not appear to me, because my spiritual director told me that these sudden appearances of Yours arouse the suspicion that You could be an illusion. And although I love You more than my own life, and know that You are my Lord and God, who are communing with me, I must above all be obedient to my confessor."

Jesus listened to her with gravity and kindness and then said to her, **Tell your confessor that I commune with your soul in such an intimate manner because you do not steal My gifts, and this is why I pour all these graces upon your soul, because I know that you will not hoard them for yourself. But as a sign that his prudence is agreeable to Me, you shall not see Me, and I will not appear to you in this way until you have given him an account of what I have just said.** (1069)

The Lord, however, continued to speak to her by means of an internal voice. On April 2, during Mass, she heard these words: **Tell your superior that I want adoration to take place here for the intention of imploring mercy for the world.** It was a very difficult thing for her to do. She knew that she was exposing herself to great sufferings by telling her superior of the Lord's request; however, she decided to be faithful to the Lord and do it, because she knew that He would sustain her with His special grace. (See 1070)

On April 3, she was given another message: **Tell the Reverend Professor that I desire that on the Feast of My Mercy he deliver a sermon about My fathomless mercy.** Most likely Jesus meant Rev. Theodore Czaputa, who was the chaplain for the sisters at Lagiewniki. She fulfilled this request but the priest did not want to acknowledge the Lord's message. When she left the confessional she heard these words: **Do as I tell you and be at peace; this matter is between him and Me. You will not be held responsible for this.** (1072)

The next day, April 4, was the first Sunday after Easter; that is, the Feast of Mercy. While Sister Faustina was immersed in the Godhead after Holy Communion; that is, united to the Three Divine Persons in such a way that when she was united to Jesus she was simultaneously united to the Father and to the Holy Spirit, her soul was flooded with inconceivable joy as she experienced the whole ocean and abyss of His fathomless mercy. "Oh, if only souls would want to understand how much God loves them!" she wrote. "All comparisons, even the most tender and the most vehement, are but a mere shadow when set against the reality." While thus united with the Lord, she came to know how many souls were glorifying God's mercy. (See 1073)

During the adoration which the Superior arranged in response to Our Lord's request, Sister Faustina heard these consoling words:

My beloved daughter, write down these words, that today My Heart has rested in this convent. Tell the world about My mercy and My love.

The flames of mercy are burning Me. I desire to pour them out upon human souls. Oh, what pain they cause Me when they do not want to accept them!

My daughter, do whatever is within your power to spread devotion to My mercy. I will make up for what you lack. Tell aching mankind to snuggle close to My merciful Heart and I will fill it with peace.

Tell [all people], My daughter, that I am Love and Mercy itself. When a soul approaches Me with trust, I fill it with such an abundance of graces that it cannot contain them within itself, but radiates them to other souls.

Souls who spread the honor of My mercy I shield through their entire life as a tender mother her infant, and at the hour of death I will not be a Judge for them, but the Merciful Savior. At that last hour, a soul has nothing with which to defend itself except My mercy. Happy is the soul that during its lifetime immersed itself in the Fountain of Mercy, because justice will have no hold on it.

Write this: Everything that exists is enclosed in the depths of My mercy, more deeply than an infant in its mother's womb. How painfully distrust of My goodness wounds Me! Sins of distrust wound Me most painfully. (1074-1076)

When Sister was saying good night to the Lord before retiring, she heard the words, **Host dear to My Heart, for your sake I bless the earth.** (1078)

On Saturday, April 10, Mother Superior handed Sister Faustina an article printed in the Vilnius *Catholic Weekly,* dated April 4, 1937. It contained a reproduction of the Image of The Divine Mercy and words that Jesus spoke to Sister, some of them quotations from her diary. When she took it into her hands, an arrow of love pierced her soul. She heard the words: **For the sake of your ardent desires, I am hastening the Feast of Mercy.** Her spirit burst into such a powerful flame of love that it seemed to her that she was totally dissolved in God. (See 1080-1082)

A Sudden Healing

The next day, Sister wrote a letter to Father Sopocko; but before she could send it, she suddenly became ill. She waited for a clear sign that it was God's will that she send it. Her illness intensified. She was forced to remain in bed. The coughing racked her so much that it seemed to her that if the attack lasted any longer, it would be the end of her. Two days later she was still in bed. Violent coughing made her so weak that she could not even walk. The next day she barely managed to get up to attend Mass. She felt more ill now than when she was in the sanatorium. There were wheezing and rattling noises in her lungs and strange pains. After she had received Holy Communion, she felt an urge to pray in this way:

> Jesus, may Your pure and healthy blood circulate in my ailing organism, and may Your pure and healthy body transform my weak body, and may a healthy and vigorous life throb within me, if it is truly Your holy will that I should set about the work in question; and this will be a clear sign of Your holy will for me. (1089)

As Faustina was praying, she suddenly felt as if something were jolting her whole organism and, in an instant, she felt completely well. Her lungs felt clear and she had no pain. It was a sign for her to set about the work of beginning the new congregation. This happened on the last day of her novena to the Holy Spirit. Jesus strongly reassured her and confirmed her as to His demands. She remained close to the Lord Jesus all that day and talked with Him about the details concerning the new congregation. Then she heard the words: **Go tell the superior that you are in good health.** In her diary she recorded the following reflection: "I asked for this health as evidence of God's will and not in order to seek relief from my suffering." (1091)

Divine Urgings

On April 23, an eight-day retreat took place and Sister took advantage of it to make her annual three-day retreat. That evening she heard in her soul: **My daughter, know that I shall speak to you in a special way through this priest, so that you may not yield to doubt concerning My wishes.**

Immediately in the first conference, the priest's words impressed her deeply. She realized more clearly that she must not oppose God's will and God's designs, whatever they might be; and that as soon as she was convinced of the certitude and authenticity of the will of God, it would be her duty to carry it out. She knew now what God wanted of her and what she ought to do. (See 1101)

On April 30, the day of the renewal of the vows, God's presence enveloped her immediately upon awaking, and divine love was poured into her soul. She clearly realized that everything that happens is dependent upon God's will. Then she heard Him speak these words: **I want to grant a plenary indulgence to the souls that will go to Confession and receive Holy Communion on the Feast of My Mercy.** (1109)

At the solemn celebration, as the sisters were renewing their vows, Sister Faustina heard angels singing in various tones, HOLY, HOLY, HOLY "with chanting so delightful," she wrote, "that no human tongue could ever match it." (1111)

Mother General was in Cracow to receive the sisters' vows and to visit the community. On May 4 Sister Faustina asked her, "Dear Mother, have you had any inspiration concerning my leaving the convent?"

Mother Michael answered, "Until the present, Sister, I have always restrained you, but now I leave you complete freedom to choose to do as you wish; you can leave the Congregation or you can stay."

Sister replied, "Very well," and thought of writing immediately to the Holy Father to release her from her vows. But, when she left the Mother General, darkness once again descended upon her soul. It seemed odd that each time she asked permission to leave, her soul became enveloped in darkness. She decided to go to Mother immediately and tell her about this strange torment and struggle.

Mother declared, "That leaving of yours is a temptation." After talking with her for a while, Sister Faustina felt some relief but the darkness remained. Mother commented, "This Divine Mercy is a beautiful thing, and it must be a great work of the Lord, since Satan opposes it so much and wants to destroy it." (1115)

The following notation in the diary reveals the extent of Sister's suffering:

> No one can understand or comprehend, nor can I myself describe, my torments. But there can be no suffering greater than this. The sufferings of the martyrs are not greater because, at such times, death would be a relief for me. There is nothing to which I can compare these sufferings, this endless agony of the soul. (1116)

On May 5, she sought help in the confessional regarding the turmoil she experienced each time she asked to leave the Congregation. The confessor told her that this may not be the right time. "You must pray and wait patiently, but it is true that great sufferings are in store for you."... (1117)

Sister also felt lost because her spiritual director, Father Andrasz, was away in Rome for a few weeks; but she firmly believed that God would not give her more than she could bear. She placed her trust in His mercy. Her soul remained in torment and darkness. Although everything in nature was throbbing with the joy of spring, her heart could not rejoice because her Beloved had hidden himself from her. (See 1118-1120)

The following day, the Feast of the Ascension, Sister experienced a complete reversal of spirit. Her soul was touched by God and she communed with the Heavenly Father for a while. Such tremendous love for the Heavenly Father enveloped her that she called this day an uninterrupted ecstasy of love. The assurance of God's love for her and the conviction that her soul pleases Him brought deep peace to her soul. Throughout that day she was unable to take any food; she felt satiated with love.

On May 20, Sister Faustina recorded that for a whole month now she had been enjoying good health. It occurred to her that she did not know which was more pleasing to the Lord: serving Him in illness or in the robust health she had asked of Him. And she said to the Lord, "Jesus, do with me as You please." That day Jesus brought her back to her previous state of ill health. (See 1125)

The Divine Tutor

It was two days later, May 22, that the following incident occurred and Sister recorded it to show the power that Jesus himself attributed to the Chaplet of The Divine Mercy that He taught her:

The heat is so intense today that it is difficult to bear. We are all thirsting for rain, and still it does not come. For several days the sky has been overcast, but there is no rain. When I looked at the plants, thirsting for the rain, I was moved with pity, and I decided to say the chaplet until the Lord would send us rain. Before supper, the sky covered over with clouds, and a heavy rain fell on the earth. I had been saying this prayer without interruption for three hours. And the Lord let me know that everything can be obtained by means of this prayer. (1128)

Important feasts of the Church followed in succession: May 23, the Feast of the Most Holy Trinity; May 27, the Feast of Corpus Christi. Each feast brought with it added joy and happiness, more illumination and understanding of God's majesty and kindness. (See 1129-1141)

It was during Mass on June 4, 1937, Feast of the Most Sacred Heart of Jesus, that Sister Faustina was given a very important message:

Apostle of My mercy, proclaim to the whole world My unfathomable mercy. Do not be discouraged by the difficulties you encounter in proclaiming My mercy. These difficulties that affect you so painfully are needed for your sanctification and as evidence that this work is Mine. My daughter, be diligent in writing down every sentence I

address to you concerning My mercy, because this is meant for a great number of souls who will profit from it. (1142)

During her monthly one-day retreat on June 6, Our Lord again spoke to her:

[Let] the greatest sinners [place] their trust in My mercy. They have the right before others to trust in My bottomless mercy. My daughter, write about My mercy towards tormented souls. Souls that make an appeal to My mercy delight me. To such souls I grant even more graces than they ask. I cannot punish even the greatest sinner if he makes an appeal to My compassion, but on the contrary, I justify him in My unfathomable and inscrutable mercy. Write: Before I come as a just Judge, I first open wide the door of My mercy. He who refuses to pass through the door of My mercy must pass through the door of My justice.... (1146)

At one time, when Sister felt hurt because she was sent to perform a task, and could not attend some special conferences with the other sisters, Jesus told her:

My daughter, why do you attach such importance to the teaching and talk of people? I myself want to teach you; that is why I arrange things so that you cannot attend those lectures. In a single moment, I will bring you to know more than others will acquire through many years of toil. (1147)

Jesus continued to teach His little novice. On June 20 she learned that "We resemble God most when we forgive our neighbors. God is Love, Goodness and Mercy." (1148)

Jesus then told her, Every soul, and especially the soul of every religious, should reflect My mercy. My heart overflows with compassion and mercy for all. The heart of My beloved must resemble Mine; from her heart must spring the fountain of My mercy for souls; otherwise I will not acknowledge her as Mine. (1148)

On June 23, as Sister was praying before the Most Blessed Sacrament, her physical sufferings suddenly ceased and she heard the voice in her soul: You see, I can give you everything in one moment. I am not constrained by any laws. (1153)

Then on June 27, the Lord granted Sister Faustina a vision of the convent of the new congregation and the persons living in it. She received light and profound understanding concerning this whole work, and not a shadow of a doubt remained in her soul. Jesus also gave her the knowledge of His will concerning the new congregation. It would consist of three branches with three different functions, yet having the same goal:

The first is that souls separated from the world will burn as an offering before God's throne and beg for mercy for the whole world... and by their entreaties they will obtain blessings for priests, and through their prayers prepare the world for the final coming of Jesus.

The second is prayer joined to the act of mercy. In particular, they will defend the souls of children against the spirit of evil. Prayer and merciful deeds are all that will be required of these souls, and even the poorest persons can be admitted to their number. And in this egoistic world they will try to rouse up love, the mercy of Jesus.

The third is prayer and deeds of mercy, without any obligation of taking vows. But by doing this, these persons will have a share in all the merits and privileges of the whole [Congregation]. Everyone in the world can belong to this group.

A member of this group ought to perform at least one act of mercy a day; at least one, but there can be many more, for such deeds can easily be carried out by anyone, even the very poorest. For there are three ways of performing an act of mercy: the merciful word, by forgiving and by comforting; secondly, if you can offer no word, then pray—that too is mercy; and thirdly, deeds of mercy. And when the Last Day comes, we shall be judged from this, and on this basis we shall receive the eternal verdict. (1155-1158)

Faustina then recorded this statement: "God's floodgates have been opened for us. Let us want to take advantage of them before the day of God's justice arrives. And that will be a dreadful day!" (1159)

At one time, when Sister asked Jesus how He could tolerate so many sins and various crimes and not punish them, the Lord replied:

> **I have eternity for punishing** [these], **and so now I am prolonging the time of mercy for the sake of** [sinners]. **But woe to them if they do not recognize this time of My visitation. My daughter, secretary of My mercy, you duty is not only to write about and proclaim My mercy, but also to beg for this grace for them, so that they too may glorify My mercy.** (1160)

Because she tried so faithfully to do the Lord's bidding, Satan admitted to Sister that she is the object of his hatred: "A thousand souls do me less harm than you do when you speak of the great mercy of the Almighty One. The greatest sinners regain confidence and return to God, and I lose everything. But what is more, you persecute me personally with that unfathomable mercy of the Almighty One." (1167)

June 29 marked the return of Father Andrasz from Rome. Because he spent two hours that afternoon with the sisters and students, recounting to them the many beautiful things he saw in Rome, there was no time for Sister Faustina to speak to him privately, although she was anxious to share with him the spiritual inspirations, as also the tribulations, she had experienced during his absence.

Sister's bitter-sweet life continued. She admitted that in spite of her profound peace of soul she was constantly struggling, and often found it was a hard battle to walk faithfully along the path Jesus intended for her to follow. Therefore, on July 4, the day of her monthly retreat, Sister wrote down the fruit of her meditation and her plan of action for the month:

> Whatever Jesus did, He did well. He went along, doing good. His manner was full of goodness and mercy. His steps were guided by compassion. Toward His enemies He showed goodness, kindness and understanding; and to those in need, help and consolation. I have resolved to mirror faithfully these traits of Jesus in myself during this month, even if this costs me much. (1175)

During adoration of the Blessed Sacrament, Sister heard the voice in her soul: **These efforts of yours, My daughter, are** pleasing to Me; they are the delight of My Heart. I see every movement of your heart with which you worship Me. (1176)

A few weeks later, Our Lord gave His secretary the following directives:

My daughter, My pleasure and delight, nothing will stop Me from granting you graces. Your misery does not hinder My mercy. My daughter, write that the greater the misery of a soul, the greater its right to My mercy; [urge] all souls to trust in the unfathomable abyss of My mercy, because I want to save them all. On the cross, the fountain of My mercy was opened wide by the lance for all souls—no one have I excluded!" (1182)

Jesus taught Sister Faustina the value of submitting to His holy will and of contemplating His Passion. She recorded the following:

... I saw the Lord upon the cross. From His hands, feet and side, the Most Sacred Blood was flowing. After some time, Jesus said to me, All this is for the salvation of souls. Consider well, My daughter, what you are doing for their salvation. I answered, "Jesus, when I look at Your suffering, I see that I am doing next to nothing for the salvation of souls." And the Lord said to me, Know, My daughter, that your silent day-to-day martyrdom in complete submission to My will ushers many souls into heaven. And when it seems to you that your suffering exceeds your strength, contemplate My wounds, and you will rise above human scorn and judgment. Meditation on My Passion will help you rise above all things. I understood many things I had been unable to comprehend before. (1184)

The Growth of Sacrificial Love

Early in July, Sister Faustina recorded:

I often pray for Poland, but I see that God is very angry with it because of its ingratitude. I exert all the strength of my soul to defend it. I constantly remind God of the promises of His mercy. When I see His anger, I throw myself trustingly into the abyss of His mercy, and I plunge all Poland in it, and then He cannot use His justice. My country, how much you cost me! There is no day in which I do not pray for you. (1188)

A few days later she heard these words:

My daughter, delight of My Heart, it is with pleasure that I look into your soul. I bestow many graces only because of you. I also withhold My punishments only because of you. You restrain Me, and I cannot vindicate the claims of My justice. You bind My hands with your love. (1193)

On July 15, Sister Faustina learned interiorly that she would be assigned to another convent. At the same time she heard a voice in her soul saying: **Do not be afraid, My daughter; it is My will that you should remain here. Human plans will be thwarted, since they must conform to My will.** (1180) Five days later she was informed that she would be transferred to the convent in Rabka, but not until after August 5. Even though she had not as yet had a chance to speak to Father Andrasz after his return from Rome, Sister Faustina asked Mother Superior to let her go to Rabka at once. Mother was surprised that she wanted to go so soon, but Sister gave her no explanation. "That will remain a secret forever," she noted in her diary. (1198)

And so it was that, on July 29, Sister Faustina left for Rabka, a village in the Carpathian Mountains where the Congregation had a rest home for the sisters and girls. Even before she departed, her soul felt hollow and dark. The warm welcome of the sisters in Rabka only doubled her suffering. While there, her health deteriorated to such an extent that she became bedridden. She was told that people with tuberculosis do not suffer sharp pains, yet she was constantly experiencing them. The chest pains were so extremely bad that she could not even move her hand. One night she had to lie quite motionless, for it seemed that, if she moved, her lungs would be torn to shreds. During that endless night she united herself with Jesus Crucified and prayed to the Heavenly Father for sinners. One of the sisters told her that she would not get better because the climate in Rabka is not beneficial to all the sick. (See 1199-1201)

Saint Joseph came to her assistance at this time. He told her that he desired that she have a constant devotion to him and requested that she say three prayers (Our Father, Hail Mary and Glory Be) and one "Memorare" to him every day. He let her know that he was supporting the work of mercy, and he promised her his special help and protection. (1203)

August 1, the day of monthly retreat, was for her a retreat day of suffering. She was incapable of any kind of prayer. The oppression of body and soul increased. She cried out to the Lord, "O my Jesus, but You do see that Your child is on the decline." (1204)

On August 6, Sister began a novena to Our Lady of the Assumption for three intentions: that she may get to see Father Sopocko, that God would hasten this work of mercy, and for the intention of Poland. (See 1206)

Four days later Sister returned to Cracow in the company of one of the sisters. She spent the next few days writing down the Novena to The Divine Mercy which Jesus had instructed her to make and write down before the Feast of Mercy. (See 1207-1229)

When the sisters began to ask her why she had returned, Sister Faustina had to arm herself with patience in order to answer each one, each time, "because I was feeling worse." It was all the more difficult because she knew that most of them were asking not in order to sympathize with her suffering but to add to it. "Jesus alone knows how much I suffer," she wrote in her diary. (1236)

Two days after her arrival, Father Sopocko was passing through Cracow and paid Sister a short visit. "My joy was very great, and I thanked God for this great grace, because it was for the greater glory of God that I wanted to see him," she wrote. (1238) Sister then revealed her perception of the mystery of the priesthood in the following notation:

> The Lord Jesus greatly protects His representatives on earth. How closely is He united with them; and He orders me to give priority to their opinion over His. I have come to know how great is that intimacy which exists between Jesus and the priest. Jesus defends whatever the priest says, and often complies with his wishes, and sometimes makes His own relationship with a soul depend on the priest's advice. O

Jesus, through a special grace, I have come to know very clearly to what extent You have shared Your power and mystery with them, more so than with the Angels. I rejoice in this, for it is all for my good. (1240)

During her meditation on August 15, God's presence again pervaded Sister Faustina's being, and she was given the grace to experience the Blessed Virgin's joy at her Assumption. The Blessed Virgin told her, *One cannot be pleasing to God without obeying His holy will.... I very much desire that you distinguish yourself in this, that is, in doing God's will faithfully....* Towards the end of a special ceremony during which the sisters elect Our Lady of Mercy as Superior General of the Congregation, Sister Faustina again saw the Blessed Virgin Mary who said to her, *O how very pleased I am with the homage of your love!* And she enveloped all the sisters of the Congregation with Her cloak. (See 1244)

The next day after Holy Communion Faustina saw Jesus who said to her, **My daughter, during the weeks when you neither saw Me nor felt My presence, I was more profoundly united to you than at times** [when you experienced] **ecstasy. And the faithfulness and fragrance of your prayer have reached Me.** After these words she was filled to overflowing with the comfort of God, and this state of deep contemplation lasted for three days. Outwardly, however, she was still able to perform her duties. (See 1246)

Sister had yet another visitation from heaven, this one on August 22:

This morning Saint Barbara, Virgin, visited me and recommended that I offer Holy Communion for nine days on behalf of my country and thus appease God's anger ... she was so beautiful that if I had not already known the Virgin Mary I would have thought it was She. Now I understand that each virgin has a special beauty all her own; a distinct beauty radiates from each of them. (1251)

During the last days of August, Father Sopocko visited at the convent in Cracow, and Sister Faustina finally received permission for a longer conversation with him. She learned that the work of mercy progressed and the matter concerning the

Feast of Mercy was far advanced, but that much prayer was still necessary for the removal of certain difficulties. Father asked her to set her mind at ease and be calm about everything. He then added that he gave the novena, litany, and chaplet to the printer, and asked her to pray that they get the approval of the Church.

Father Sopocko left on the morning of August 30. When Faustina became deeply absorbed in a prayer of thanksgiving for having seen him, she found herself intimately united with the Lord, who said to her:

He is a priest after My own Heart; his efforts are pleasing to Me. You see, My daughter, that My will must be done, and that which I had promised you, I shall do. Through him I spread comfort to suffering and careworn souls. Through him it pleased Me to proclaim the worship of My mercy. And through this work of mercy more souls will come close to Me than otherwise would have, even if he had kept giving absolution day and night for the rest of his life, because by so doing, he would have labored for only as long as he lived; whereas, thanks to this work of mercy, he will be laboring till the end of the world. (See 1254-1256)

However, during her conversations with Father Sopocko, Sister Faustina discerned that his was an anguished soul. It resembled the Crucified Savior. Where he could duly expect comfort, he found a cross. He lived among friends, but had no one but Jesus. This is how God strips the soul He especially loves. (See 1259)

On September 1, 1937, Sister wrote that she saw Jesus as a King of great majesty, severely looking down at the earth, but because of His Mother's intercession, He again prolonged the time of His mercy. However, on exactly the same day but two years later, and one year after Sister Faustina's death, the chastisement began with the invasion of Poland by the Nazis and the beginning of World War II. (See 1261)

On the first Friday of September, Faustina was inspired during Holy Communion to make what she called the "Act of total abandonment to the will of God." It reads as follows:

Act of Oblation

Jesus Host, whom I have this very moment received into my heart, in this union with You I offer myself to the Heavenly Father as a sacrificial host, abandoning myself totally and completely to the most merciful holy will of my God. From today onward, Your will, Lord, is my food. You have my whole being; dispose of me as You please. Whatever Your fatherly hand gives me, I will accept with submission, peace, and joy. I fear nothing, no matter in what direction You lead me; helped by Your grace I will carry out everything You demand from me. I no longer fear any of Your inspirations, nor do I probe anxiously to see where they will lead me. Lead me, O God, along whatever roads You please; I have placed all my trust in Your will which is, for me, love and mercy itself.

Bid me to stay in this convent, I will stay; bid me to undertake the work, I will undertake it; leave me in uncertainty about the work until I die, be blessed; give me death when, humanly speaking, my life seems particularly necessary, be blessed. Should You take me in my youth, be blessed; should You let me live to a ripe old age, be blessed. Should You give me health and strength, be blessed; should You confine me to a bed of pain for my whole life, be blessed. Should You give failures and disappointments in life, be blessed. Should You allow my purest intentions to be condemned, be blessed. Should You enlighten my mind, be blessed. Should You leave me in darkness and all kinds of torments, be blessed.

From this moment on, I live in the deepest peace, because the Lord Himself is carrying me in the hollow of His hand. He, Lord of unfathomable mercy, knows that I desire Him alone in all things, always and everywhere. (1264)

Prayer. O Jesus, stretched out upon the cross, I implore You, give me the grace of doing faithfully the most holy will of Your Father, in all things, always and everywhere. And when this will of God will seem to me very harsh and difficult to fulfill, it is then I beg You, Jesus, may power and strength flow upon me from Your wounds and may my lips keep repeating, "Your will be done, O Lord." O Savior of the world, Lover of man's salvation, who in such terrible torment and pain forget Yourself to think only of the salvation of souls, O most compassionate Jesus, grant me the grace to forget myself that I may live totally for souls, helping You in the work of salvation, according to the most holy will of Your Father. (1265)

She had reached the stage of holy indifference and was now prepared to accept God's will in its fullest.

Gatekeeper

Because of her poor health, Sister Faustina was transferred on September 6, 1937, from gardener to gatekeeper. She thanked the Lord and asked for His blessing and grace to faithfully discharge this new duty assigned to her. Immediately, unpleasant situations arose for her. She was late for dinner because she was detained at the gate by extra duties. The sister in the kitchen let her know how displeased she was with her tardiness. Sister Faustina humbly and quietly accepted this. Later that day, she felt so ill that she needed to rest. When she went to ask another sister to replace her at the gate, she again received a scolding: "What! You're so fatigued that you must lie down again! Confound you with that lying around." Sister Faustina listened patiently to all this also, but it was not yet the end of it. She still had to ask the sister who was in charge of the sick to bring her a meal. That sister ran out of the chapel into the hallway, calling after Sister, "Why are you going to lie down, etc...." Sister Faustina begged her not to bring her anything. She wrote in her diary that she had no intention of writing about these incidents but did it only because she wished that other sick sisters would not be treated in the same way:

> ... for this is displeasing to the Lord. In a suffering soul we should see Jesus Crucified, and not a loafer or burden to the community. A soul who suffers with submission to the will of God draws down more blessings on the whole convent than all the working sisters. Poor indeed is a convent where there are no sick sisters. God often grants many and great

graces out of regard for the souls who are suffering, and He withholds many punishments solely because of the suffering souls. (1268)

O my Jesus, when shall we look upon souls with higher motives in mind? When will our judgments be true? You give us occasions to practice deeds of mercy, and instead we use the occasions to pass judgment. In order to know whether the love of God flourishes in a convent, one must ask how they treat the sick, the disabled, and the infirm who are there. (1269)

The Lord compensated Faustina for the insensitivities of her sisters. When she learned how dangerous it was to be at the gate in those days of revolutionary disturbances and how evil people hated convents, she spoke to the Lord and asked Him so to arrange it that no evil person would dare come to the gate. Then she heard the words: **My daughter, the moment you went to the gate I set a Cherub over it to guard it. Be at peace.** When she returned to her duty after this conversation with the Lord, she saw a little white cloud and, in it, a Cherub with folded hands. His countenance was like lightning, and she realized that the fire of the love of God was burning in that glance. (1271)

On September 14, Jesus said to her, **My daughter, do you think you have written enough about My mercy? What you have written is but a drop compared to the ocean. I am Love and Mercy itself. There is no misery that could be a match for My mercy, neither will misery exhaust it, because as it is being granted—it increases. The soul which will trust in My mercy is most fortunate, because I myself take care of it.** (1273)

My secretary, write that I am more generous toward sinners than toward the just. It was for their sake that I came down from heaven; it was for their sake that My Blood was spilled. Let them not fear to approach Me; they are most in need of My mercy. (1275)

Atonement for Abortions

Under the date of September 16, 1937, Sister Faustina recorded a surprising revelation concerning some of her unusual sufferings:

I wanted very much to make a Holy Hour before the Blessed Sacrament today, but God's will was otherwise. At eight o'clock I was seized with such violent pains that I had to go to bed at once. I was convulsed with pain for three hours; that is, until eleven o'clock at night. No medicine had an effect on me, and whatever I swallowed I threw up. At times, the pain caused me to lose consciousness. Jesus had me realize that in this way I took part in His Agony in the Garden, and that He himself allowed these sufferings in order to offer reparation to God for the souls murdered in the wombs of wicked mothers. I have gone through these sufferings three times now. They always start at eight o'clock in the evening and last until eleven. No medicine can lessen these sufferings. When eleven o'clock comes, they cease by themselves, and I fall asleep at that moment. The following day, I feel very weak.

This happened to me for the first time when I was at the sanatorium. The doctors couldn't get to the bottom of it, and no injection or medicine helped me at all nor did I myself have any idea of what these sufferings were about. I told the doctor that never before in my life had I experienced such sufferings, and he declared he does not know what sort of pains they are. But now I understand the nature of these pains, because the Lord himself made this known to me.... Yet, when I think that I may perhaps suffer in this way again, I tremble. But I don't know whether I'll ever again suffer in this way; I leave that to God. What it pleases God to send, I will accept with submission and love. If only I could save even one soul from murder by means of these sufferings! (1276)

Mystical Graces

Although Sister Faustina was asked to suffer much, she also had many days in which she was filled with God's grace of mystical union, as the continuing pages of her Diary reveal:

I receive Holy Communion in the manner of the angels, so to speak. My soul is flooded with God's light and nourishes itself from Him. My feelings are as if dead. This is a purely spiritual union with God; it is a great predominance of spirit over nature. (1278)

The Lord gave me knowledge of the graces which He has been constantly lavishing on me. This light pierced me through and through, and I came to understand the inconceivable favors that God has been bestowing on me. I stayed in my cell for a long act of thanksgiving, lying face down on the ground and shedding tears of gratitude. I could not rise from the ground because, whenever I tried to do so, God's light gave me new knowledge of His grace. It was only after the third attempt that I was able to get up. As His child, I felt that everything the Heavenly Father possessee was equally mine. He himself lifted me up from the ground up to His Heart. I felt that everything that existed was exclusively mine; but I had no desire for it all, because God alone is enough for me. (1279)

The following day, still filled with profound gratitude, Sister wrote a poem of thanksgiving for the many graces lavished upon her: for her creation, for each of the Holy Sacraments she had received, for the grace of being called to His exclusive service, for perpetual vows and the union of pure love. It was in poetry that she was able to give vent to the feelings she was experiencing, but so much is lost in translation! (See 1286)

Although she led a rich spiritual life, she was not exempt from leading the ordinary life of a lay sister. In the duty of gatekeeper, Sister Faustina found many occasions to exercise the virtue of love of neighbor, the exterior manifestation of the love of God. Whenever the same poor people returned to the gate, Sister treated them with even greater kindness in order not to embarrass them. She never let on that she knew that they were there once before. Thus they spoke to her more freely about their problems and needs.

Many times the sister who helped Faustina at the gate would tell her, "One should not deal with beggars in this way," and she would slam the door shut before Faustina was able to greet the stranger. But, whenever she was alone, Sister Faustina always treated these forsaken people as her Master would have done. She wrote, "Sometimes more is given when giving nothing, than when giving much in a rude manner." (See 1282)

On September 19 the Lord told Sister Faustina, **My daughter, write that it pains Me very much when religious souls receive the Sacrament of Love merely out of habit, as if they did not distinguish this food. I find neither faith nor love in their hearts. I go to such souls with great reluctance. It would be better if they did not receive Me.** (1288)

Sister's immediate response was, "Most sweet Jesus, set on fire my love for You and transform me into Yourself. Divinize me that my deeds may be pleasing to You. May this be accomplished by the power of the Holy Communion which I receive daily. Oh, how greatly I desire to be wholly transformed into You, O Lord!" (1289)

Jesus was pleased with these desires. He assured Sister Faustina that she never committed a mortal sin. However, human frailties were still part of her makeup. On September 21 she wrote of an incident from which she gleaned a valuable lesson about God's mercy:

> It so happened that I fell again into a certain error, in spite of a sincere resolution not to do so—even though the lapse was a minor imperfection and rather involuntary— and at this I felt such acute pain in my soul that I interrupted my work and went to the chapel for a while. Falling at the feet of Jesus, with love and a great deal of pain, I apologized to the Lord, all the more ashamed because of the fact that in my conversation with Him after Holy Communion this very morning I had promised to be faithful to Him. Then I heard these words: **If it hadn't been for this small imperfection, you wouldn't have come to Me. Know that as often as you come to Me, humbling yourself and asking My forgiveness, I pour out a superabundance of graces on your soul, and your imperfection vanishes before My eyes, and I see only your love and your humility. You lose nothing but gain much.** (1293)

Mother Irene's Role

On September 25, 1937, Mother Irene, the Superior of the convent, was going into town. As Sister Faustina opened the gate for her, she discerned that Mother's trip had something to do with the work of mercy. She was right. Two days later she was asked to accompany Mother to see the man who was to print the Chaplet and Litany of The Divine Mercy on the back of a holy card bearing the image. On September 1, Father Sopocko had obtained the approval of the Church for it. The publisher was also preparing a pamphlet entitled *Christ King of Mercy.* It would contain the novena, litany and chaplet. A larger image, copied from the original by a woman artist in Vilnius, was to be used on the cover. It was being touched up by the printer, and Sister Faustina happily noted that it closely resembled the original. When she looked at that image, she was penetrated by such a strong love of God that, for a moment, she did not know where she was.

Having settled that matter, they both attended Mass at the Church of the Most Holy Virgin Mary. During the Mass, the Lord revealed to Sister Faustina how great will be the number of souls who will find salvation through this work. She then immersed herself in prayer, thanking Jesus for letting her see the spread of the devotion to His Divine Mercy.

Sister Faustina was also grateful for Mother Irene's efforts on behalf of this work of mercy. Mother became Faustina's Superior in Vilnius, just two years after the first revelation of Jesus to her in Plock. While in Vilnius, she went with Sister Faustina to the artist who was to paint the image. And now, in Cracow, Mother Irene was settling matters concerning the printing of the holy cards and pamphlet. Sister Faustina knew how dear this person was to the Lord, and that it was He who so arranged it that, in these critical times, she would be in Mother Irene's care, inasmuch as she had undertaken most of the hardships connected with the work of The Divine Mercy. "Thank you, Lord, for such superiors who live in the love and fear of the Lord." (See 1300-1301.)

Hidden Mysteries

Sister Faustina continued to live out her unusual life in the usual hidden way. On September 29 she noted in her diary the following special grace:

Today I have come to understand many of God's mysteries. I have come to know that Holy Communion remains in me until the next Holy Communion. A vivid and clearly felt presence of God continues in my soul. The awareness of this plunges me into deep recollection, without the slightest effort on my part. My heart is a living tabernacle in which the living Host is reserved. I have never sought God in some far-off place, but within myself. It is in the depths of my own being that I commune with my God. (1302)

The sisters with whom she lived were not aware of the fact that this humble sister, who continued to work faithfully and quietly at her duty as gatekeeper, was a chosen victim soul. On the contrary, many of them were positive that she was feigning illness in order to have more time for prayer. According to the following notation in Sister's diary, written at this time, how wrong they were!

When one is ill and weak, one must constantly make efforts to measure up to what others are doing as a matter of course. But even those matter-of-course things cannot always be managed. Nevertheless, thank You, Jesus, for everything, because it is not the greatness of the works, but the greatness of the effort that will be rewarded. What is done out of love is not small, O my Jesus, for Your eyes see everything. I do not know why I feel so terribly unwell in the morning; I have to muster all my strength to get out of bed, sometimes even to the point of heroism. The thought of Holy Communion gives me back a little more strength. And so, the day starts with a struggle and ends with a struggle. When I go to take my rest, I feel like a soldier returning from the battlefield. You alone, my Lord and Master, know what this day has contained. (1310)

At the end of September a haggard young man, barefoot and bareheaded, his clothes in tatters, came to the gate. Hungry and very cold from the dampness of the day, he asked for something to eat. Sister Faustina went to the kitchen, but found nothing set aside for the poor. After much search, she was able to find some soup. She heated it, crumbled some bread into it, and handed it to the starved youth. As she was taking the empty cup from him, he revealed himself as the Lord of heaven and earth. When she recognized Him, He vanished from her sight. Returning to the building and reflecting on what happened at the gate, Sister Faustina heard these words in her soul: **My daughter, the blessings of the poor who bless Me as they leave this gate reached My ear. I was pleased with your mercy which is within the bounds of obedience and that is why I came down from My throne to taste the fruit of your mercy.** (1313)

From that moment, her heart was kindled with an even purer love towards the poor and needy. How happy she was that the Superiors have given her this duty! She understood that mercy is manifold; one can do good always and everywhere and at all times. But, she again had to admit that this was not an easy task for her: "Oh, what great efforts I must make to carry out my duties well when my health is so poor! This will be known to You alone, O Christ." (See 1314)

Soon after this, Jesus said to Sister: **Daughter, I need sacrifice lovingly accomplished because that alone has meaning for Me. Enormous indeed are the debts of the world which are due to Me; pure souls can pay them by their sacrifice, exercising mercy in spirit.**

Sister answered, "I understand Your words, Lord, and the magnitude of the mercy that ought to shine in my soul." (1316)

Jesus responded, **I know, My daughter, that you understand it and that you do everything within your power. But write this for the many souls who are often worried because they do not have the material means with which to carry out acts of mercy. Yet, spiritual mercy, which requires neither permissions nor storehouses, is much more meritorious and is within the grasp of every soul. If a soul does not exercise mercy in some way, it will not obtain My mercy on the day of judgment. Oh, if only souls knew how to gather eternal treasure for themselves, they would not be**

judged, for they would forestall My judgment with their mercy.
(1317)

On October 10, as Sister Faustina conversed with Jesus, she
learned a valuable lesson which she recorded thus:

O my Jesus, in thanksgiving for Your many graces I
offer You my body and soul, intellect and will, and all the
sentiments of my heart. Through the vows, I have given
myself entirely to You; I have then nothing more which I can
offer You. Jesus said to me, **My daughter, you have not
offered Me that which is really yours.** I probed deeply into
myself and found that I love God with all the faculties of my
soul and, unable to see what it was that I had not yet given to
the Lord, I asked, "Jesus, tell me what it is, and I will give it
to You at once with a generous heart." Jesus said to me with
kindness, **Daughter, give Me your misery, because it is your
exclusive property.** At that moment, a ray of light illumined
my soul, and I saw the whole abyss of my misery. In that
same moment I nestled close to the Most Sacred Heart of
Jesus with so much trust that even if I had the sins of all the
damned weighing on my conscience I would not doubt
God's mercy but with a heart crushed to dust, I would throw
myself into the abyss of Your mercy. I believe, O Jesus, that
You would not reject me, but would absolve me with the
hand of Your representative." (1318)

The Hour of Great Mercy

On this day also, Sister Faustina received instruction from
the Lord concerning another principal element of the devotion to
The Divine Mercy; namely, The Hour of Great Mercy:

**At three o'clock, implore My mercy, especially for
sinners; and, if only for a brief moment, immerse yourself in
My Passion, particularly in My abandonment at the
moment of agony. This is the hour of great mercy for the
whole world. I will allow you to enter into My mortal
sorrow. In this hour I will refuse nothing to the soul that
makes a request of Me in virtue of My Passion....** (1320)

Just before the above entry, Sister recorded a prayer, which could be prayed as part of this devotion:

You expired, Jesus, but the source of life gushed forth for souls, and the ocean of mercy opened up for the whole world. O Fount of Life, unfathomable Divine Mercy, envelop the whole world and empty Yourself out upon us. (1319)

The Making of a Saint

On October 20, Sister Faustina expressed in writing her complete submission to the Will of God, especially in reference to the fulfillment of the role He had assigned to her:

O my God, let everything that is in me praise You, my Lord and Creator; and with every beat of my heart I want to praise Your unfathomable mercy. I want to tell souls of Your goodness and encourage them to trust in Your mercy. That is my mission, which You Yourself have entrusted to me, O Lord, in this life and in the life to come. (1325)

That same day she began her last eight-day retreat in common with the other sisters. Realizing she had less than a year to live, she wrote:

...I desire to come out of this retreat a saint, even though human eyes will not notice this, not even those of the superiors. I abandon myself entirely to the action of Your grace. Let Your will be accomplished entirely in me, O Lord. (1326)

Jesus told His "apostle" Faustina on the first day of the retreat:

My daughter, this retreat will be an uninterrupted contemplation. I will bring you into this retreat as into a spiritual banquet. Close to My merciful Heart you will meditate upon all the graces your heart has received, and a deep peace will accompany your soul. I want the eyes of your soul to be always fixed on My holy will, since it is in this way that you will please Me most. No sacrifices can be

compared to this. Throughout all the exercises you will remain close to My Heart. You shall not undertake any reforms, because I will dispose of your whole life as I see fit. The priest who will preach the retreat will not speak a single word which will trouble you. (1327)

Humbly she responded: "Jesus, You yourself have deigned to lay the foundations of my sanctity, as my cooperation has not amounted to much. You have taught me to set no store on the use of created things, because my heart is, of itself, so weak. And this is why I have asked You, O my Master, to take no heed of the pain of my heart, but to cut away whatever might hold me back from the path of love. I did not understand You, Lord, in times of sorrow, when You were effecting Your work in my soul; but today I understand You and rejoice in my freedom of spirit." (1331)

And she continued writing on the theme of becoming a saint:

...In spite of all my defeats, I want to go on fighting like a holy soul and to comport myself like a holy soul. I will not be discouraged by anything, just as nothing can discourage a soul who is holy. I want to live and die like a holy soul, with my eyes fixed on You, Jesus, stretched out on the Cross, as the model for my actions. I used to look around me for examples and found nothing which sufficed, and I noticed that my state of holiness seemed to falter. But from now on, my eyes are fixed on You, O Christ, who are for me the best of guides. I am confident that You will bless my efforts. (1333)

One day during the retreat, Sister Faustina prayed before the Blessed Sacrament, greeting the five wounds of Jesus. At each salutation of a wound she felt a stream of grace rushing into her soul, giving her a foretaste of heaven and complete trust in Divine Mercy. As she began to write about this, she could hear Satan's cry: "She's writing everything, she's writing everything, and because of this we are losing so much! Do not write about the goodness of God; He is just!" And with a howl of fury the evil spirit vanished. (1337-1338) She extolled The Divine Mercy with these words:

O merciful God, You do not despise us but lavish Your graces upon us continuously. You make us fit to enter Your kingdom, and in Your goodness You grant that human beings may fill the places vacated by the ungrateful angels. O God of great mercy, who turned Your sacred gaze away from the rebellious angels and turned it upon contrite man, praise and glory be to Your unfathomable mercy, O God who do not despise the lowly heart. (1339)

Jesus reminded Sister, **Bear in mind that when you come out of this retreat, I shall be dealing with you as with a perfect soul. I want to hold you in My hand as a pliant tool, perfectly adapted to the completion of My works.** (1359)

To this Sister Faustina replied, "O Lord, You who penetrate my whole being and the most secret depths of my soul, You see that I desire You alone and only for the fulfillment of Your holy will, paying no heed to difficulties or sufferings or humiliations or of what others might think." (1360)

Jesus replied, **This firm resolution to become a saint is exremely pleasing to Me. I bless your efforts and will give you opportunities to sanctify yourself. Be watchful that you lose no opportunity that My providence offers you for sanctification. If you do not succeed in taking advantage of an opportunity, do not lose your peace, but humble yourself profoundly before Me and, with great trust, immerse yourself completely in My mercy. In this way, you gain more than you have lost, because more favor is granted to a humble soul than the soul itself asks for...**(1361)

On the seventh day of the retreat, Faustina received interior certainty of her destiny—that she will attain sanctity. This profound knowledge filled her soul with gratitude to God, and to Him she gave all the glory, for she knew what she was of herself. With childlike simplicity she recorded the great things the Lord had done for her during this retreat:

I am coming out of this retreat thoroughly transformed by God's love. My soul is beginning a new life, earnestly and courageously; although outwardly my life will not change, and no one will notice it, nevertheless, pure love is [now] the guide of my life and, externally, it is mercy which is its fruit. I feel that I have been totally imbued with God and, with this

God, I am going back to my everyday life, so drab, tiresome and wearying, trusting that He whom I feel in my heart will change this drabness into my personal sanctity.

In profound silence, close to Your merciful Heart, my soul is maturing during this retreat. In the clear rays of Your love, my soul has lost its tartness and has become a sweet and ripe fruit.

Now I can be wholly useful to the Church by my personal sanctity, which throbs with life in the whole Church, for we all make up one organism in Jesus. That is why I endeavor to make the soil of my heart bear good fruit. Although the human eye will perhaps never see it, there will nevertheless come a day when it will become apparent that many souls have been fed and will continue to be fed with this fruit. (1363-1364)

On the eighth day of the retreat, as she recalled all the benefits and graces she received from the Lord, Sister Faustina felt the need to give special thanks to God. She desired to continue in a prayer of thanksgiving before the Majesty of God for the next seven days and seven nights. Exteriorly, she would fulfill her assigned tasks; interiorly, her spirit would remain constantly before the Lord, and all her spiritual exercises would be permeated with this spirit of thankfulness. (See 1367)

To be certain that this plan would be pleasing to God, and to remove even a shadow of a doubt from her mind, Sister Faustina presented these desires to Father Andrasz in confession and received his permission for everything except that she was not to exert herself at prayer should she awaken during the night. The next day, October 29, beginning with the renewal of her vows, Sister began this "great thanksgiving." (See 1368-1369)

From the following entry in her Diary, we find that the thought of becoming a saint was not just a recent desire:

My Jesus, You know that from my earliest years I have wanted to become a great saint; that is to say, I have wanted to love You with a love so great that there would be no soul who has hitherto loved You so. At first these desires of mine were kept secret, and only Jesus knew of them. But today I cannot contain them within my heart; I would like to cry out to the whole world, "Love God, because He is good and great is His mercy!" (1372)

O humdrum days, filled with drabness, I look upon you with a solemn and festive eye. How great and solemn is the time that gives us the chance to gather merits for eternal heaven! I understand how the saints made use of it. (1373)

A week after the retreat, on the morning of November 5, 1937, one of the sisters at the gate met with a dangerous, frightening situation. Five unemployed men demanded entrance. Unable to resolve the situation, she hurried to the chapel to inform the Mother Superior, who, in turn, told Sister Faustina to go to them. She left a record of the event:

...When I was still a good way from the gate I could hear them banging loudly. At first, I was overcome with doubt and fear, and I did not know whether to open the gate or, like Sister N., to answer them through the little window. But suddenly I heard a voice in my soul saying, **Go and open the gate and talk to them as sweetly as you talk to Me.**

I opened the gate at once and approached the most menacing of them and began to speak with such sweetness and calm that they did not know what to do with themselves. And they too began to speak gently and said, "Well, it's too bad that the convent can't give us work." And they went away peacefully. I felt clearly that Jesus, whom I had received in Holy Communion just an hour before, had worked in their hearts through me. O, how good it is to act under God's inspiration! (1377)

A few hours after this incident, Sister Faustina began to feel sick. She approached Mother Superior with the intention of asking her for permission to lie down. Instead she was given a new assignment: to manage by herself at the gate because the girl, who usually helped her, was needed to work in the garden. When Sister Faustina took up her assignment at the gate, she felt unusually strong and remained at her post feeling strong and well all day. She attributed this incident, as well as all her successes in the various duties that have been assigned her, to holy obedience. (See 1378)

On November 10, Mother Irene showed Sister Faustina a

copy of the booklet *Christ King of Mercy* which the Cebulski Co. had printed for Father Sopocko. Sister asked if she could glance through it. As she was doing so, she heard Jesus say, **Already there are many souls who have been drawn to My love by this image. My mercy acts in souls through this work.** (1379)

Source of Strength in Suffering

On November 19, Our Lord's secretary recorded a message Jesus gave her that day after Holy Communion:

I desire to unite Myself with human souls; My great delight is to unite Myself with souls. Know, My daughter, that when I come to a human heart in Holy Communion, My hands are full of all kinds of graces which I want to give to the soul. But souls do not even pay attention to Me; they leave Me to Myself and busy themselves with other things. O, how sad I am that souls do not recognize Love! They treat Me as a dead object. (1385)

Faustina answered Jesus, "O treasure of my heart, the only object of my love and entire delight of my soul, I want to adore You in my heart as You are adored on the throne of Your eternal glory. My love wants to make up to You at least in part for the coldness of so great a number of souls. Jesus, behold my heart which is for You a dwelling place to which no one has entry. You alone repose in it as in a beautiful garden. O my Jesus, farewell; I must go already to take up my tasks. But I will prove my love for You with sacrifice, neither neglecting nor letting any chance for practicing it slip by." (1385-1386)

Throughout that day, Sister had an exceptional number of opportunities for sacrifice. She neglected none of them, owing to the strength of spirit she drew from Holy Communion. Her love for this sacrament is revealed in the following notation:

All the good that is in me is due to Holy Communion. I owe everything to it. I feel that this holy fire has transformed me completely. Oh, how happy I am to be a dwelling place for You, O Lord! My heart is a temple in which You dwell continually.... (1392)

Hidden Jesus, in You lies all my strength. From my most tender years, the Lord Jesus in the Blessed Sacrament has attracted me to Himself. Once, when I was seven years old, at a Vesper Service conducted before the Lord Jesus in the monstrance, the love of God was imparted to me for the first time and filled my little heart; and the Lord gave me understanding of divine things. From that day until this, my love for the hidden God has been growing constantly to the point of closest intimacy. All the strength of my soul flows from the Blessed Sacrament. I spend all my free moments in conversation with Him. He is my Master. (1404)

During her day of monthly recollection, November 26, Sister Faustina learned more profoundly the value of suffering. She learned that sufferings likened her to Jesus. If there were another and better way, Jesus would have shown it to her. Amidst suffering she enjoyed profound peace, but the peace did not lessen the suffering she experienced. "Although my face is often bowed to the ground and my tears flow profusely," she wrote, "at the same time my soul is filled with profound peace and happiness." (See 1394)

That same day Jesus told His faithful secretary:

O, if sinners knew of My mercy, they would not perish in such great numbers. Tell sinful souls not to be afraid to approach Me; speak to them of My great mercy.... The loss of each soul plunges Me into mortal sadness. You always console Me when you pray for sinners. The prayer most pleasing to Me is prayer for the conversion of sinners. Know, My daughter, that this prayer is always heard and answered. (1396-1397)

Since the season of Advent was again approaching, the ever-vigilant Sister Faustina resolved, on that day of monthly recollection, to prepare her heart for the coming of the Lord Jesus by keeping silence and recollection, uniting herself with the Blessed Mother, especially by faithfully imitating her silence.

A letter from Father Sopocko came on November 21. He told her that God was demanding prayer and sacrifice from her, rather than action. He was referring to her desire to begin the new congregation. From what she wrote in her diary, it is clear that

Sister was not disappointed in his answer:

Yesterday I received a letter from Father Sopocko. I learned that God's work is progressing, however slowly. I am very happy about this, and I have redoubled my prayers for this entire work. I have come to learn that, for the present, so far as my participation in the work is concerned, the Lord is asking for prayer and sacrifice. Action on my part could indeed thwart God's plans, as Father Sopocko wrote in yesterday's letter. O my Jesus, grant me the grace to be an obedient instrument in Your hands. I have learned from this letter how great is the light which God grants to this priest. This confirms me in the conviction that God will carry out this work through him despite the mounting obstacles. I know well that the greater and the more beautiful the work is, the more terrible will be the storms that rage against it. (1401)

God, in His unfathomable decrees, often allows it to be that those who have expended most effort in accomplishing some work do not enjoy its fruit here on earth; God reserves all their joy for eternity. But for all that, God sometimes lets them know how much their efforts please Him. And such moments strengthen them for further struggles and ordeals. These are the souls that bear closest resemblance to the Savior who, in the work which He founded here on earth, tasted nothing but bitterness. (1402)

Sister Faustina now had to contend with spiritual struggles. On the evening of November 30, 1937, she was suddenly overcome by an unusual distaste for everything that had to do with God. Then she heard Satan who said to her, "Think no more about this work. God is not as merciful as you say He is. Do not pray for sinners, because they will be damned all the same, and by this work of mercy you expose your own self to damnation. Talk no more about this mercy of God with your confessor and especially not with Father Sopocko and Father Andrasz." At this point, the voice changed into the figure of Sister Faustina's Guardian Angel. Immediately she said, "I know who you are: the father of lies." She made the sign of the cross and the angel flew into a rage and vanished. The next day the Lord let her know that

He would not abandon her, that no one could touch even a hair of her head without His will. (See 1405-1406.)

One day in December, while she was receiving Holy Communion, Sister Faustina noticed that in the ciborium there was only one "Live Host" which the priest gave to her. When she returned to her place she asked the Lord, "Why was one Host alive, since You are equally alive under each of the species?"

The Lord answered her, **That is so. I am the same under each of the species, but not every soul receives Me with the same living faith as you do, My daughter, and therefore I cannot act in their souls as I do in yours.** (1407)

Soon after this, Sister attended a Mass celebrated by Father Sopocko. During the Mass she saw the Infant Jesus, who touching the priest's forehead with one of His fingers, said to her, **His thought is closely united to Mine, so be at peace about what concerns My work. I will not let him make a mistake, and you should do nothing without his permission.**

Her soul was then filled with great calm concerning the entire work. In the days that followed she was made even more aware of the Lord's tender love and care for her. He let her understand more profoundly how everything depends on His will, how He allows certain difficulties solely for our merit, so that our faithfulness would be openly manifest. And with this she had also been granted strength for suffering and self-denial. (See 1408-1409)

Love for Mary Immaculate

With great zeal Sister Faustina had been preparing for the celebration of the Feast of the Immaculate Conception of the Mother of God. She spent the days in greater recollection, thanking God for the great privilege granted to Mary, and her heart was completely immersed in Hers. She prepared not only by taking part in the novena in which the entire Congregation participated, but for nine days, she personally greeted Mary by saying a thousand Hail Marys daily in her honor. This was the third time that she had made such a novena: twice at her duty— without taking away from it but performing it meticulously—and not during Mass, spiritual exercises or recreation; and once while lying in bed in the sanatorium. To honor the Immaculate One this was not too much, she said, although she admitted that it took a lot of concentration and effort.

God blessed these endeavors. Already at the midday meal on the eve of the feast, December 7, the Lord in an instant gave Faustina knowledge of the greatness of her destiny; that is, His closeness, which for all eternity will not be taken away from her. It was all so vivid and clear that she remained wrapped in His living presence for a long time.

Of the feast day itself, Sister wrote:

... Before Holy Communion I saw the Blessed Mother inconceivably beautiful. Smiling at me She said to me, *My daughter, at God's command I am to be, in a special and exclusive way your Mother; but I desire that you, too, in a special way, be My child.*

I desire, My dearly beloved daughter, that you practice the three virtues that are dearest to Me—and most pleasing to God. The first is humility, humility, and once again humility; the second virtue, purity; the third virtue, love of God. As My daughter, you must especially radiate with these virtues. When the conversation ended She pressed me to Her Heart and disappeared. When I regained the use of my senses, my heart became so wonderfully attracted to these virtues; and I practice them faithfully. They are as though engraved in my heart.

This has been a great day for me. During this day I remained as though in unceasing contemplation; the very thought of this grace drew me into further contemplation; and throughout the whole day I continued in thanksgiving which I never stopped, because each recollection of this grace caused my soul ever anew to lose itself in God...

O my Lord, my soul is the most wretched of all, and yet You stoop to it with such kindness! I clearly see Your greatness and my littleness, and therefore I rejoice that You are so powerful and without limit, and so I rejoice greatly at being so little.

O suffering Christ, I am going out to meet You. As Your bride, I must resemble You. Your cloak of ignominy must cover me too. O Christ, You know how ardently I desire to become like You. Grant that Your entire Passion be my lot. May all Your sorrow be poured into my heart. I trust that You will complete this in me in the way You deem most fitting. (1414-1418)

On the first Thursday of the month, Sister Faustina was too weak to participate in the nocturnal adoration of the Blessed Sacrament. However, she united herself with the sisters who were in adoration. Between four and five o'clock in the morning she was suddenly awakened and she heard a voice telling her to join those sisters who were still adoring. She was given to know that among them was someone who was praying for her. As she prayed she was transported in spirit to the chapel and saw the Lord Jesus exposed in the monstrance. In place of the monstrance she saw the Glorified Face of Jesus who said to her, **What you see in reality, these souls see through faith. Oh, how pleasing to Me is their great faith! You see, although there appears to be no trace of life in Me, in reality it is present in its fullness in each and every Host. But for Me to be able to act in a soul, the soul must have faith. O how pleasing to Me is living faith!** (1420)

It was Mother Irene who was at adoration at that time with some other sisters. Sister Faustina was given to know that Mother's prayers were rousing heaven. It gladdened her to know that there were souls so pleasing to God.

Suffering for Souls

Physical as well as mystical pains increased, and with them Faustina's desire for souls. After having experienced for a short but very painful moment the pain of the crown of thorns, she wrote:

Christ, give me souls. Let anything You like happen to me, but give me souls in return. I want the salvation of souls. I want souls to know Your mercy. I have nothing left for myself, because I have given everything away to souls, with the result that on the day of judgment I will stand before You empty-handed, since I have given everything away to souls. Thus You will have nothing on which to judge me, and we shall meet on that day: Love and mercy. (1426)

From the following diary excerpt we learn that Sister's physical pain was intense. But, in imitation of the Lord, hidden under the species of bread in the Holy Eucharist, her true physical state remained hidden from others.

> For a month now I have been feeling worse. Every time I cough, I feel my lungs disintegrating. It sometimes happens that I feel the complete decay of my own corpse. It is hard to express how great a suffering this is. Although I fully agree to this with my will, it is nevertheless a great suffering for nature, greater than wearing a hairshirt or a flagellation to the point of blood. I have felt it especially when I was going to the refectory. It took great effort for me to eat anything because food made me sick. I also started at this time to suffer from pains in my intestines. All highly seasoned dishes caused me such immense pain that I spent many nights writhing in pain and in tears, for the sake of sinners.

> However, I asked my confessor what to do: whether I should continue to suffer this for the sake of sinners or ask the superiors for an exception by way of milder food. He decided that I should ask the superiors for milder food. And thus I followed his directions, seeing that this humiliation was more pleasing to God.

> One day I began to doubt as to how it was possible to feel this continual decaying of the body and at the same time to be able to walk and work. Perhaps this was some kind of an illusion. Yet it cannot be an illusion, because it causes me such terrible pains. As I was thinking about this, one of the sisters came to converse with me. After a minute or two, she made a terribly wry face and said, "Sister, I smell a corpse here, as though it were all decaying. Oh, how dreadful it is! I said to her, "Do not be frightened, Sister, that smell of a corpse comes from me." She was very surprised and said she could not stand it any longer. After she had gone, I understood that God had allowed her to sense this so that I would have no doubt, but that He was no less than miraculously keeping the knowledge of this suffering from

the whole community. O my Jesus, only You know the full depth of this sacrifice.

Nevertheless, when in the refectory, I still had to bear being the object of the frequent suspicion that I was being fussy [about my food]. At such times, as always, I hasten to the Tabernacle, bow before the ciborium and there draw strength to accept God's will. That which I have written is not yet everything. (1428-1431)

Christmas 1937

In silence, in suffering, but in God's strength and mercy Sister Faustina continued to live from day to day. A few days before Christmas she went to confession to Father Andrasz who, breaking the wafer spiritually with her, expressed these wishes for her: "Be as faithful as you can to the grace of God; secondly, beg God's mercy for yourself and for the whole world, because we are all in great need of God's mercy." (1432)

Two days before Christmas, as the words "Tomorrow is the Birth of Jesus Christ according to the flesh" were being read in the dining room, Sister Faustina's soul was pierced by the light and love of God and she gained a deeper knowledge of the Mystery of the Incarnation. "How great is the mercy of God contained in the Mystery of the Incarnation of the Son of God!" (1433) And that same day she made the following entry in the diary:

> Today, the Lord gave me knowledge of His anger toward mankind which deserves to have its days shortened because of its sins. But I learned that the world's existence is maintained by chosen souls; that is, the religious orders. Woe to the world when there will be a lack of religious orders! (1434)

It was the Vigil of Christmas. After Holy Communion the Mother of God let Sister experience the anxious concern of Her heart with regard to the Son of God. "But this anxiety was permeated with such a fragrance of abandonment to the will of God that I should call it rather a delight than an anxiety," she wrote. "I understood how my soul ought to accept the will of God in all things...." (See 1437)

It pleased the Lord very much when Sister Faustina, before going to the vigil supper, made a visit to the chapel, in order to share the wafer spiritually with her loved ones and those dear to her heart who were far away. She first steeped herself in prayer, and then asked the Lord to lavish graces upon them all as a group, and then on each one individually. She learned how much this pleased the Lord, and her soul was filled with even greater joy when she saw that God loves in a special way those whom we love. (See 1438)

During the reading in the dining room, her entire being was steeped in God. In spirit, she saw God's pleasing gaze upon them all. She remained alone with the Heavenly Father. In that moment she had a deeper knowledge of the Three Divine Persons, "whom we shall be contemplating throughout eternity and, after millions of years, shall discover that we have just barely begun our contemplation." She further reflected, "Oh, how great is the mercy of God, who allows man to participate in such a high degree in His divine happiness! At the same time, what great pain pierces my heart [at the thought] that so many souls have spurned this happiness." (See 1439)

At the sharing of the wafer before the vigil supper, sincere mutual love prevailed. Mother Irene's wishes to her were: "Sister, the works of God proceed slowly, so do not be in a hurry." Generally, all the sisters sincerely wished her great love, that which she most desired. Only one sister had some hidden malice in her wishes, which Sister easily overlooked because her soul was overflowing with God; but she was enlightened as to why God communicates so little with such a soul. She learned that such a one is always seeking herself, even in holy things. She reflected, "Oh, how good the Lord is in not letting me go astray! I know that He will guard me, even jealously, but only as long as I remain little, because it is with such that the great Lord likes to commune. As to proud souls, He watches them from afar and opposes them." (See 1440)

Before Midnight Mass, Sister Faustina intended to keep watch but fell asleep at once even though she felt very ill. However, as soon as the bell rang for the Mass, she arose immediately, but dressed with great effort, because she felt sick again and again. She left an account of what she experienced that night and during the holiday season:

> When I arrived at Midnight Mass, from the very beginning I steeped myself in deep recollection, during which time I saw the stable of Bethlehem filled with great radiance. The Blessed Virgin, all lost in the deepest of love, was wrapping Jesus in swaddling clothes, but Saint Joseph was still asleep. Only after the Mother of God put Jesus into the manger, did the light of God awaken Joseph, who also prayed. But after a while, I was left alone with the Infant Jesus who stretched out His little hands to me, and I understood that I was to take Him in my arms. Jesus pressed His head against my heart and gave me to know, by His profound gaze, how good He found it to be next to my heart. At that moment Jesus disappeared and the bell was ringing for Holy Communion.

> My soul was languishing from joy. But toward the end of the Mass, I felt so weak that I had to leave the chapel and go to my cell, as I felt unable to take part in the community tea. But my joy throughout the whole Christmas Season was immense, because my soul was unceasingly united with the Lord. I have come to know that every soul would like to have divine comforts, but is by no means willing to forsake human comforts, whereas these two things cannot be reconciled.

> During this Christmas season, I have sensed that certain souls have been praying for me. I rejoice that such spiritual union and knowledge exist already here on earth. O my Jesus, praise be to You for all this! (1442-1444)

During the greatest sufferings of the soul, Sister Faustina found herself alone with Jesus. No person came to her aid. There was a time when it bothered her that no one understood her heart; but now, she was not concerned, even when her intentions were wrongly interpreted or condemned. "People do not know how to perceive the soul," she wrote. "They see the body and judge according to the body. But as distant as heaven is from earth, so distant are God's thoughts from our thoughts." (1445)

Jesus continued to teach His secretary: **It should be of no concern to you how anyone else acts; you are to be My living reflection, through love and mercy.**

She answered, "Lord, but they often take advantage my goodness."

That makes no difference, My daughter. That is no concern of yours. As for you, be always merciful toward other people, and especially toward sinners.

Oh, how painful it is to Me that souls so seldom unite with Me in Holy Communion. I wait for souls, and they are indifferent toward Me. I love them tenderly and sincerely, and they distrust Me. I want to lavish My graces on them, and they do not want to accept them. They treat Me as a dead object, whereas My heart is full of love and mercy. In order that you may know at least some of My pain, imagine the most tender of mothers who has great love for her children, while those children spurn her love. Consider her pain. No one is in a position to console her. This is but a feeble image and likeness of My love.

Write, speak of My mercy. Tell souls where they are to look for solace; that is, in the Tribunal of Mercy [The Sacrament of Reconciliation]. **There the greatest miracles takes place** [and] **are incessantly repeated. To avail oneself of this miracle, it is not necessary to go on a great pilgrimage or to carry out some external ceremony; it suffices to come with faith to the feet of My representative and to reveal to him one's misery, and the miracle of Divine Mercy will be fully demonstrated. Were a soul like a decaying corpse so that from a human standpoint, there would be no** [hope of] **restoration and everything would already be lost, it is not so with God. The miracle of Divine Mercy restores the soul in full. Oh, how miserable are those who do not take advantage of this miracle of God's mercy! You will call out in vain, but it will be too late.** (1446-1448)

That was Jesus' last message to Sister Faustina in 1937. Two days before the New Year she was feeling so ill that she was forced to stay in bed. A terrible cough, constant pain in her intestines, and nausea exhausted her. The sisters were awakened at eleven p.m. to keep watch and greet the New Year. She tried to unite spiritually with the community in the services that were being held to end the old year; but, writhing in pain from twilight to midnight, she only was able to add her sufferings to the prayers of the sisters who kept vigil in the chapel, atoning to God for the insults of sinners. (See 1451.)

When the clock struck twelve, Faustina's soul became steeped in even deeper contemplation, and she heard in her soul the words: **Do not fear, My little child, you are not alone. Fight bravely, because My arm is supporting you; fight for the salvation of souls, exhorting them to trust in My mercy, as that is your task in this life and in the life to come.**

"After these words," wrote Sister, "I received a more profound understanding of divine mercy. Only that soul who wants it will be damned, for God condemns no one." (1452)

TOTAL SUBMISSION (1938)

Acceptance of More Suffering

On January 1, 1938, Sister wrote, "I am ending the old year with suffering and beginning the new one with suffering as well." And she continued:

Welcome to you, New Year, in the course of which my perfection will be accomplished. Thank You in advance, O Lord, for everything Your goodness will send me. Thank You for the cup of suffering from which I shall daily drink. Do not diminish its bitterness, O Lord, but strengthen my lips that, while drinking of this bitterness, they may know how to smile for love of You, my Master. I thank You for Your countless comforts and graces that flow down to me daily like the morning dew, silently, imperceptibly, which no curious eye may notice, and which are known only to You and me, O Lord. For all this, I thank You as of today because, at the moment when You hand me the cup, my heart may not be capable of giving thanks. (1449)

So, today I submit myself completely and with loving consent to Your holy will, O Lord, and to Your most wise decrees, which are always full of clemency and mercy for me, though at times I can neither understand nor fathom them. O my Master, I surrender myself completely to You, who are the rudder of my soul; steer it Yourself according to Your divine wishes. I enclose myself in Your most compassionate Heart, which is a sea of unfathomable mercy. (1450)

That morning Sister Faustina barely managed to receive Holy Communion. To go to Mass was out of the question. Her thanksgiving rose from her bed of pain.

The Sister Infirmarian reprimanded Sister Faustina for not having attended Mass on so great a holy day, and even returned to take her temperature. Since Sister Faustina had no fever, she was forced to listen to yet another sermon on how she should not give in to illness. Left alone, Sister again repeated the words, "Welcome New Year, welcome cup of bitterness."

After dinner Mother Irene briefly looked in on her. Afraid to scandalize, Sister Faustina did not ask for Father Andrasz to hear her confession. She was also afraid that she would have been unable to confess because she was too emotionally fragile. Later that day a sister rebuked her for not taking some milk with butter which was left for her in the community's kitchen. Faustina only replied that there was no one to bring it to her. At nightfall, the physical sufferings increased and she agonized until eleven o'clock. For all this suffering Sister found a remedy:

> I went in spirit to the Tabernacle and uncovered the ciborium, leaning my head on the rim of the cup, and all my tears flowed silently toward the Heart of Him who alone understands what pain and suffering is. And I experienced the sweetness of this suffering, and my soul came to desire this sweet agony, which I would not have exchanged for all the world's treasures. The Lord gave me strength of spirit and love towards those through whom these sufferings came. This then was the first day of the year. (1454)

On January 2, as Sister Faustina prepared to receive Holy Communion, Jesus requested that she write more, not only about the graces He bestowed upon her, but also about other matters, since all this was for the consolation of many souls. At His command she continued to write candidly of her experiences.

> After that night of suffering, when the priest entered my cell with the Lord Jesus, such fervor filled my whole being that I felt that if the priest had tarried a little longer, Jesus himself would have leaped out of his hand and come to me. (1458)

> After Holy Communion the Lord said to me, **If the priest had not brought Me to you, I would have come Myself under the same species. My daughter, your suffering of this night obtained the grace of mercy for an immense**

number of souls. (1459)

Jesus also told Faustina that morning that He was displeased that out of human respect she had not asked for Father Andrasz to hear her confession in her cell. Greatly humbled, she begged the Lord's pardon and added: "O my Master, rebuke me; do not overlook my faults, and do not let me err." (1460)

On January 6, the chaplain brought Sister Holy Communion, and Jesus gave her to know that many bishops and one lay person were considering the proposed Feast of Mercy. Some were enthusiastic about this Work of God, while others regarded it with disbelief. In spite of everything, the result would be great glory for the work of God. (See 1463)

On the eve of First Friday, Sister's health seemed to improve. She was happy because she would be able to pray better during the Holy Hour. At that she heard the voice say, **You will not be in good health. Do not put off the Sacrament of Penance, because this displeases Me. Pay little attention to the murmurs of those around you.** (1464)

Surprised at these words because she felt better, Faustina gave them no more thought. When the sister put out the light, Faustina began her Holy Hour. However, something went wrong with her heart. Until eleven o'clock, she suffered quietly. But when the pain increased, she awakened the sister next to her. The medication she gave her eased the pain enough for Faustina to lie down. Now she understood the Lord's warning and resolved to call for any priest the next day.

That was not all. As Sister Faustina lay there, praying and offering her pains for sinners, she was attacked by the Evil Spirit who could not stand that. He told her, "Do not pray for sinners, but for yourself, for you will be damned." Taking no notice of Satan, she kept on praying with redoubled zeal for sinners. Enraged, the evil one howled, "Oh, if I had power over you!" and disappeared. She realized that her suffering and prayer restrained Satan and pulled many souls out of his clutches. (See 1465)

The next morning during Mass, Sister Faustina saw the suffering Christ and was struck by the fact that Jesus was so peaceful in the midst of such great suffering. She understood that He was teaching her how to behave externally in the face of diverse sufferings.

As happened every Friday, Sister suffered the pains in her hands, feet and side. This time the suffering lasted longer. Suddenly she saw a certain sinner who, having benefited from her suffering, drew closer to the Lord. "All this for starving souls that they may not die of starvation," she wrote. (1468)

That day Faustina had the opportunity for confession, and she thanked Jesus for the comfort she received through the chaplain, His representative. "O my Mother, Church of God, you are a true Mother who understands her children," she wrote, and added:

> O how good it is that Jesus will judge us according to our conscience and not according to people's talk and judgments. O inconceivable goodness, I see You full of goodness in the very act of judgment.
>
> Although I am feeling weak, and my nature is clamoring for rest, I feel the inspiration of grace telling me to take hold of myself and write, write for the comfort of souls, whom I love so much and with whom I will share all eternity. And I desire eternal life for them so ardently that that is why I use all my free moments, no matter how short, for writing in the way that Jesus wishes of me. (See 1469-1471)

At Mass on January 8, Sister Fautina was given interior knowledge that the efforts of Father Sopocko and her own were joint efforts that gave much glory to God. Although distance separated them, they were often together because a common goal united them.

Already far advanced in the spiritual life, Sister nevertheless continued to strive for the greatest perfection possible in order to be useful to the Church. She noted in her diary:

> ... Greater by far is my bond to the Church. The sanctity or the fall of each individual soul has an effect upon the whole Church. Observing myself and those who are close to me, I have come to understand how great an influence I have on other souls, not by any heroic deeds, as these are striking in themselves, but by small actions like a movement of the hand, a look, and many other things too numerous to mention, which have an effect on and reflect in the souls of others, as I myself have noticed. (1475)

During vespers when the sisters sang the "Magnificat," at the words "He has shown the might of His arm," Sister's soul became enveloped in profound contemplation. She recognized and understood that the Lord would soon complete His work in her soul and she was no longer surprised that Jesus had not disclosed everything to her sooner. (See 1477)

That same day Sister asked the Lord, "Why are You sad today, Jesus? Tell me, who is the cause of Your sadness?"

Jesus answered her, **Chosen souls who do not have My spirit, who live according to the letter and have placed the letter above My spirit, above the spirit of love. I have founded My whole law on love, and yet I do not see love, even in religious orders. This is why sadness fills My Heart.** (1478)

While on her bed of suffering Sister Faustina was not idle. Mindful of Jesus' requests—that she keep writing about His mercy for the consolation and benefit of souls—and of the confirmation of these by her spiritual directors, Sister wrote, between January 8 and 15, a series of conversations between the Merciful God and a sinful soul, a despairing soul, a suffering soul, a soul striving for perfection and a perfect soul. These conversations contain many of her own poignant experiences and feelings which she reveals to a tender, compassionate God. He, in turn, makes known His own unbounded love and mercy, and priceless direction, not only for her benefit, but for all people. Since this was the period of a great illness, what effort must have gone into the writing of these precious spiritual gems! (See 1485-1489.)

By January 17, Sister Faustina seemed unable to hold on to the reassurance given her by Jesus just a few days ago when He said, **My daughter, do not be afraid of what will happen to you. I will give you nothing beyond your strength. You know the power of My grace; let that be enough.** (1491) From early morning, darkness enveloped her. She felt abandoned by Jesus, yet knew that turning to creatures would be of no avail. When in spirit she tried to join the sisters who were praying Vespers, she became immersed in even greater darkness. She felt discouraged about everything. Then she heard the voice of Satan: "See how contradictory everything is that Jesus gives to you: He tells you to found a convent, and then He gives you sickness; He tells you to set about establishing the Feast of Mercy while the whole world does not at all want such a feast. Why do you pray for this feast? It is so inopportune." Sister Faustina did not enter into conversation with the spirit of darkness, but a strange disinclination to life enveloped her, and she had to exert her will to consent to live.

Again the tempter spoke: "Ask for death for yourself, tomorrow after Holy Communion. God will hear you, for He has heard you so many times before and has given you what you have asked for." Sister remained silent, forcing herself meanwhile to pray to God not to abandon her at this time. It was already eleven at night, all the sisters were asleep, but her soul continued to struggle.

The tempter continued: "Why should you bother about other souls? You ought to be praying only for yourself. As for sinners, they will be converted without your prayers. I see that you are suffering very much at this moment. I'm going to give you a piece of advice on which your happiness will depend: never speak about God's mercy and, in particular, do not encourage sinners to trust in God's mercy, because they deserve a just punishment. Another very important thing: do not tell your confessors, and especially this extraordinary confessor and the priest in Vilnius, about what goes on in your soul. I know them; I know who they are, and so I want to put you on your guard against them. You see, to live as a good nun, it is sufficent to live like all the others. Why expose yourself to so many difficulties?" (See 1496-1497)

Sister Faustina remained silent. Out of sheer will power, she remained in the presence of God, though a moan was escaping from her heart. At last the tempter left her and the tired Sister immediately fell asleep. The next day she received Holy Communion in the neighboring cell, returned to her own cell, fell to her knees and renewed her act of total submission to the most holy will of God, asking for help in the struggle. At that moment she saw Jesus who said to her, **I am pleased with what you are doing. And you can continue to be at peace if you always do the best you can in respect to this work of mercy. Be absolutely as frank as possible with your confessor. Satan gained nothing by tempting you, because you did not enter into conversation with**

him. Continue to act in this way. You gave Me great glory today by fighting so faithfully. Let it be confirmed and engraved in your heart that I am always with you, even if you don't feel My presence at the time of battle. (1499) After this, she wrote what follows:

> Today the love of God is transporting me into the other world. I am immersed in love; I love and I sense that I am loved, and with full consciousness I experience this. My soul drowns in the Lord, realizing the great Majesty of God and its own littleness; but through this knowledge my happiness increases... This awareness is so vivid in the soul, so powerful and, at the same time, so sweet. (1500)

When the following nights became sleepless ones, due to pain, Sister Faustina visited various churches and chapels in spirit, and in each one made a short adoration before the Blessed Sacrament. Then she returned to her own convent chapel where she prayed for the priests who preached and made known The Divine Mercy, for the intentions of the Holy Father, and for mercy for sinners.

On January 20, Sister penned some thoughts and inspirations concerning the virtue of humility, fidelity to God's will, and the Divine Mercy. As to the latter, she wrote:

> O incomprehensible God, my heart dissolves in joy that You have allowed me to penetrate the mysteries of Your mercy! Everything begins with Your mercy and ends with Your mercy. All grace flows from mercy and the last hour abounds with mercy for us. Let no one doubt concerning the goodness of God; even if a person's sins were as dark as night, God's mercy is stronger than our misery. One thing alone is necessary: that the sinner set ajar the door of his heart, be it ever so little, to let in a ray of God's merciful grace, and then God will do the rest. But poor is the soul who has shut the door on God's mercy, even at the last hour. It was just such souls who plunged Jesus into deadly sorrow in the Garden of Olives; indeed, it was from His Most Merciful Heart that divine mercy flowed out. (1506-1507)

The Providence of God allowed that the infirmarian in charge of Sister Faustina was Sister Chrysostom. She and Sister Faustina were together in Vilnius. While there, Sister Chrysostom heard a few things about Sister Faustina's spirituality, but did not want to believe them. Instead, she believed the disreputable rumors. That accounted for the callous way in which she was treating Sister Faustina in the present situation. In addition, the sister who was appointed to clean Sister Faustina's cell was deathly afraid of contracting tuberculosis so she kept away for weeks at a time. Sister recorded the following observations in regard to her lingering illness:

January 21, 1938. Jesus, how truly dreadful it would be to suffer if it were not for You. But it is You, Jesus, stretched out on the cross, who give me strength and are always close to the suffering soul. Creatures will abandon a person in his suffering, but You, O Lord, are faithful...

It often happens when one is ill, as in the case of Job in the Old Testament, that as long as one can move about and work, everything is fine and dandy; but when God sends illness, somehow or other, there are fewer friends about. But yet, there are some. They still take interest in our suffering and all that, but if God sends a longer illness, even those faithful friends slowly begin to desert us. They visit us less frequently, and often their visits cause suffering. Instead of comforting us, they reproach us about certain things, which is an occasion of a good deal of suffering. And so the soul, like Job, is alone; but fortunately it is not alone, because Jesus-Host is with it.

After having tasted the above sufferings and spent a whole night in bitterness, the next morning, when the chaplain brought me Holy Communion, I had to control myself by sheer effort of will to keep from crying out at the top of my voice, "Welcome, my true and only Friend." Holy Communion gives me strength to suffer and fight.

I wish to speak of one more thing that I have experienced: when God gives neither death nor health, and [when] this lasts for many years, people become accustomed to this and consider the person as not being ill. Then there begins a whole series of silent sufferings. Only God knows how many sacrifices the soul makes.

One evening, when I was feeling so bad that I wondered how I would get back to my cell, I came across the Sister Assistant, who was asking one of the sisters of the first choir to go to the gate with a certain message. But when she saw me, she said to her, "No, Sister, you need not go, but Sister Faustina will, because it is raining heavily." I answered, "All right," and went and carried out the order, but only God knows the whole of it. This is just one example among many. Sometimes it would seem that a sister of the second choir is made of stone, but she also is human and has a heart and feelings...

At such times, God Himself comes to our rescue, for otherwise the soul would not be able to bear these crosses of which I haven't even begun to write, nor do I intend to do so now. But when I will feel the inspiration to do so, I will write about them... (1508-1511)

During this difficult time, Faustina's Novice Master, Jesus, continued to instruct her. At Mass on the following day, she saw the Lord Jesus suffering, as if dying on the cross. He said to her, **My daughter, meditate frequently on the sufferings which I have undergone for your sake, and then nothing of what you suffer for Me will seem great to you. You please Me most when you meditate on My sorrowful Passion. Join your little sufferings to My sorrowful Passion, so that they may have infinite value before My majesty.** And again He reminded her, **You often call Me your Master. That is pleasing to My Heart; but do not forget, My disciple, that you are a disciple of a crucified Master. Let that one word be enough for you. You know what is contained in the cross.** (1512-1513)

Sister Faustina was too ill to go to chapel for the night adoration. As she could not sleep the whole night through, she spent it with Jesus in the dark dungeon. Jesus gave her knowledge of the sufferings He endured there on Holy Thursday night. "The world will learn about them on the day of Judgment," she wrote. Then she recorded the following message of Jesus:

My daughter, tell souls that I am giving them My mercy as a defense. I Myself am fighting for them and am bearing

the just anger of My Father.

Say, My daughter, that the Feast of My Mercy has issued forth from My very depths for the consolation of the whole world. (1516-1517)

Devotion to The Divine Mercy

Before Holy Communion on or about January 23, Jesus told Sister Faustina, **My daughter, today talk openly to the Superior [Mother Irene] about My mercy because, of all the superiors, she has taken the greatest part in proclaiming My mercy.** (1519)

And it so happened that Mother Irene visited her that afternoon and they spoke about the Divine Mercy Devotion. Mother told her that sales for the holy cards went very slowly. She herself was distributing them and doing as much as she could to further the devotion. After Mother's departure, the Lord told Sister how very dear Mother was to Him. He then continued to reveal further His message of mercy:

I have opened My Heart as a living fountain of mercy. Let all souls draw life from it. Let them approach this sea of mercy with great trust. Sinners will attain justification, and the just will be confirmed in good. Whoever places his trust in My mercy will be filled with My divine peace at the hour of death.

My daughter, do not tire of proclaiming My mercy. In this way you will refresh this Heart of Mine, which burns with a flame of pity for sinners. Tell My priest that hardened sinners will repent on hearing their words, when they will speak about My unfathomable mercy, about the compassion I have for them in My Heart. To priests who will proclaim and extol My mercy, I will give wondrous power, and I will anoint their words and touch the hearts of those to whom they will speak. (1520-1521)

A few days later, Sister Faustina saw Father Andrasz at prayer, interceding for her to the Lord. She was now keeping herself somewhat in the background, as if the work of mercy did not interest her. But although she stopped speaking about it, she constantly prayed, asking God to hasten the day of the Feast of

Mercy. "And I see," she wrote, "that Jesus is acting, and is Himself giving the directives as to how this is to be carried out. Nothing happens by accident." (See 1530)

However, very soon after this, Sister said to the Lord, "Do You see how many difficulties there are to be overcome before they believe that You yourself are the author of this work? And even now, not everyone believes in it."

Jesus answered her, **Be at peace, My child; nothing can oppose My will. In spite of the murmuring and hostility of the sisters, My will shall be in you in all its fullness, down to the last detail of My wishes and My designs. Do not become sad about this; I too was a stumbling stone for some souls.** (1531)

That same day Sister was given special knowledge concerning the fate of Poland:

> I saw the anger of God hanging heavy over Poland. And now I see that if God were to visit our country with the greatest chastisements, that would still be great mercy because, for such grave transgressions, He could punish us with eternal annihilation. I was paralyzed with fear when the Lord lifted the veil a little for me. Now I see clearly that chosen souls keep the world in existence to fulfill the measure [of justice]. (1533; see also II Maccabees 6:12-16)

On Thursday, January 27, Sister made her usual Holy Hour adoration. At that time Jesus complained, **In return for My blessings, I get ingratitude. In return for My love, I get forgetfulness and indifference. My Heart cannot bear this.** (1537)

"At that moment," wrote Sister Faustina, "love for Jesus was enkindled so strongly in my heart that, offering myself for ungrateful souls, I immersed myself completely in Him. When I came to my senses, the Lord allowed me to taste a little of the ingratitude which flooded His Heart. This experience lasted for a short while." (1538)

In the course of her conversation with Jesus, Sister Faustina asked, "When will You take me to Yourself? I've been feeling so ill and I've been waiting for Your coming with such longing!"

Jesus answered, **Be always ready; I will not leave you in this exile for long. My holy will must be fulfilled in you.**

"O Lord, if Your holy will has not yet been entirely fulfilled in me, here I am, ready for everything that You want, O Lord! O my Jesus, there is only one thing which surprises me; namely, that You make so many secrets known to me; but that one secret—the hour of my death—You do not want to tell me."

The Lord answered, **Be at peace; I will let you know, but not just now.**

"Ah, my Lord, I beg Your pardon for wanting to know this. You know very well why, because You know my yearning heart, which is eagerly going out to You. You know that I would not want to die even a minute before the time which You have appointed for me before the ages." Jesus listened to her outpourings with unusual kindness. (See 1529)

On January 28, Jesus gave His "secretary" some very important messages to record:

> **My daughter, write down these words: All those souls who will glorify My mercy and spread its worship, encouraging others to trust in My mercy, will not experience terror at the hour of death. My mercy will shield them in that final battle...**

> **My daughter, encourage souls to say the chaplet which I have given to you. It pleases me to grant everything they ask of Me by saying the chaplet. When hardened sinners say it, I will fill their souls with peace, and the hour of their death will be a happy one.**

> **Write this for the benefit of distressed souls: when a soul sees and realizes the gravity of its sins, when the whole abyss of the misery into which it immersed itself is displayed before its eyes, let it not despair, but with trust let it throw itself into the arms of My mercy, as a child into the arms of its beloved mother. These souls have a right of priority to My compassionate Heart, they have priority to My mercy. Tell them that no soul that has called upon My mercy has been disappointed or brought to shame. I delight particularly in a soul which has placed its trust in My goodness.**

> **Write that when they say this chaplet in the presence of the dying, I will stand between My Father and the dying person, not as the just Judge but as the merciful Savior.** (1540-1541)

Jesus then made her aware of His jealous love for her: **Even among the sisters you will feel lonely. Know then that I want you to unite yourself more closely to Me. I am concerned about every beat of your heart. Every stirring of your love is reflected in My Heart. I thirst for your love.**

Faustina responded, "Yes, O Jesus, but my heart would not be able to live without You, either; for even if the hearts of all creatures were offered to me, they would not satisfy the depths of my heart." (1542)

That evening the Lord said to her:

> **Entrust yourself completely to Me at the hour of death, and I will present you to My Father as My bride. And now I recommend that you unite, in a special way, even your smallest deeds to My merits, and then My Father will look upon them with love as if they were My own.**

> **Do not change your particular examen which I have given you through Father Andrasz; namely, that you unite yourself with Me continually. That is what I am clearly asking of you today. Be a child toward My representatives, because I borrow their lips to speak to you, so that you will have no doubts about anything.** (1543-1544)

By the end of January, Sister Faustina was able to rejoin the sisters in the dining room and the chapel, but unable as yet to resume her duties. She remained in her cell, crocheting lace for the altar. She wrote:

> I enjoy this work very much, but still, even with such light work, I tire easily. I see how feeble I am. There are no indifferent moments in my life, since every moment of my life is filled with prayer, suffering and work. If not in one way, then in another, I glorify God; and if God were to give me a second life, I do not know whether I would make better use of it... (1545)

Jesus let her know how pleased He was with her: **I am delighted with your love. Your sincere love is as pleasing to My Heart as the fragrance of a rosebud at morningtide, before the sun has taken the dew from it. The freshness of your heart captivates Me; that is why I unite Myself with you more closely than with**

any other creature... (1546)

Weakness did not prevent Sister Faustina from making her monthly day of retreat. At this time she made heroic resolutions, and during her meditation on death she asked to experience now those feelings that she would have at the actual moment of death. As she prepared herself to receive the next morning's Holy Communion as a "Viaticum" (Eucharist given to a dying person), she heard these words: **As you are united with Me in life, so will you be united at the hour of death.**" She wrote:

> After these words, such great trust in God's great mercy was awakened in my soul that, even if I had had the sins of the whole world, as well as the sins of all the condemned souls weighing on my conscience, I would not have doubted God's goodness but, without hesitation, would have thrown myself into the abyss of divine mercy, which is always open to us; and, with a heart crushed to dust, I would have cast myself at His feet, abandoning myself totally to His holy will, which is mercy itself. (1552)

Sacrificial Host

The next day, February 1, Sister Faustina's condition became worse. Yet she went to the spiritual exercises, to the dining room and to recreation with the rest of the sisters. Her great efforts were known to Jesus alone. In fact, on this day she thought she would not last until the end of the dinner. Every spoonful caused her untold pain.

Just last week, she recalled, Mother Irene visited her and told her, "You catch every sickness, Sister, because your system is so weak, but that is not your fault. In fact, if any other sister had that same sickness, she would certainly be walking around; whereas you, Sister, must stay in bed!!"

Sister noted in her diary, "These words did not hurt me, but it is better not to make such comparisons with very sick persons, because their cup is full enough as it is...."

How was it possible that such things could be happening in a convent? How could Sister so heroically accept all that was happening to her? Perhaps the following notation found in her diary will help one to understand:

> When I had gone to the chapel for a moment, the Lord gave me to know that, among His chosen ones, there are some who are especially chosen, and whom He calls to a higher form of holiness, to exceptional union with Him. These are seraphic souls [so called after the the angels of high rank, the Seraphim, who are considered purifying ministers of God] from whom God demands greater love than He does from others. Although all live in the same convent, yet He sometimes demands of a particular soul a greater degree of love. Such a soul understands this call, because God makes this known to it interiorly, but the soul may either follow this call or not. It depends on the soul itself whether it is faithful to these touches of the Holy Spirit, or whether it resists them. (See 1556)

Sister Faustina had answered the call to be a sacrificial host, a whole-burnt offering for souls, so she accepted the opportunities for suffering which, through God's permissive will, living in community provided.

A Lesson in Humility

But the Lord was asking much more of His chosen one. On February 2, Feast of the Presentation of the Lord in the Temple, Sister Faustina's soul was plunged into darkness. Her mind seemed impaired. She understood neither herself nor those who spoke to her. Terrible temptations against faith assailed her. She said she dared not describe them in detail for fear of scandalizing those who will read about them. "O hurricane, what are you doing with the boat of my heart?" she cried. The storm persisted all day and night. When Mother Superior asked if she would like to go to confession, since Father Andrasz would be in the house administering the sacrament, Sister refused, fearing that even he would not understand her and she would be unable to confess. From the following entry in her diary, we see that her tribulations were not unlike the sufferings endured by the mystics:

> I spent the whole night with Jesus in Gethsemane.

From my breast there escaped one continuous moan. A natural dying will be much easier, because then one is in agony and will die; while here, one is in agony, but cannot die. O Jesus, I never thought such suffering could exist. Nothingness: that is the reality. O Jesus, save me! I believe in You with all my heart. So many times have I seen the radiance of Your Face, and now, where are You, Lord?... I believe, I believe, and again I believe in You, Triune God, Father, Son and Holy Spirit, and in all the truths which Your holy Church gives me to believe... But the darkness does not recede and my spirit plunges into even greater agony. And at that moment, such terrible torment overwhelmed me that now I am amazed at myself that I did not breathe my last, but this was for only a brief instant.

At that moment I saw Jesus, and from His Heart there issued those same two rays, which enveloped me, whole and entire. At the same moment, all my torments vanished. **My daughter,** the Lord said, **know that of yourself you are just what you have gone through, and it is only by My grace that you are a participant of eternal life and all the gifts I lavish on you.** And with these words of the Lord, there came to me a true knowledge of myself. Jesus is giving me a lesson in deep humility and, at the same time, one of total trust in Him. My heart is reduced to dust and ashes, and even if all people were to trample me under their feet, I would still consider that a favor. I feel and am, in fact, very deeply permeated with the knowledge that I am nothing, so that real humiliations will be a refreshment for me. (1558-1559)

After Holy Communion the next day, the good Master continued to teach His novice Faustina, giving her the following directives:

First, do not fight against a temptation by yourself, but disclose it to the confessor at once, and then the temptation will lose all its force. Second, during these ordeals do not lose your peace; live in My presence; ask My Mother and the Saints for help. Third, have the certitude that I am looking at you and supporting you. Fourth, do not fear either struggles of the soul or any temptations, because I am supporting you; if only you are willing to fight, know that

the victory is always on your side. **Fifth, know that by fighting bravely you give Me great glory and amass merits for yourself. Temptation gives you a chance to show Me your fidelity.**

And now I am going to tell you something that is most important for you: boundless sincerity with your spiritual director. If you do not take advantage of this grace according to My instructions, I will take him away from you, and then you will be left to yourself; and all the torments, which you know very well, will return to you. It displeases Me that you do not take advantage of the opportunity when you are able to see him and talk with him. Know that it is a great grace on My part when I give a spiritual director to a soul. Many souls ask Me for this, but it is not to all that I grant this grace. From the moment I gave you this priest as spiritual director, I endowed him with new light so that he might easily know and understand your soul... (1560-1561)

After this exhortation she recorded what follows:

O my Jesus, my only mercy, allow me to see contentment in Your Face as a sign of reconciliation with me, because my heart cannot bear Your seriousness; if this continues a moment longer my heart will burst with grief. You see that I am even now crushed to dust. (1562)

And at that very moment I saw myself in some kind of a palace; and Jesus gave me His hand, sat me at His side, and said with kindness, **My bride, you always please me by your humility. The greatest misery does not stop Me from uniting Myself to a soul, but where there is pride, I am not there.** (1563)

When she came to, and reflected on what had happened in her heart, she thanked God for His love and the mercy He had shown her. This deepened knowledge of humility evoked the following prayer:

Jesus, hide me; just as You have hidden Yourself under the form of the white Host, so hide me from human eyes, and particularly hide the gifts which You so kindly grant me.

May I not betray outwardly what You are effecting in my soul. I am a white host before You, O Divine Priest. Consecrate me Yourself, and may my transubstantiation be known only to You. I stand before You each day as a sacrificial host and implore Your mercy upon the world. In silence, and unseen, I will empty myself before You; my pure and undivided love will burn, in profound silence, as a holocaust. And may the fragrance of my love be wafted to the foot of Your throne. You are the Lord of lords, but You delight in innocent and humble souls. (1564)

Very soon after this, Jesus petitioned Sister Faustina, **My daughter, help me to save a certain dying sinner. Say the chaplet that I have taught you for him.** She recorded what transpired:

When I began to say the chaplet, I saw the man dying in the midst of terrible torment and struggle. His Guardian Angel was defending him, but he was, as it were, powerless against the enormity of the soul's misery. A multitude of devils was waiting for that soul. But while I was saying the chaplet I saw Jesus just as He is depicted in the Image. The rays which issued from Jesus' Heart enveloped the sick man, and the powers of darkness fled in panic. The sick man peacefully breathed his last. When I came to myself, I understood how very important the chaplet was for the dying. It appeases the anger of God. (1565)

A Blessing for a "Saintly" Secretary

Within the first week of February, Sister Faustina, after taking a pen into her hand and invoking the Holy Spirit, said, "Jesus, bless this pen so that everything You order me to write may be for the glory of God."

Then she heard the voice: **Yes, I bless [it], because this writing bears the seal of obedience to your superior and confessor, and by that very fact I am already given glory, and many souls will be drawing profit from it. My daughter, I demand that you devote all your free moments to writing about My goodness and mercy. It is your office and your assignment throughout your life to continue to make known to souls the great**

mercy I have for them and to exhort them to trust in My bottomless mercy. (1567)

Just a short while ago Mother Irene told Sister Faustina to write more about the Divine Mercy. To Sister this was a confirmation of Jesus' request. She understood now that when Jesus wants something He also inspires the superiors to give the necessary permissions., "... even though it sometimes happens," she wrote, "that we do not receive permission at once, and our patience is often put to the test...." (1568)

With no introduction, Sister Faustina wrote the following prayer calling for Divine Mercy upon mankind:

O Greatly Merciful God, Infinite Goodness, today all mankind calls out from the abyss of its misery to Your mercy—to Your compassion, O God; and it is with its mighty voice of misery that it cries out. Gracious God, do not reject the prayer of this earth's exiles! O Lord, Goodness beyond our understanding, Who are acquainted with our misery through and through, and know that by our own power we cannot ascend to You, we implore You: anticipate us with Your grace and keep on increasing Your mercy in us, that we may faithfully do Your holy will all through our life and at death's hour. Let the omnipotence of Your mercy shield us from the darts of our salvation's enemies, that we may with confidence, as Your children, await Your final coming—that day known to You alone. And we expect to obtain everything promised us by Jesus in spite of all our wretchedness. For Jesus is our Hope: Through His merciful Heart, as through an open gate, we pass through to heaven. (1570)

Sister next recalled that ever since she entered the community the one charge that was constantly leveled against her was that she was a "saint." Because this was said sarcastically, it hurt her much at first. But with time she was able to rise above it, and it bothered her only when it also hurt someone else. When she then complained to Jesus, He answered, **Are you sad because of this? Of course you are a saint. Soon I Myself will make this manifest in you, and they will pronounce that same word** *saint,* **only this time it will be with love.**

The Hour of Great Mercy

After February 3, Sister Faustina did not date her entries. But some time before February 10, Jesus again reminded her of a devotion dear to His Heart, a devotion He first mentioned on October 20, 1937 (See 1320):

> **I remind you, My daughter, that as often as you hear the clock strike the third hour, immerse yourself completely in My mercy, adoring and glorifying it; invoke its omnipotence for the whole world, and particularly for poor sinners; for at that moment mercy was opened wide for every soul. In this hour you can obtain everything for yourself and for others for the asking; it was the hour of grace for the whole world—mercy triumphed over justice.**
>
> **My daughter, try your best to make the Stations of the Cross in this hour, provided that your duties permit it; and if you are not able to make the Stations of the Cross, then at least step into the chapel for a moment and adore, in the Blessed Sacrament, My Heart which is full of mercy; and should you be unable to step into the chapel, immerse yourself in prayer there where you happen to be, if only for a very brief instant. I claim veneration for My mercy from every creature, but above all from you, since it is to you that I have given the most profound understanding of this mystery.** (1572)

Sister Faustina took this message to heart. Several sisters and students reported a few years later that, often at three o'clock, they had seen Sister Faustina lying prostrate in the chapel or in some out-of-the-way place. She was committed to the task Jesus gave her—the salvation of souls—as the following prayer discloses:

> O my Jesus, may the last days of my exile be spent totally according to Your most holy will. I join my sufferings, my bitterness and my last agony itself to Your Sacred Passion; and I offer myself for the whole world to implore an abundance of God's mercy for souls, and in particular for the souls who are in our homes.... (See 1574)

As the Lord continued to reveal to her the depths of His

mercy, she, His faithful secretary, continued to record His messages:

> **Tell souls not to place within their hearts obstacles to My mercy, which so greatly wants to act within them. My mercy works in all those hearts which open their doors to it. Both the sinner and the righteous person have need of My mercy. Conversion, as well as perseverance, is a grace of My mercy.**
>
> **Let souls who are striving for perfection particularly adore My mercy, because the abundance of graces which I grant them flows from My mercy. I desire that these souls distinguish themselves by boundless trust in My mercy. I Myself attend to the sanctification of such souls. I will provide them with everything they will need to attain sanctity. The graces of My mercy are drawn by means of one vessel only, and that is—trust. The more a soul trusts, the more it will receive. Souls that trust boundlessly are a great comfort to Me, because I pour all the treasures of My graces into them. I rejoice that they ask for much, because it is My desire to give much, very much. On the other hand, I am sad when souls ask for little, they constrict their hearts.** (1577-1578)

On Calvary with Jesus

One day Sister Faustina clearly saw that through all the phases of her life she had been following Jesus: childhood, youth, vocation, apostolic work, Mount Tabor, and the Garden of Olives. Now she felt that she was already with Him on Calvary. She told Jesus:

> I have willingly allowed myself to be crucified, and I am indeed already crucified; although I can still walk a little, I am stretched out on the cross, and I feel distinctly that strength is flowing to me from Your Cross, that You and You alone are my perseverance. Although I often hear the voice of temptation calling to me, "Come down from the cross!", the power of God strengthens me. Although loneliness and darkness and sufferings of all kinds beat

against my heart, the mysterious power of God supports and strengthens me. I want to drink the cup to the last drop. I trust firmly that Your grace, which has sustained me when I was in the Garden of Olives, will sustain me also now that I am on Calvary. (1580)

And now, forgetful of self, Sister poured forth her innermost desires as if in a last will and testament:

O Jesus, my Master, I unite my desires to Your desires which You had on the cross: I desire to fulfill Your holy will; I desire the conversion of souls; I desire that Your mercy be adored; I desire that the triumph of the Church be hastened; I desire the Feast of Mercy to be celebrated all over the world; I desire sanctity for priests; I desire that there be a saint in our Congregation; I desire that our whole Congregation have a great spirit of zeal for the glory of God and for the salvation of souls; I desire that souls who live in our homes not offend God, but persevere in good; I desire that the blessing of God descend upon my parents and my whole family; I desire that God give special light to my spiritual directors, and in particular to Father Andrasz and Father Sopocko; I desire a special blessing for Superiors under whose direction I have been, and in particular for Mother General, for Mother Irene, and for the Directress Mother Joseph. (1581)

O my Jesus, I now embrace the whole world and ask You for mercy for it. When You tell me, O God, that it is enough, that Your holy will has been completely accomplished, then, my Savior, in union with You, I will commit my soul into the hands of the Heavenly Father, full of trust in Your unfathomable mercy. And when I stand at the foot of Your throne, the first hymn that I will sing will be one to Your mercy. Poor earth, I will not forget you. Although I feel that I will be immediately drowned in God as in an ocean of happiness, that will not be an obstacle to my returning to earth to encourage souls and incite them to trust in God's mercy. Indeed, this immersion in God will give me the possibility of boundless action. (1582)

While Sister Faustina was writing, the devil stood by,

grinding his teeth. He could not bear the Divine Mercy and kept banging things in her cell. Filled with God's power, she did not mind the fury of the enemy of our salvation, but quietly kept on writing and extolling the Divine Mercy.

That same week Sister had a vision of Our Lady holding the Child Jesus on Her left arm. She looked kindly at Sister and said, *I am the Mother-of-God of Priests.* At that, She lowered Jesus to the ground, and raising her right hand heavenward, She said, *O God, bless Poland, bless priests.* And again She said to Sister, *Tell the priests what you have seen.* Although she had never seen Our Lady like that, and could understand nothing of this vision, Sister made a resolution to tell Father Andrasz at the first opportunity. (See 1585)

It was about February 9 that Sister heard the following words:

> **In the Old Covenant I sent prophets wielding thunderbolts to My people. Today I am sending you with My mercy to the whole of mankind. I do not want to punish aching mankind, but I desire to heal it, pressing it to My Merciful Heart. I use punishment when they themselves force Me to do so; My hand is reluctant to take up of the sword of justice. Before the Day of Justice I am sending the Day of Mercy.**

Sister answered, "O my Jesus, You speak to souls Yourself, because my words are insignificant." (1588)

Moments of Respite

Some of the sisters finally recognized Sister Faustina's uniqueness and her close union with God. They began to visit her and to ask her advice in matters spiritual, and she would give good advice to all of them. On February 10, Sister recorded:

> One of the sisters came into my cell for a little while. After a short conversation on the subject of obedience, she said to me, "Oh, now I understand how the saints acted. Thank you, Sister; a great light has entered my soul. I have profited much." (1594)

O my Jesus, this is Your work. It is You who have spoken thus to that soul, because this sister came in when I was completely immersed in God, and it was at that moment when this deep recollection left me. O my Jesus, I know that, in order to be useful to souls, one has to strive for the closest possible union with You, who are Eternal Love. One word from a soul united to God effects more good in souls than eloquent discussions and sermons from an imperfect soul. (1595)

On another occasion Jesus told Sister Fautina how much He desires the perfection of chosen souls:

Chosen souls are, in My hand, lights which I cast into the darkness of the world and with which I illumine it. As stars illumine the night, so chosen souls illumine the earth. And the more perfect a soul is, the stronger and the more far-reaching is the light shed by it. It can be hidden and unknown, even to those closest to it, and yet its holiness is reflected in souls even to the most distant extremities of the world. (1601)

Jesus also told her:

Daughter, when you go to confession, to this fountain of My mercy, the Blood and Water which came forth from My Heart always flows down upon your soul and ennobles it. Every time you go to confession, immerse yourself entirely in My mercy, with great trust, so that I may pour out the bounty of My grace upon your soul. When you approach the confessional, know this, that I Myself am waiting for you there. I am only hidden by the priest, but I myself act in your soul. Here the misery of the soul meets the God of mercy. Tell souls that from this fount of mercy souls draw graces solely with the vessel of trust. If their trust is great, there is no limit to My generosity. The torrents of grace inundate humble souls. The proud remain always in poverty and misery, because My grace turns away from them to humble souls. (1602)

During adoration on February 14, Sister began to repeat the prayer, "Holy God, Holy Mighty One, Holy Immortal One, have mercy on us." As she did so, she was transported into heaven before the majesty of God and experienced how the Angels and Saints give glory to God. She could not find words to describe what she saw. She dared not try, for she did not want people to think that what she wrote was everything. Recalling her own way of praising God, she could only exclaim: "Oh, how miserable it is! And what a tiny drop it is in comparison to that perfect heavenly glory. O my God, how good You are to accept my praise as well, and to turn Your Face to me with kindness and let us know that our prayer is pleasing to You." (1604)

One day Jesus said to Sister Faustina, **Write down about My goodness whatever occurs to you.**

She answered, "What do You mean, Lord, what if I write too much?"

The Lord replied, **My daughter, even if you were to speak at one and the same time in all human and angelic tongues, even then you would not have said very much, but on the contrary, you would have sung in only a small measure the praises of My goodness—of My unfathomable mercy.**

"O my Jesus, do You Yourself put words into my mouth that I may worthily praise You," she exclaimed.

Jesus said, **My daughter, be at peace; do as I tell you. Your thoughts are united to My thought, so write whatever comes to your mind. You are the secretary of My mercy. I have chosen you for that office in this life and the next life. That is how I want it to be in spite of all the opposition they will give you. Know that My choice will not change.** (1605)

At that moment Sister steeped herself in deep humility. However, the more she humbled herself, the more the presence of God pervaded her.

When on February 20 the Lord said to Sister Faustina, **I have need of your sufferings to rescue souls,** she answered, "O my Jesus, do with me as You please." But she had no courage to ask the Lord Jesus for greater sufferings, because just the previous night she had suffered so much that she would not be able to bear a drop more than what Jesus himself gave her. She wrote:

Almost all night I was in such violent pain that it seemed all my intestines were torn to pieces. I threw up the medicine I had taken. When I bowed my head down to the ground, I lost consciousness, and I stayed like that for some time, with my head on the floor. When I came to, I became aware that my whole body was pressing on my head and face, and that I was covered with vomit. I thought it would be the end of me. Dear Mother Superior [Irene] and Sister Tarcisia were trying to help me as best they could. Jesus demanded suffering, but not death. O my Jesus, do with me as You please. Only give me strength to suffer. Since Your power supports me, I shall bear everything. O souls, how I love you! (1612-1613)

The sisters in the infirmary, as well as visitors, felt that Faustina was dying. Sister Amelia Socha, a dear friend who came to help her at this time, was suffering from tuberculosis of the bones. Fearing to be a burden to the community, she asked Sister Faustina to intercede with Jesus for the grace of an early death. Sister Faustina told her that she would die a year after her (and so it happened).

That February many sisters had the flu. Sister Faustina went to the neighboring dormitory to visit the sisters who were ill. One of them said, "Sister, when you die I will not fear you at all. Come to see me after you die, because I want to confide to you a secret concerning my soul, something I want you to settle for me with the Lord Jesus. I know you can obtain this from Him."

Because she was speaking publicly, Sister Faustina answered her in this way: "The Lord Jesus is very discreet. And so He never betrays to anyone a secret that is between Him and a soul." (1615)

Sisters from the various homes of the community began to write to Sister Faustina, asking for her intercession when she dies. Those who visited her were struck by the peace, the joy, and the smile she had for them, despite the sufferings that were ravaging her. She herself prayed, "O my Lord, thank you for conforming me to Yourself through immolation. I see that this earthly vessel is beginning to crumble. I rejoice in this, because soon I will be in my Father's house." (1616)

Father Andrasz heard Sister's confession on February 27. She was simple as a child, just as Jesus wanted her to be. After confession her soul was deeply illumined and she heard the voice say, **Because you are a child, you shall remain close to My Heart.**

Your simplicity is more pleasing to Me than your mortifications.
(1617)

In the School of Suffering

During the last two carnival days before Ash Wednesday, Sister's sufferings increased. She united even more closely with the Suffering Savior, asking for mercy for the world gone mad in its malice. The pain from the crown of thorns remained with her all day, and she could not put her head on the pillow when she tried to lie down. About ten o'clock at night the pain disappeared and she fell asleep, but the next day she felt completely exhausted. She revealed the source of her stamina:

Jesus-Host, if You Yourself did not sustain me, I would not be able to persevere on the cross. I would not be able to endure so much suffering. But the power of Your grace maintains me on a higher level and makes my sufferings meritorious. You give me strength to always move forward and to gain heaven by force and to have love in my heart for those from whom I suffer adversities and contempt. With Your grace one can do all things. (1620)

On March 1, the day before Ash Wednesday, Sister Faustina made her monthly one-day retreat. She resolved to be a host in Jesus' hand throughout Lent. She prayed, "Make use of me that You may enter into sinners Yourself. Demand anything You like; no sacrifice will seem too much for me when souls are at stake." Sister offered all her Masses and Holy Communions during March for the intention of Father Andrasz, asking God to give him an even deeper understanding of His love and mercy. (1622-1623)

She began Lent as Jesus wished, relying completely on His holy will and accepting all in love. "I cannot practice any greater mortifications because I am so very weak. This long illness has sapped my strength completely," she wrote. "I am uniting myself with Jesus through suffering. When I meditate on His painful Passion, my physical sufferings are lessened." (1625)

Jesus instructed Sister, **I am taking you into My school for the whole of Lent. I want to teach you how to suffer.**

She answered, "With You, Lord, I am ready for everything."

The Lord replied, "You are allowed to drink from the cup from which I drink. I give you that exclusive privilege today." Sister Faustina felt Jesus' Passion in her whole body that day and the Lord gave her knowledge of the conversion of certain souls. (See 1626-1627)

The teaching began during Holy Mass. She saw Jesus crucified who said to her, **My pupil, have great love for those who cause you suffering. Do good to those who hate you.**"

She replied, "O my Master, You see very well that I feel no love for them, and that troubles me."

Jesus answered her, **It is not always within your power to control your feelings. You will recognize that you have love if, after having experienced annoyance and contradiction, you do not lose your peace, but pray for those who have made you suffer and wish them well.** (1628)

During this period, Sister Faustina wrote a poem beginning with the line, "I am a host in Your hand," to remind her that she offered herself as a victim host. In another poem written at this time, Sister confessed that her heart's desires are so great and beyond comprehension that nothing can fill the abyss formed by them, not even the most beautiful beings gathered from the whole earth. Because the earth holds no love equal to hers, she has turned her gaze toward the eternal world; her heart seeks the love of The Immortal One. (See 1629, 1632.)

On March 10, Sister recorded that her sufferings were continuous. She was on the cross with Jesus. Just a little while ago, Mother Superior told her, "It is a lack of love of neighbor on your part, Sister, that you eat something and then you suffer and disturb the others during their night's rest." After that remark, she resolved to suffer in secret and not ask for help because it was of no use, anyway. She was certain that her pain was not caused by food. Dr. Silberg confirmed this. Rather, it was an act of God. The pains were so severe that they rendered her unconscious. Then she would get drenched in a cold sweat, and gradually the pain would go away. She managed to suffer through several bouts known only to Jesus. "If I accept the delights and raptures of love to the point of becoming oblivious to what is going on around me," she reasoned, "it is also right that I should accept with love these sufferings which cause me to faint." (See 1633)

The doctor came to examine the sick sisters in the parlor. Sister Faustina could not go down and asked that he come to her cell. After the examination he said, "I will tell everything to the Sister Infirmarian." After his departure, the infirmarian came in, showing great displeasure.

"Sister, what did the doctor say about these pains?" asked Faustina.

She replied, "He said nothing. He said that it was nothing. The patient was just sulking." With that she left the room and did not return for another week. But the sufferings returned with great violence and once it seemed it would be the end.

The superiors then decided to approach Dr. Adam Silberg who had treated Sister Faustina at the Sanatorium on Pradnik. He found that the condition was serious and told Sister Faustina, "It will not be possible to restore you to good health. We can remedy your condition partially, but complete recovery is out of the question." The medicine he prescribed would ward off major attacks, but he very much wanted her to go to the sanatorium "to try to patch up your health somehow, if that is still possible." (See 1634)

Several unpleasant episodes, stemming from her going for this treatment, occurred. Sister left an account of these because, she wrote, "Jesus orders me to write all of this for the consolation of other souls who will often be exposed to similar sufferings." In short, her companion to the sanatorium showed her displeasure by trying to vex her. When Sister Faustina saw that her unruffled peace was getting on her companion's nerves, she began to pray for her and to offer it all up to obtain mercy for poor sinners. Then, when they returned home, she felt she needed to go to confession and to ask advice of her spiritual director. Usually the novices went first. She would have to get permission from the Directress of the Novices to go before them. Not having enough strength to go and look for the Directress, she waited her turn. By the time she went in to make her confession, she was feeling so weak that she barely managed just to confess.

On that day there also arose some misunderstandings between the Superior and herself. She could have revealed the truth by a single word, but she didn't because it was a secret.

For the next several days the sufferings persisted day and night. Sister Faustina offered them for a soul dying in despair, and for poor, hardened sinners in order to obtain Divine Mercy for them.

On Friday March 25, Sister saw the suffering Jesus, who leaned over her and whispered quietly, **My daughter, help me to save sinners.** At that, a burning desire to save souls filled her to the point of ecstasy; and when she came to, she knew in what way she was to save souls. And she prepared for greater sufferings. In addition to the increase of sufferings, she patiently endured the wounds in her hands, feet and side. She could feel the anger of the enemy of souls but he did not touch her. (See 1645-1646)

On April 1, First Friday, Sister Faustina was burning up with fever. Unable to eat solid food, she wished she had something refreshing to drink, but it so happened that she did not have any water in her pitcher. Just as she renewed her intention with the words, "All this, O Jesus, to obtain mercy for souls," a novice entered and gave her a big orange from the Directress of Novices, Sister Callista. She wrote:

> I saw the Lord's hand in this. The same thing happened again, several times. During this time, although my needs were known, I never received anything refreshing to eat, even though I had asked for it. However, I knew that God was demanding suffering and sacrifices. I am not writing in detail about these refusals, because these are delicate matters, and difficult to believe. Yet, God can demand even such sacrifices. (1647)

When Mother Superior visited her that day, Sister Faustina was about to ask permission to have something brought to her cell to quench her great thirst. But before she managed to ask, Mother said, "Sister, let's make an end of this illness once and for all, one way or another. You'll have to undergo regular treatment or something. Things can't go on like this any longer."

When Mother left, Sister knelt and prayed, "May Your holy will be done in my regard. Do with me, Jesus, as You please." At that moment she felt completely alone and was attacked by various temptations. In earnest prayer she found peace and light, and she realized that the Superior had only been testing her. (See

1648.)

Later that same day, after she read the account of the canonization of St. Andrew Bobola, Sister Faustina wept like a child, because there was as yet no saint in her community. And she said to the Lord, "I know Your generosity, and yet it seems to me that You are less generous toward us."

The Lord answered, **Don't cry. You are that saint.** Her soul was flooded with light and she was given to know how much more she would still have to suffer.

She asked the Lord, "How will that come about? You have been speaking to me about another congregation."

The Lord answered, **It is not for you to know how this will come about. Your duty is to be faithful to My grace and to do always what is within your power and what obedience allows you to do...** (1650)

What her heart felt overflowed on paper. In verse after verse she glorified the Divine Mercy, revealed her joy in the knowledge that she would soon be leaving this earth and going to the eternal banquet to meet Love Eternal, her Father in heaven, her Betrothed. She was certain that heaven was her destiny, but she promised to remember mankind and to obtain Divine Mercy for all, especially those dear to her heart. In one verse she prophesied:

> I know the moment will come when all will understand the work of God in my soul.
> I know that such is Your will.—So be it. (1653)

Also in verse form she confessed her inability to struggle and suffer on her own:

> I would not know how to suffer without You, O Christ.
> Of myself I would not be able to brave adversities.
> Alone, I would not have the courage to drink from Your cup;
> But You, Lord, are always with me, and you lead me along mysterious paths. (1654)

And she admitted:

> O Christ, if my soul had known, all at once, what it was going to have to suffer during its lifetime, it would have died of terror at the very sight; it would not have touched its lips

to the cup of bitterness. But as it has been given to drink a drop at a time, it has emptied the cup to the very bottom. O Christ, if You Yourself did not support the soul, how much could it do of itself? We are strong, but with Your strength; we are holy, but with Your holiness. And of ourselves what are we?—less than nothing... (1655)

Holy Week and Easter

On April 10, Palm Sunday and her last Holy Week, Sister Faustina managed to go to Mass but had no strength to go receive the palm. In fact, weakened by a drenching, shivering fever, she could hardly persevere through the Mass. During Mass, as Jesus revealed to her how the shouts of "Hosanna" echoed painfully in His most Sacred Heart, each "Hosanna" likewise pierced her heart and soul. Also inundated by a sea of bitterness, she was drawn close to Him. She heard Jesus say, **My daughter, your compassion for Me refreshes Me. By meditating on My Passion, your soul acquires a distinct beauty.** (1657)

The following day, weakness forced Sister to receive Holy Communion upstairs with the other sick sisters. The priest who celebrated Mass brought Holy Communion and gave it first to the three sisters, and then to her. Thinking she was the last one, he gave Sister Faustina two Hosts. A novice who was lying in the adjoining cell did not receive any. While the priest went back to get the Holy Communion for the novice, Jesus said to Faustina, **I enter that heart unwillingly. You received those two Hosts, because I delayed My coming into this soul who resists My grace. My visit to such a soul is not pleasant for Me.** Immediately, Sister's soul was drawn into His presence, and she received a deep interior illumination of the entire plan of mercy. "It was like a flash of lightning," she wrote, "but more distinct than if I had watched it for hours with the eyes of my body." (See 1658)

No words could completely convey the joyous feeling in her soul. She wrote:

> ... The glory of The Divine Mercy is resounding, even now, in spite of the efforts of its enemies and of Satan himself, who has a great hate for God's mercy. This work will snatch

a great number of souls from him, and that is why the spirit of darkness sometimes tempts good people violently, so that they may hinder the work. But I have clearly seen that the will of God is already being carried out, and that it will be accomplished to the very last detail. The enemies' greatest efforts will not thwart the smallest detail of what the Lord has decreed. No matter if there are times when the work seems to be completely destroyed; it is then that the work is being all the more consolidated. (1659)

On Holy Thursday, Sister Faustina felt strong enough to take part in the Church ceremonies. During Mass Jesus said to her, **Look into My Heart and see there the love and mercy which I have for humankind, and especially for sinners. Look, and enter into My Passion.** In an instant, she experienced the entire Passion in her own heart. "I was surprised that these tortures did not deprive me of my life," she wrote. (See 1663)

That evening during her Holy Hour Sister heard these words: **You see My mercy for sinners, which at this moment is revealing itself in all its power. See how little you have written about it; it is only a single drop. Do what is in your power, so that sinners may come to know My goodness.** (1665)

On Good Friday the tortured but not yet crucified Jesus appeared to Sister and said, **You are My Heart. Speak to sinners about My mercy.** And as she received interior knowledge of the whole abyss of His mercy for souls, she realized that what she had written so far was truly but a drop. (See 1666)

During adoration on Holy Saturday Jesus told Sister: **Be at peace, My daughter. This work of mercy is Mine; there is nothing of you in it. It pleases Me that you are carrying out faithfully what I have commanded you to do, not adding or taking away a single word.** And by interior enlightenment Sister learned that not a single word was hers. "...despite difficulties and adversities, I have always, always fulfilled His will, as He has made it known to me," she wrote that day. (See 1667)

The next morning before the Mass of the Resurrection, Sister felt so weak that she lost all hope of participating in the procession in the church with the rest of the sisters. She said to the Lord, "Jesus, if my prayers are pleasing to You, give me the strength for this moment that I may take part in the procession."

At that same instant, she felt strong, and was certain that she could go along with the sisters. (See 1668)

During the procession, Jesus appeared to her in a brightness greater than the light of the sun, looked at her with love and said, **Heart of My Heart, be filled with joy.** Instantly her spirit was drowned in Him and when she came to, she was still walking in procession while her soul was totally immersed in Him. (1669)

As she thanked the Lord Jesus for the Redemption and the gift of His love, that is, of Himself in the Holy Eucharist, she was drawn into the bosom of the Most Holy Trinity and immersed in the love of the Father, the Son and the Holy Spirit. "These moments are difficult to describe," she wrote. (See 1670)

During recreation next day one of the sisters said, "Sister Faustina is doing so poorly that she can hardly walk; but may she die soon because she is going to be a saint."

Then one of the sister directresses retorted, "That she is going to die, we know; but whether she is going to be a saint, that is another question." Sharp gibes on the subject ensued. Throughout the talk, Sister Faustina remained silent. (See 1672)

In the meantime Faustina was beginning to receive letters from some of the sisters who were her companions in the novitiate. Many, similar to the one which follows, often amused her to the point of laughter:

"Dear Sister Faustina, we are very sorry you are so gravely ill, but we are very happy that, when the Lord Jesus takes you away, you will pray for us, for you have a lot of influence with the Lord."

One of the sisters put it this way: "When you die, Sister, please take me under your special care, for certainly you can do that for me."

Another sister wrote, "How I am waiting for the time when the Lord Jesus will take you, because I know what will happen then; and I greatly desire death for you." Sister Faustina was tempted to ask her what she thinks will happen, but instead she answered her, "The same thing will happen to me, a sinner, as happens to all sinners, if God's mercy does not shield me." (See 1673)

Return to the Sanatorium

Sister Faustina learned that on Thursday, April 21, she would be returning to the Sanatorium on Pradnik. She was to remain there for two months or longer. The day before her departure she worried that she would be placed in a ward and exposed to much unpleasantness. That evening she went to the little chapel for a long talk with Jesus and poured out before Him all her worries and fears. Jesus listened with loving kindness and then said, **Be at peace, My child, I am with you. Go in great peace. All is ready; I have ordered, in My own special way, a private room to be prepared for you.**" Calmed and filled with gratitude she retired. (See 1674)

Sister Felicia drove Faustina to the sanatorium, where, indeed, a private room was made ready for her. She wrote:

> ... When we entered the room, we were surprised that everything had been prepared so beautifully: all was clean and neat, covered with tablecloths and bedecked with flowers; a pretty Easter Lamb had been placed on the night table by the Sisters. At once, three Sacred Heart Sisters, who work at the sanatorium, my old acquaintances, came and greeted me warmly. Sister Felicia was surprised at all this. We bid a warm farewell to each other, and she left. When I was alone, with just the Lord Jesus and myself, I thanked Him for this great grace. (1675)

That evening, the sister who was her nurse came and said to her, "Tomorrow you will not receive the Lord Jesus, Sister, because you are very tired; later on, we shall see." Although very hurt, Sister Faustina resigned herself to God's will and tried to sleep. In the morning, after her meditation, she prepared for Holy Communion even though she was not going to receive the Lord Jesus. She recorded what happened then:

> ... When my love and desire had reached a high degree, I saw at my bedside a Seraph, who gave me Holy Communion, saying these words: "Behold the Lord of Angels." When I received the Lord, my spirit was drowned in the love of God and in amazement. This was repeated for thirteen days, although I was never sure he would bring me Holy

Communion the next day. Yet, I put my trust completely in the goodness of God, but did not even dare to think that I would receive Holy Communion in this way on the following day.

The Seraph was surrounded by a great light, the divinity and love of God being reflected in him. He wore a golden robe and, over it, a transparent surplice and a transparent stole. The chalice was crystal, covered with a transparent veil. As soon as he had given me the Lord, he disappeared. (1676)

Once Sister Faustina had a certain doubt and asked the Seraph, "Could you perhaps hear my confession?"

He answered, "No spirit in heaven has that power." And at that instant, the Sacred Host rested on her lips. (1677)

On Sunday, the priest brought her Holy Communion. After two weeks or so, Sister received permission to get up. She was able now to go to Mass and spend time with the Lord in the chapel.

At the first examination, Dr. Adam Silberg found Sister's condition grave, just as she had suspected. "But Almighty God can do all things," he told her. Back in her room she was so thankful for all that the Lord sent her throughout her lifetime, so peaceful and joyful, that "if death had come at that moment," she wrote, "I would not have said to it, 'Wait, for I still have some matters to attend to.' No, I would have welcomed it with joy, because I am ready for the meeting with the Lord, not only today, but ever since the moment when I placed my complete trust in the Divine Mercy, resigning myself totally to His most holy will, full of mercy and compassion. I know what I am of myself..." (See 1679)

On the First Sunday after Easter, the day on which Jesus desired the Feast of Mercy to be celebrated, Sister wrote in her diary:

> Today I again offered myself to the Lord as a holocaust for sinners. My Jesus, if the end of my life is already approaching, I beg You most humbly, accept my death in union with You as a holocaust which I offer You today, while I still have full possession of my faculties and a fully

conscious will, and this for a threefold purpose:

Firstly: that the work of Your mercy may spread throughout the whole world and that the Feast of The Divine Mercy may be solemnly promulgated and celebrated.

Secondly: that sinners, especially dying sinners, may have recourse to Your mercy and experience the unspeakable effects of this mercy.

Thirdly: that all the work of Your mercy be realized according to Your wishes, and for a certain person who is in charge of this work...

Accept, most merciful Jesus, this, my inadequate sacrifice, which I offer to You today before heaven and earth. May Your Most Sacred Heart, so full of mercy, complete what is lacking in my offering and offer it to Your Father for the conversion of sinners. I thirst after souls, O Christ. (1680)

At that moment Sister Faustina felt she was God's exclusive property, and she felt the greatest spiritual freedom of which she had no previous experience. She also saw at that same moment the glory of The Divine Mercy and a multitude of souls who were praising His goodness. Immersed in God, she heard these words: **You are My well-beloved daughter.** His vivid presence remained with her that entire day.

The evening of May 1, Jesus asked Sister Faustina, **My daughter, do you need anything?**

She answered, "O my Love, when I have You I have everything."

And the Lord replied: **If souls would put themselves completely in My care, I Myself would undertake the task of sanctifying them, and I would lavish even greater graces on them. There are souls who thwart My efforts, but I have not given up on them; as often as they turn to Me, I hurry to their aid, shielding them with My mercy, and I give them the first place in My compassionate Heart.**

Write for the benefit of religious souls that it delights Me to come to their hearts in Holy Communion. But if there is anyone else in such a heart, I cannot bear it and quickly leave that heart, taking with Me all the gifts and graces I have prepared for the soul. And the soul does not even notice My going. After some

time, the inner emptiness and dissatisfaction will come to her attention. Oh, if only she would turn to me then, I would help her to cleanse her heart, and I would fulfill everything in her soul; but without her knowledge and consent, I cannot be the Master of her heart. (1683)

In her meditations and Holy Hours, Jesus continued to counsel His novice:

My daughter, faithfully live up to the words which I speak to you. Do not value any external thing too highly, even if it were to seem very precious to you. Let go of yourself, and abide with Me continually. Entrust everything to Me and do nothing on your own, and you will always have great freedom of spirit. No circumstances or events will ever be able to upset you. Set little store on what people say. Let everyone judge you as they like. Do not make excuses for yourself; it will do you no harm. Give away everything at the first sign of a demand, even if they were the most necessary things. Do not ask for anything without consulting Me. Allow them to take away even what is due you—respect, your good name—let your spirit rise above all that. And so, set free from everything, rest close to My Heart, not allowing your peace to be disturbed by anything. My pupil, consider the words which I have spoken to you. (1685)

In a symbolic vision on May 8, Sister Faustina saw two enormous pillars that were implanted in the ground with much strain, fatigue and effort—one by herself and the other by S.M. It is not known who Sister had in mind by these initials. When she marveled how she could have done this with her own strength, she learned that she accomplished this only with the power that came from above.

The Image of The Divine Mercy hung very high on these two pillars. In an instant, on these two pillars stood a huge temple, within and without. She saw the hand but not the person who was completing this temple. There was a great multitude of people inside and outside the temple and the rays issuing out of the compassionate Heart of Jesus flowed down upon everyone. (See 1689.)

That same day after Holy Communion Jesus told Sister, **My daughter, give me souls. Know that it is your mission to win souls for Me by prayer and sacrifice, and by encouraging them to trust in My mercy.** (1690)

On another day, while she was writing in glowing terms about Jesus hidden in the Blessed Sacrament and about His great intimacy with her, Sister Faustina saw Jesus lean over her and ask, **My daughter, what are you writing?**

Sister answered, "I am writing about You, Jesus, about Your being hidden in the Blessed Sacrament, about Your inconceivable love and mercy for people."

And Jesus said, **Secretary of My most profound mystery, know that yours is an exclusive intimacy with Me. Your task is to write down everything that I make known to you about My mercy, for the benefit of those who by reading these things will be comforted in their souls and will have the courage to approach Me. I therefore want you to devote all your free moments to writing.**

"But, O Lord, shall I always have a moment, at least a brief one, in which to write?" she asked.

And Jesus replied, **It is not for you to think about that. Only do as much as you can and I will always arrange things so that you will easily be able to do what I ask of you...** (1693)

Sister rarely dated her notes from then on, and her thoughts seemed to be random ones; but she was being obedient, writing down everything that Jesus let her know about His mercy.

One Thursday, Sister Faustina was happy because she was feeling better and felt she could make a Holy Hour. However, as soon as she began the Holy Hour, her physical sufferings intensified to such an extent that she was unable to pray. When the Holy Hour ended, so did her sufferings. When she complained to Jesus that her sufferings kept her from immersing herself in His sorrowful passion, Jesus answered her, **My daughter, know that if I allow you to feel and have a more profound knowledge of My sufferings, that is a grace from Me. But when your mind is dimmed and your sufferings are great, it is then that you take an active part in My Passion, and I am conforming you more fully to Myself. It is your task to submit yourself to My will at such times, more than at others...** (1697)

Even before she entered the convent, Sister Faustina's favorite practice was to go to the bedside of a dying person and, by prayer, obtain trust in The Divine Mercy for him. As already mentioned, she continued this practice in the sanatorium. At first, she was physically present to the dying person; and then, when forbidden by her superior, she accompanied the dying person in spirit. She wrote the following about dying sinners:

> ... God's mercy sometimes touches the sinner at the last moment in a wondrous and mysterious way. Outwardly, it seems as if everything were lost, but it is not so. The soul, illumined by a ray of God's powerful final grace, turns to God in the last moment with such a power of love that, in an instant, it receives from God forgiveness of sin and punishment, while outwardly it shows no sign either of repentance or of contrition, because souls [at that stage] no longer react to external things. Oh, how beyond comprehension is God's mercy! But—horror!—there are also souls who voluntarily and consciously reject and scorn this grace! Although a person is at the point of death, the merciful God gives the soul that interior vivid moment, so that if the soul is willing, it has the possibility of returning to God. But sometimes, the obduracy in souls is so great that consciously they choose hell; they [thus] make useless all the prayers that other souls offer to God for them and even the efforts of God Himself... (1698)

When one day Sister Faustina asked Jesus to teach her about the interior life, He answered:

> ... I was your Teacher, I am and I will be; strive to make your heart like unto My humble and gentle Heart. Never claim your rights. Bear with great calm and patience everything that befalls you. Do not defend yourself when you are put to shame, though innocent. Let others triumph. Do not stop being good when you notice that your goodness is being abused. I Myself will speak up for you when it is necessary. Be grateful for the smallest of My graces, because your gratitude compels Me to grant you new graces... (1701)

One day when Sister almost finished making the Stations of

the Cross, Jesus complained to her about the lack of love in chosen souls. He told her, **I will allow convents and churches to be destroyed.**

Sister answered, "Jesus, but there are so many souls praising You in convents."

The Lord responded, **That praise wounds My Heart, because love has been banished from convents.... The great sins of the world are superficial wounds of My Heart, but the sins of a chosen soul pierce My Heart through and through....** (1702)

Unable to find anything to justify those chosen souls, Sister Faustina began to weep bitterly. The Lord looked at her graciously and comforted her with these words: **Do not cry. There are still a great number of souls who love Me very much, but My Heart desires to be loved by all and, because My love is great, that is why I warn and chastise them.** (1703)

On another occasion, Sister entered the chapel for a moment. Her heart became immersed in a prayer of adoration and she praised God's incomprehensible goodness and mercy. Then she heard these words in her soul: **I am and will be for you such as you praise Me for being. You shall experience My goodness, already in this life and then, to the full, in the life to come.** (1707)

She responded, "O Christ, I am most delighted when I see that You are loved, and that Your praise and glory resound, especially the praise of Your mercy. O Christ, to the last moment of my life, I will not stop glorifying Your goodness and mercy. With every drop of my blood, with every beat of my heart, I glorify Your mercy. I long to be entirely transformed into a hymn of Your glory. When I find myself on my deathbed, may the last beat of my heart be a loving hymn in praise of Your unfathomable mercy. (1708)

On May 26, as Sister contemplated the Ascension of Our Lord into Heaven, she saw herself in the midst of a huge crowd of disciples and apostles, together with the Mother of God. Jesus was telling them to go out to the whole world and teach in His Name. He then lifted up His hands, blessed them and disappeared in a cloud. She saw that Our Lady longed after Jesus with the whole force of Her love, but was so peaceful and so dependent on God that there was not a stir in her heart but for what God wanted. Sister remained alone with Our Lady who instructed her concerning the interior life. The Mother of God told her, *The soul's true greatness is in loving God and in humbling oneself in His presence, completely forgetting oneself and believing oneself to be nothing; because the Lord is great, but He is well-pleased only with the humble; He always opposes the proud.* (1711)

The Power of Union with God

One day after Holy Communion, when Sister Faustina had welcomed Jesus into her heart she said to Him, "My Love, reign in the most secret recesses of my heart, there where my most secret thoughts are conceived, where You alone have free access, in this deepest sanctuary where human thought cannot penetrate. May You alone dwell there, and may everything I do exteriorly take its origin in You. I ardently desire, and I am striving with all the strength of my soul, to make You, Lord, feel at home in this sanctuary." (1721)

She then heard these words: **If you did not tie my hands, I would send down many punishments upon the earth. My daughter, your look disarms My anger. Although your lips are silent, you call out to Me so mightily that all heaven is moved. I cannot escape from your requests, because you pursue Me, not from afar but within your own heart.** (1722)

Several days after the Feast of the Ascension, Jesus told Sister Faustina:

Write: I am Thrice Holy, and I detest the smallest sin. I cannot love a soul that is stained with sin; but when it repents, there is no limit to My generosity toward it. My mercy embraces and justifies it. With My mercy, I pursue sinners along all their paths, and My Heart rejoices when they return to Me. I forget the bitterness with which they fed My Heart and rejoice at their return.

Tell sinners that no one shall escape My hand; if they run away from My merciful Heart, they will fall into My just hands. Tell sinners that I am always waiting for them, that I listen intently to the beating of their heart... when will it beat for Me? Write, that I am speaking to them through their

remorse of conscience, through their failures and sufferings, through thunderstorms, through the voice of the Church. And if they bring all My graces to naught, I begin to be angry with them, leaving them alone and giving them what they want. (1728)

Sister knew that despite the diligent care of her superiors and the efforts of the doctors, her health was failing. "But I rejoice greatly at Your call, my God, my Love," she wrote, "because I know that my mission will begin at the moment of my death...." (1729) And she again affirmed her belief in the mercy of God:

.... Although my misery is great, and my offenses are many, I trust in Your mercy, because You are the God of mercy; and, from time immemorial, it has never been heard of, nor do heaven or earth remember, that a soul trusting in Your mercy has been disappointed. O God of compassion, You alone can justify me, and You will never reject me when I, contrite, approach Your merciful Heart, where no one has ever been refused, even if he were the greatest sinner. (1730)

One night toward the end of May, Sister Faustina was awakened by a great storm. She described the incident:

Today I was awakened by a great storm. The wind was raging, and it was raining in torrents, thunderbolts striking again and again. I began to pray that the storm would do no harm, when I heard the words, **Say the chaplet I have taught you, and the storm will cease.** I began immediately to say the chaplet and hadn't even finished it when the storm suddenly ceased, and I heard the words: **Through the chaplet you will obtain everything, if what you ask for will be compatible with My will.** (1731)

Was this storm a portent of another great storm which in a year's time was to rage over her beloved country? Sister Faustina knew that a long and terrible war, full of adversities, was about to occur. For this reason, she intensified her prayers for Poland. One day as she prayed, she heard these words: **I bear a special love for Poland, and if she will be obedient to My will, I shall exalt her in might and holiness. From her will come forth the spark that will prepare the world for My final coming.** (1732)

During her stay in the sanatorium, Sister Faustina was never idle. She continued to live in close intimacy with God, praying for sinners, counseling the patients who visited her, and interceding for the dying and for the souls in purgatory, who came to her for help. She was also inspired to record a series of reflections which she interspersed with original poems and prayers, all in praise of God's mercy as manifested in His plan of creation and redemption. These can be read in their entirety in the Diary itself. (See 1741-1751.)

On June 2, Sister began a three-day retreat under the direct guidance of Jesus, her Retreat Master. He Himself told her to make the retreat and appointed the three days before the Feast of Pentecost for this purpose. Sister agreed to it, but only after she received the permission of her superior. Jesus directed the entire retreat. Each day the Lord gave her the topics to consider during her first and second meditations, and each day He preached a conference. In addition, Jesus gave her specific readings from the Gospel of St. John: the first day she was to read, very slowly, Chapter 15; the second day, not just with her lips but with her heart, Chapter 19; and on the third day she was told to experience Chapter 21, more with her heart than with her mind. On the last day of the retreat, the Lord gave Sister Faustina the following conference, which could be called "The Testament of Mercy":

My daughter, know that My Heart is mercy itself. From this sea of mercy, graces flow out upon the whole world. No soul that has approached Me has ever gone away unconsoled. All misery gets buried in the depths of My mercy, and every saving and sanctifying grace flows from this fountain. My daughter, I desire that your heart be an abiding place of My mercy. I desire that this mercy flow out upon the whole world through your heart. Let no one who approaches you go away without that trust in My mercy which I so ardently desire from souls.

Pray as much as you can for the dying. By your entreaties, obtain for them trust in My mercy, because they have most need of trust, and have it the least. Be assured that the grace of eternal salvation for certain souls in their final moment depends on your prayer. You know the whole abyss

of My mercy, so draw upon it for yourself and especially for poor sinners. Sooner would heaven and earth turn into nothingness than would My mercy not embrace a trusting soul. (See 1752-1779.)

Sister Faustina made only one resolution after this extraordinary retreat—the same one she had been making for several years now: Union with Christ-Mercy. At the end of the retreat she said to Jesus, "Thank You, Eternal Love, for Your inconceivable kindness to me, that You would occupy Yourself so directly with my sanctification."

Jesus replied, My daughter, let three virtues adorn you in a particular way: humility, purity of intention and love. Do nothing beyond what I demand of you, and accept everything that My hand gives you. Strive for a life of recollection so that you can hear My voice, which is so soft that only recollected souls can hear it... (1779)

On the Feast of Pentecost, Sister Faustina arose earlier than usual, even though she did not fall asleep until midnight because she was so deeply moved at the thought of renewing her vows the next day. She went to the chapel and immersed herself in the love of God. Before receiving Holy Communion, she renewed her religious vows privately. After Holy Communion, the infinite love of God swept over her. "My soul was in communion with the Holy Spirit, who is the same Lord as the Father and the Son," she wrote. "His breath filled my soul with such delight that it would be useless for me to try to give even a faint idea of what my heart experienced." (1781)

Several days later, in a longer conversation, the Lord said to Sister:

How very much I desire the salvation of souls! My dearest secretary, write that I want to pour out My divine life into human souls and to sanctify them, if only they were willing to accept My grace. The greatest sinners would achieve great sanctity, if only they would trust in My mercy. The very inner depths of My being are filled to overflowing with mercy, and it is being poured out upon all I have created. My delight is to act in a human soul and to fill it with My mercy and to justify it. My kingdom on earth is My

240

life in the human soul. Write, My secretary, that I Myself, am the spiritual guide of souls—and I guide them indirectly through the priest, and lead each one to sanctity by a road known to Me alone. (1784)

On June 17, which was the Friday after the Feast of Corpus Christi, Sister Faustina was so ill that she was certain the longed-for moment was approaching. She was very feverish and spewed up much blood during the night. Though she was still able to go to Holy Communion, she was too weak to remain for the Mass. That afternoon her temperature dropped and she felt as if everything inside her were dying. But when she became immersed in deep prayer she understood that "it was not yet the moment of deliverance, but only a closer call from my Bridegroom." (See 1786)

At her next meeting with the Lord she said, "You are fooling me, Jesus; You show me the open gate of heaven, but again You leave me on earth."

The Lord answered, **When, in heaven, you see these present days, you will rejoice and will want to see as many of them as possible. I am not surprised, My daughter, that you cannot understand this now, because your heart is overflowing with pain and longing for Me. Your vigilance pleases me. Let My word be enough for you; it will not be long now.** And once again her soul remained in exile. (1787)

In June, Mother Irene paid her a brief visit. When she looked around the room she told Sister, "Everything is too pretty here." Sister Faustina agreed, but noted in her diary:

It is true, the sisters are trying to make my stay in the sanatorium pleasant. But all this beauty does not lessen my sacrifice, which God alone can see and which will cease only when my heart stops beating. Neither the beauty of the whole earth, nor even of heaven itself, can blur the torture of my soul, which is real at each moment though so deeply interior. It will end when You Yourself, Author of my suffering, say, "Enough." There is nothing that could lessen my sacrifice. (1785)

Mother Michael, the Mother General, visited Sister Faustina in July. She enjoyed this last visit with Sister Faustina who gave her lively accounts of the various episodes of her life in the hospital. Just before they parted Sister Faustina told her joyfully, "Oh, Mother, what beautiful things Jesus is telling me!" And pointing to the notebooks she added, "Mother will read all that."

In August, when Mother Michael received the news that Sister Faustina's condition worsened, she wrote her a private letter in which she assured Sister Faustina of her sympathy and remembrance. Mother added that Father Sopocko will be attending a synod at Czestochowa, and would undoubtedly visit her. This pleased Sister very much. At the end of August, Sister Faustina wrote to Mother General:

Dearest Mother, it seems to me that this is our last conversation on earth. I am very weak, and am writing with trembling hand. I am suffering as much as I can stand. Jesus does not give beyond our strength. I rely completely on God and His holy will. An ever greater yearning for God encompasses me. Death does not frighten me; my soul abounds in deep peace. I still make all my spiritual exercises. I also rise for Mass, but do not remain to the end because I begin to feel ill. But I take advantage of the graces Jesus left us in His Church as best I can.

Dearest Mother, I thank you, from a heart overwhelmed with deep gratitude, for all the good I received in the Community, from the first moment I entered until now. I especially thank you, Mother, for your heartfelt compassion and direction in difficult times, seemingly impossible to endure. May God repay you abundantly!

And now, in the spirit of religious humility, I most humbly beg pardon of you, Dearest Mother, for my inexact keeping of the rules, for any bad example I may have given to the Sisters, for lack of zeal in my entire religious life, for all the troubles and sufferings I may have unknowingly caused you, Mother. Your goodness was my strength, loving Mother, in trying times....

Good-bye, Dearest Mother, we shall see each other in heaven at the foot of God's throne.

And now, may The Divine Mercy be glorified in us and through us...

The greatest misery and nothingness,
Sr. Faustina

The Lord gave Sister Faustina, perhaps for her consolation, a glimpse into the future. She wrote, without giving the precise date:

Today I saw the glory of God which flows from the image. Many souls are receiving graces, although they do not speak of it openly. Even though it has met up with all sorts of vicissitudes, God is receiving glory because of it; and the efforts of Satan and of evil men are shattered and come to naught. In spite of Satan's anger, The Divine Mercy will triumph over the whole world and will be worshiped by all souls. (1789)

Through her Lord and Master, Sister Faustina had learned a most valuable lesson:"I have come to know that, in order for God to act in a soul, it must give up acting on its own; otherwise, God will not carry out His will in it." (1790)

Sister then recorded two more incidents that emphasize the great power of the Chaplet of The Divine Mercy:

When a great storm was approaching, I began to say the chaplet. Suddenly I heard the voice of an Angel: "I cannot approach in this storm, because the light which comes from her mouth drives back both me and the storm." Such was the Angel's complaint to God. I then recognized how much havoc he was to have made through this storm; but I also recognized that this prayer was pleasing to God, and that this chaplet was most powerful. (1791)

Today the Lord came to me and said, **My daughter, help me to save souls. You will go to a dying sinner, and you will continue to recite the chaplet, and in this way you will obtain for him trust in My mercy, for he is already in despair.**

Suddenly I found myself in a strange cottage where an elderly man was dying amidst great torments. All about the bed was a multitude of demons and the family, who were crying. When I began to pray, the spirits of darkness fled, with hissing and threats directed at me. The soul became calm and, filled with trust, rested in the Lord. At that same moment, I found myself in my own room. How this happens... I do not know. (1797-1798)

Faustina recorded yet another vision: "Today I saw the Sacred Heart of Jesus in the sky, in the midst of a great brilliance. The rays were issuing from the Wound [in His side] and spreading over the entire world." (1796)

While in the hospital, Sister Faustina edified all with her gentleness, modesty, and love of order; as well as with her respect, submission, and obedience to the hospital personnel. All those who came in contact with her loved her. Although she herself spoke little, her entire person and bearing spoke volumes to all. Dr. Adam Silberg, director of the hospital, often visited with Sister and spoke with her about spiritual matters. He was newly baptized in the faith, and had many questions to ask of this unusual patient.

The Last Days

On August 24, Mother Irene was informed that Sister Faustina had taken a turn for the worse. The superior rushed to the hospital to be at her bedside. On the following day, August 25, 1938, which marked Sister Faustina's thirty-third birthday, Father Theodore Czaputa, the Sisters' chaplain at Jozefow, administered the Sacrament of Anointing of the Sick. Sister's health did not improve.

On August 28, Father Sopocko visited Sister Faustina. Then again, on September 2, after spending some time with her, he left; but, realizing that he forgot to leave some newly printed holy cards with her, he returned to her room and found her in ecstasy. He did not disturb her.

Sister Alfreda, the new infirmarian in the Cracow house, saw that Sister Faustina was gravely ill so she asked her if she would like to be taken home to die in the community.

A joyful smile was Sister's answer; but, on further reflection, Sister Faustina said, "I won't die yet, so please let me stay here. I would be a burden to the Community, because a sister would have to be with me constantly." Yet after a while, she added, "But, please, do what you think is best, and what the superiors wish."

Two weeks later, on September 17, Sister Alfreda arrived at the sanatorium to take Sister home. Dr. Silberg asked Sister Faustina to let him have the holy card of St. Therese which stood on the night table. He wanted to hang it over the bed of his six-year-old son. Sister Alfreda, a little worried, suggested that the holy card be disinfected. The doctor answered, "I have no fear of contamination. I am convinced that Sister Faustina is a saint, and saints do not contaminate."

The trip back to the convent was a difficult one for Sister Faustina. Seeing how faint she was, Sister Alfreda became alarmed. Faustina calmed her with the words, "Sister, please don't worry, because I will not die on the way."

Back in a private room at St. Joseph's in Lagiewniki, Sister Faustina was given tender, loving care by Sister Amelia. Because of her physical deterioration, she could no longer partake of food. Her life slowly ebbed away. On September 22, according to convent custom, Sister Faustina asked pardon of the entire community for all her unintentional shortcomings. Then she quietly awaited the coming of her Bridegroom.

On September 26, Father Michael Sopocko paid Faustina what was to be his last visit. He found she no longer had need to speak to him. She was engaged in communion with the Heavenly Father. In his memoirs he noted, "She gives the impression of an unearthly being. I no longer have the least doubt that what is found in her diary, concerning Holy Communion being administered to her by an Angel, is true." It was on this day that she told Father Sopocko the date of her impending death as revealed to her by Jesus.

Several days before her death, the Sister Gardener visited the emaciated Sister Faustina. "Aren't you afraid of death, Sister?" she asked.

"Why?" answered Sister Faustina. "All my sins and imperfections will be consumed like straw in the fire of the Divine Mercy." Then the conversation turned to talk of war. The Sister

Gardener claimed it would be a short war.

"Oh, no," replied Sister Faustina. "The war will be terribly long, long, long. There will be much misfortune; terrible sufferings will come upon the people."

"Will Poland still exist?" inquired the gardener.

"Oh, Poland will exist, but there will be few people left because many will perish. And they will love each other much and will desire to see each other."

This was not the first time that Sister Faustina spoke of a war. She frequently asked her fellow sisters and the girls to pray for Poland, affirming that a long and terrible war was soon to come. Their disbelief did not discourage her and she kept insisting that it would be a terrible, a dreadful war. Father Sopocko recalled that she lamented Poland's fate but he confessed that he paid little attention to what she was saying about the war. He did not ask for any particulars and she offered none, but he remembered the time she sighed and covered her face as if trying to obliterate some terrible scene.

The sisters likewise could not understand her constant concern about an approaching war. In fact, when she mentioned to Sister Anna, an elderly sister who took kindly to her, that "There will be a terrible war but the sisters will not leave this place," Sister Anna thought that a person on her deathbed should be thinking of her soul and not of some future war.

During the long war, which began a year after Sister Faustina's death, the sisters were indeed threatened three times with eviction by the Nazis. Then they recalled Sister Faustina's words. Each time this crisis occurred, the sisters hurried to Faustina's grave to ask her intercession with The Divine Mercy so that they be left in peace. The threats were not carried out, and the sisters remained in Lagiewniki as Sister Faustina had predicted.

All her earthly affairs having been taken care of, Sister Faustina peacefully awaited her Beloved, edifying her fellow sisters to the end. Those who still remained antagonistic toward her were later very sorry that they did not partake of the special graces that illumined her last moments. The majority of the sisters, however, did give in to her spiritual charm; and her last words with them were deeply imbedded in their minds even though not many were recorded. When the former Sister

Infirmarian, the one who caused her added suffering, came and saw the skeleton-like figure before her, she burst into tears and cried out, "Sister, just look at you!"

Sister Faustina answered, "What's that in the face of God's love?"

In these last days, Mother Irene looked forward to her visits with Sister Faustina. "She had so much peace and unusual charm, this sick one. And how she changed! Where before she was frustrated and agitated about this work of Divine Mercy, in the end, she took everything calmly, relying completely on God's will," she recalled.

During one visit, Sister Faustina told her, "There will be a Feast of The Divine Mercy, I know that; I only want God's will." At other times she spoke about the common work of the Sister Directors and the Sister Coadjutors, recalling the names of the sisters who knew how to include the Sister Coadjutors in their work, by sharing with them the concerns and worries they encountered in their classes with the girls. In her simplicity she once told Mother Irene, "You will see that the Congregation will have much joy because of me." When asked if she was glad to be dying in this community, she answered, "Yes. For all the trials and tribulations I encountered because of that work [the founding of the New Community], you will have much happiness, Mother, already here on earth."

When Mother Irene visited her shortly before her death, Sister Faustina raised herself somewhat, beckoned to Mother to draw nearer and said to her, "The Lord Jesus wants to elevate me and make me a saint."

Mother Irene later declared, "She said this with such gravity that I had the strange feeling that Sister Faustina was accepting this assurance as a gift of The Divine Mercy, without a shade of pride. When I left Sister, I was strangely moved by the remark, but not fully aware of the importance of those words."

On October 5, Sister Faustina whispered to Sister Felicia, "The Lord will take me today." At four o'clock in the afternoon Father Joseph Andrasz came to hear her last confession. She was suffering immensely. A few hours later she asked for an injection to ease the pain, but then decided not to take it in order to fulfill God's will to the end.

At nine o'clock the sisters gathered at her bedside, and together with the chaplain, Father Czaputa, prayed for the dying Sister. She was conscious and grateful for the presence of those dear to her, above all, to her Mother Superior, faithful witness to her visions. The agony was not yet evident, so the sisters dispersed. Only Sister Liguoria remained at her bedside. At 10:45 p.m., while Sister Liguoria ran for Mother Irene, Sister Faustina, eyes raised heavenwards as if in ecstasy, quietly and peacefully went to her reward.

Almost immediately, Sister Faustina's emaciated body seemed to take on an unearthly beauty. This need not surprise anyone. Her prayer, "Divinize me that my deeds may be pleasing to You. May this be accomplished by the power of the Holy Communion which I receive daily," was now fulfilled.

Sister Faustina's little notebook entitled "My Preparation for Holy Communion" was found some time later. She wrote in the introduction:

> The most solemn moment of my life is the moment when I receive Holy Communion. I long for each Holy Communion, and for every Holy Communion I give thanks to the Most Holy Trinity. If the Angels were capable of envy, they would ency us for two things: one is the receiving of Holy Communion, and the other is suffering. (1804)

An entry in this notebook reveals that while Sister prepared one day for the coming of Jesus as King, she became acutely aware that He was not just another king but rather the King of kings and Lord of lords before Whom all Powers and Dominions tremble. When she invited Him in, and He entered the dwelling of her heart, she was filled with so much reverence that she fainted with fear, falling at His feet. Jesus held out His hand to her, and kindly let her take a seat beside Him. He calmed her and said, **See, I have left My heavenly throne to become united with you. What you see is just a tiny part and already your soul swoons with love. How amazed your heart will be when you see Me in all My glory.**

But I want to tell you that eternal life must begin already here on earth through Holy Communion. Each Holy Communion makes you more capable of communing with God throughout eternity. (1810-1811)

How glorious must have been the heavenly welcome of this tremendous lover of the Eucharist, that even her mortal remains seemed to have been transformed!

Sister Faustina's funeral took place on October 7, 1938, Feast of Our Lady of the Rosary and the First Friday of the month. Besides the chaplain Father Czaputa, three Jesuits—two priests and a cleric—took part in the funeral. At 8:30 a.m. the Matins were sung. Then Father Wojton, S.J., celebrated the funeral Mass at the main altar while Father Chabrowski, S.J., celebrated in white vestments at the altar of the Sacred Heart, where the famous Image of The Divine Mercy is presently situated. In order to spare her family the expense of travel, Sister Faustina asked that they not be informed of her terminal illness and death. For this reason, no one from her family was present. After the Mass, her fellow sisters and the girls carried the coffin on their shoulders and laid Sister Faustina to rest in the community's common grave in Lagiewniki.

EPILOGUE

Very few of the community members had any inkling of the extraordinary mystical experiences of Sister Faustina. She was hardly mentioned for two years following her death. Then, the devotion to The Divine Mercy began to spread in Vilnius, and Sister's name was being mentioned in connection with it. News of this reached the sisters in the various houses of the congregation, and they began to ask questions. Therefore, in 1941, Mother Michael Moraczewska, who was still the Superior General of the Congregation, felt this was the opportune time to officially acquaint her sisters with Sister Faustina's mission. She did this while visiting the houses to which she had access during the Nazi occupation of Poland.

The sisters were filled with amazement. "She was so simple," said one, "she did not stand out among us; she was one of us but more virtuous, more recollected, and more united to God. When after her death we learned what great things God accomplished in her and through her, we could not believe it!" But, of course, they were overjoyed that the Patroness of their Congregation, Our Lady of Mercy, obtained for them, and commissioned through Sister Faustina, the great gift of reminding the poor, sinful world of God's Divine Mercy.

The devotion itself was familiar to the sisters and the girls under their care. Father Sopocko's booklet, containing the Novena, the Litany and the Chaplet to The Divine Mercy, was being used by them for almost two years; but they had no idea that Sister Faustina was the author of those prayers. The holy cards of the image, with the chaplet printed on the reverse side, were also commonly known; Mother Irene had distributed them to the sisters.

Although Mother Irene was cautious about spreading the devotion, when she became superior in Cracow, in September

1937, she obtained a small Image of The Divine Mercy and placed it on the altar of St. Joseph. Seeing that the sisters and girls referred to it with great respect and devotion, she decided to obtain a large image for the chapel. In 1938, on the Sunday after Easter, the day Jesus chose for the Feast of Mercy, the image was placed on the side altar of the Sacred Heart. That same Sunday, Mass was celebrated at that altar, and a special homily on The Divine Mercy was preached. Sister Faustina who was then in the sanatorium, most probably did not know about this celebration, for she would have mentioned this important fact in her diary.

Sister Faustina's mission truly did begin after her death, just as she had said it would. During the war, the convent chapel was open to the public. From then on, her grave was being constantly visited by people from all segments of society, who wished to ask for her intercession, or thank her for a grace received, or just simply to pray. In Lagiewniki, the devotion to The Divine Mercy became very strongly related to the person of Sister Faustina. Those who came to pray before the image in the convent chapel inevitably went to Sister's grave also. The devotion spread almost spontaneously throughout Poland. The dominant cause was, no doubt, the felt need of the time. Sister Faustina's message met that need in a special way. The sisters and girls recalled her love and concern for Poland. They related her predictions of war to the people who visited the grave and the chapel. The visitors, in turn, told others about them.

The convent in Lagiewniki became the chief center of the devotion to The Divine Mercy. The faithful came to the convent for holy cards, novenas, chaplets and litanies to The Divine Mercy. With the permission of the church authorities, special devotions to The Divine Mercy were held every third Sunday of the month, and the Sunday after Easter was celebrated as the Feast of Mercy. More and more solemn enthronements of the Image of The Divine Mercy took place in various churches and Catholic Institutions. Permission was granted by the bishops of the various dioceses of Poland to publish holy cards and prayers to The Divine Mercy. By 1951, there were 130 centers of this devotion in Poland alone.

During World War II from 1940 on, the Devotion to The Divine Mercy became a shield of strength and hope for many, especially for those in the numerous concentration camps throughout Poland, and even beyond its borders. Eventually, it was carried by soldiers and refugees to all parts of the world. The novena, litany and chaplet were soon translated into many other languages. The most dynamic centers sprang up in France, the United States, and Australia. The Pallotine and Marian Congregations were the chief promoters, thanks to graces received by some of their members.

The growing success and expansion of the devotion into the mid 1950s seemed to be a contradiction to a prophecy Sister Faustina recorded in her diary in 1935:

> Once, as I was talking with my spiritual director, I had an interior vision—quicker than lightning—of his soul in great suffering, in such agony that God touches very few souls with such fire. The suffering arises from this work. There will come a time when this work, which God is demanding so very much, will be as though utterly undone. And then God will act with great power, which will give evidence of its authenticity. It will be a new splendor for the Church, although it has been dormant in it from long ago. That God is infinitely merciful, no one can deny. He desires everyone to know this before He comes again as Judge. He wants souls to come to know Him first as the King of Mercy. When this triumph comes, we shall already have entered the new life in which there is no suffering. But before this, your soul [of the spiritual director] will be surfeited with bitterness at the sight of the destruction of your efforts. However, this will only appear to be so, because what God has once decided upon, He does not change. But although this destruction will be such only in outward appearance, the suffering will be real. When will this happen? I do not know. How long it will last? I do not know. But God has promised a great grace especially to you and to all those... **who will proclaim My great mercy. I shall protect them Myself at the hour of death, as My own glory. And even if the sins of souls will be as dark as night, when the sinner turns to My mercy he gives Me the greatest praise and is the glory of My Passion. When a soul praises My goodness, Satan trembles before it and flees to the very bottom of hell.** (378)

The first section of this prophecy was almost literally fulfilled when the Holy See, acting upon inaccurate and insufficient data concerning the revelations, by a notification dated March 6, 1959, prohibited the spreading of the Devotion to The Divine Mercy in the forms proposed by Sister Faustina. The removal of images of The Divine Mercy from churches, where they might have been already exposed for public veneration, was left to the prudence of the Bishops.

As a result, the images were removed from many churches, and some priests stopped preaching about The Divine Mercy. Father Sopocko himself was severely admonished by the Holy See, and suffered many other tribulations in connection with the spreading of the devotion. The Congregation of the Sisters of Our Lady of Mercy was also forbidden to spread the devotion. In consequence, the images, the chaplet, the novena and whatever might suggest propagation of the devotion were withdrawn. It appeared that the work of mercy, so urgently recommended by the Lord to Sister Faustina, was completely destroyed.

The Sisters of Our Lady of Mercy in Lagiewniki, in view of the Holy See's ban, addressed the Ordinary of the Archdiocese of Cracow, Archbishop Baziak, inquiring what should be done with the image which hung in the side altar, covered with many votive offerings, and what should they do about the celebrations in praise of The Divine Mercy. In answer, the Archbishop ordered that the image remain where it was, and the faithful be allowed to pray for graces before it. He also ordered the existing celebrations to be maintained. In this way, the devotion to The Divine Mercy survived the test in this small community center in Cracow, where the body of Sister Faustina was buried.

Meanwhile, in 1963, Cardinal Ottaviani, Prefect of the Holy Office, showed great interest in furthering the mission of Sister Faustina. He told Archbishop Karol Wojtyla, promoter of the cause of beatification of Sister Faustina, to act quickly before all the witnesses die. Therefore, twenty-seven years after the death of Sister Faustina, on October 21, 1965, Bishop Julian Groblicki, specially delegated by Archbishop Wojtyla, began with a solemn session The Process of Information regarding the life and virtues of Sister Faustina, who from then on bore the title—"Servant of God." As part of this process, Sister Faustina's remains were exhumed and transferred from the cemetery to the convent chapel on November 25, 1966. The newly elevated Karol Cardinal Wojtyla concluded the Process of Information in the Diocese of Cracow with a solemn session on September 20, 1967. The Acts of the Process of Information were received in Rome by the Sacred Congregation for the Causes of Saints on January 26, 1968, and by a Decree of the same Sacred Congregation, on January 31, 1968, the Process of Beatification of the Servant of God Sister Faustina Kowalska was formally inaugurated.

On April 15, 1978, after a thorough examination of original documents which were previously unavailable to it, the Holy See completely reversed its Notification of 1959. After a ban of twenty years, it again permitted the spreading of the devotion to The Divine Mercy, according to the forms proposed by Sister Faustina. The person primarily responsible for the reversal of the ban was Karol Cardinal Wojtyla, the Archbishop of Cracow, who six months later on October 16, 1978, was elevated to the See of Peter as Pope John Paul II. Thus, the second part of the above-mentioned prophecy began to be fulfilled. In May of 1938, Sister Faustina wrote in her diary:

> As I was praying for Poland, I heard the words: **I bear a special love for Poland, and if she will be obedient to My will, I will exalt her in might and holiness. From her will come forth the spark that will prepare the world for My final coming.** (1732)

Is the Devotion to The Divine Mercy the "new splendor for the Church, though it has been dormant in it from long ago?" Is this devotion the spark that will come out of Poland to prepare the world for His Second Coming?" If so, then one more request of the Lord—made at least fourteen times as recorded by Sister Faustina—has yet to be realized: that a Feast of The Divine Mercy on the first Sunday after Easter be officially established in the Church, and that the Image of The Divine Mercy be blessed and publicly venerated on that day.

Sister Faustina knew the urgency of such a feast and, as has been noted earlier, prayed fervently for its establishment. On April 10, 1937, as Sister Faustina took into her hands an article on The Divine Mercy, published in the Vilnius *Weekly* and sent to her by Father Sopocko, an arrow of love pierced her soul. She heard the words, **For the sake of your ardent desires, I am hastening the Feast of Mercy.** (1082)

For the world's sake, let us ardently pray for the fulfillment of this promise. MARANA THA! COME, LORD JESUS!— THE DIVINE MERCY INCARNATE!

JESUS I TRUST IN YOU

BIBLIOGRAPHY

Borkiewicz, O. Izydor, OFMConv. "Kowalska, Helena (Siostra M. Faustyna)," in *Hagiografia Polska,* Vol. I, pp. 837-849. Poznan: 1971.

Kowalska, Sister Faustina, ZMBM, *Dzienniczek.* Krakow Stockbridge Rzym: 1981.

Piekut, Sister M. Beata, ZMBM, *Kalendarzyk Zycia Slugi Bozej s. M. Faustyny Kowalskiej.* Krakow: 1973.

Szymanski, Rev. Stanislaus, S.J. *W Sluzbie Bozego Milosierdzia.* Siostra Faustyna Kowalska. London: 1978.

Archives of Sister Faustina:
Recollections of Sister Faustina's family members.
Recollections of Marcianna Sadowska.
Recollections of Aldona Lipszyc.
Recollections of Rev. Michael Sopocko.
Comments of the Sisters of the Congregation of Our Lady of Mercy.
Comments of the girls from the various institutes of the Sisters of Our Lady of Mercy.

256

*Places where Sister Faustina
lived and worked*

ABOUT THE AUTHOR...

Sister Sophia Michalenko, a member of the Community of the Mother of God of Tenderness, currently works for the Marian Helpers Center in Stockbridge, Massachusetts. Sister holds a master's degree in English from St. John's University, Jamaica, Long Island, New York.

For many years, Sister was an educator in the New England and Middle Atlantic States. During the past six years she has devoted her efforts primarily to Divine Mercy ministries, especially through research, translating, and editing Divine Mercy materials. Chief among these was the preparation of both the Polish (1981) and English texts of the definitive diary of Sister Faustina (forthcoming).

CORRECTIONS

PAGE

31   delete other "the" L 16

49   "worldly" L 26

51   language "was" L 25

62   "justly" L 30

69   "intense" L 19

87   Jesus "gave" L 6

98   On "another" L 1

106   interior "thoughts" L 5

119   of "the" L 22

123   battle "that" L 26

193   miracles "take" L 21

198   Sister "Faustina" L 22

200   "sufficient" L 25

204   sales "of" L 11

227   "enemy's" L 5

229   Sanatorium "in" L 2

229   delete quote mark L 10

246   whole page should be standard type.